AF753943

Aspects of Urbanization in China

IIAS PUBLICATIONS SERIES

International Institute for Asian Studies

The *IIAS Publications Series* consists of Monographs and Edited Volumes. The Series publishes results of research projects conducted at the International Institute for Asian Studies. Furthermore, the aim of the Series is to promote interdisciplinary studies on Asia and comparative research on Asia and Europe.

The *International Institute for Asian Studies* (IIAS) is a postdoctoral research centre based in Leiden and Amsterdam, the Netherlands. Its objective is to encourage the interdisciplinary and comparative study of Asia and to promote national and international cooperation. The institute focuses on the humanities and social sciences and, where relevant, on their interaction with other sciences. It stimulates scholarship on Asia and is instrumental in forging research networks among Asia scholars worldwide.

IIAS acts as an international mediator, bringing various parties together, working as a clearinghouse of knowledge and information. This entails activities such as providing information services, hosting academic organisations dealing with Asia, constructing international networks, and setting up international cooperative projects and research programmes. In this way, IIAS functions as a window on Europe for non-European scholars and contributes to the cultural rapprochement between Asia and Europe.

For further information, please visit www.iias.nl.

Aspects of Urbanization in China

Shanghai, Hong Kong, Guangzhou

Edited by

Gregory Bracken

Amsterdam University Press

IIAS International Institute for Asian Studies

Publications Series

Edited Volumes 6

DSD Delft School of Design

TU Delft Delft University of Technology

The publication of this book is co-financed by the Delft School of Design (DSD) and the Delft University of Technology (TU Delft).

Cover photo: Gregory Bracken

Cover design: Maedium, Utrecht
Layout: The DocWorkers, Almere

ISBN 978 90 8964 398 8
e-ISBN 978 90 4851 306 2 (pdf)
e-ISBN 978 90 4851 561 5 (ePub)
NUR 758

Table of Contents

List of Tables and Illustrations

List of Tables

List of Illustrations

Acknowledgements

First of all, I would like to thank the contributors, without whom there would be no book. This book would not have come about if it had not been for the suggestion of Paul van der Velde and Martina van den Haak at the International Institute for Asian Studies, Leiden, so thanks to you, too. I would also like to thank the International Institute for Asian Studies in general, especially Deputy Director Manon Osseweijer and Director Philippe Peycam, for giving me the opportunity to work there in the first place and engage in this interesting research – your support is very much appreciated. I would also like to thank the Delft School of Design (DSD) at the Technical University of Delft, especially founding director Arie Graafland and current director Deborah Hauptmann, as well as the DSD's very generous financial support of this book. I would also like to make special mention of Annemieke Bal-Sanders and Patrick Healy, both colleagues at the DSD, who have given me invaluable assistance, each in their different ways, over the life of this project. Finally, I would also like to particularly thank the book's peer reviewers, whose insightful analysis and constructive criticism helped form the project into what it is today, something that I feel confident we can all be proud of.

INTRODUCTION

1 Aspects of Urbanization in China: Shanghai, Hong Kong, Guangzhou

Gregory Bracken

Urbanization is as old as civilization. As societies change and develop, urbanization tends to be part and parcel of that development. In fact, the evolution of the city has mirrored human development in a symbiotic way. Mankind's chief glory has always been its cities. They represent all that is best in human endeavor: the ability to plan, to construct, and to live together in comity. Cities are evidence of mankind's ability to reshape the environment to better suits its needs, and to exhibit the best that can be produced by human hands and minds, not just in engineering terms but in architecture and the arts as well. Cities also act as crucibles of change; the way a society will develop is often first discerned in a city. They have been the birthplace of art, culture, and commerce and have enabled us to be who we are today.

There have been waves of urbanization throughout history, from ancient Egypt and Mesopotamia to the flowering of the Greek city-states, through the rigorous planning of the Romans to the ad hoc mercantilist zeal of the Renaissance. The nineteenth century, with its staggering technological development, saw the Western empires establish new cities all over the world, invariably founded to control the flows of goods and people.

At the end of the twentieth century there was a seismic shift of wealth, power, and influence back to the East. Asia is experiencing its own renaissance as a center of world power, and now it is China's turn to engage in city building. China, of course, has a long and venerable history of urban development. Beginning as far back as the second millennium BCE, Chinese cities were ritual centers surrounded by artisan workshops in service to royal courts. The creation of a united empire under the Zhou Dynasty, around 1110 BCE, saw the development of large walled towns, and it was in the Han and the Tang Dynasties that followed that a pattern of centralized control was first devised that enjoyed an unparalleled duration and thoroughness. For more than a millennium, China's capitals of Loyang, Chang'an, and Kaifeng were among the world's largest cities.

China is now a world power politically, militarily, and economically, and is increasingly being seen as a rival to the United States. China's economy is now second only to that of the United States, the result of almost 10 percent growth per annum for over three decades. A number of countries in the early stages of economic development and/or reform have experienced rapid growth, but nothing has ever come close to the speed of achievement in China in recent years, and one significant factor in China's remarkable economic growth has been its rapid and massive urbanization.

This book examines some of the aspects of this urbanization in China. This will necessarily be an incomplete picture, which is why the book has been called 'Aspects of Urbanization in China', as aspects are all we can hope to look at in such a vast country with so many cities, and all undergoing such rapid change. The papers have been written by academics from different disciplines, primarily architecture and urbanism (indeed some of the contributors have been trained as architects and are still in private practice), but there are also contributions from fields as diverse as social science, area studies and geography. The point of departure for their investigations is always the city – in this case the cities of Shanghai, Hong Kong, and Guangzhou – and their papers represent ongoing processes of research and exploration which, taken together, give us a useful snapshot of such a rapidly developing discourse.

Split into three parts, the book deals with cities' global ambitions as well as their cultural and architectural expression. Part One examines the role of the architectural icon in the business of city-branding. It also looks at certain specific cities' efforts to brand themselves in an increasingly globalized world – in this case Shanghai (via the 2010 World Expo) and Guangzhou.

Leslie Sklair's chapter 'Towards an Understanding of Architectural Iconicity in Global Perspective' in Part One has a wider breadth of scope than most of the other chapters in the book. In it, he explores the role of icons, especially architectural icons, in a city's identity-building. Sklair posits the idea that certain types of architecture can be hegemonic in a class sense, so that alongside their recognized aesthetic qualities they can also serve specific class interests. Iconic architecture, defined by Sklair in terms of a particular building's fame, is often achieved by rendering it with a distinctive aesthetic or symbolic significance. Historically, this sort of architecture tended to be driven by the state and/or religious elites, but in an era of capitalist globalization it is those who are in control of capital flows – the transnational capitalist class – that have become increasingly implicated in the production of iconic architecture, particularly in service to their own narrow and specific class interests.

Jacob Dreyer's chapter 'Shanghai and the 2010 Expo: Staging the City' explores issues in Shanghai's urbanism, particularly the question of why architecture is the language through which the contemporary spirit of cities tends to express itself. In Shanghai, these concepts can be seen in the futuristic skyline, enormous neon-lit highways, and the 2010 World Expo. Dreyer sees Shanghai as the symbolic outlier of China, a space fundamentally out of step with the rest of the country because it was always ahead of it. The city's clearly expressed aim of becoming (once again) a world city makes use of events like the World Expo as a way of fusing its rich historical legacy with a contemporaneity so fresh that, as Dreyer puts it, it almost seems to be the future rather than the present.

'Guangzhou's Special Path to Global City Status' by Xiangmin Guo and Changtao Liu is the last paper in Part One and looks at this city's long and proud history of foreign trade, where for most of China's imperial history it was the only point of contact with the outside world. During the century or so that it had treaty port status (from 1842 onwards), Guangzhou stayed ahead of its inland competitors by turning itself into a highly cosmopolitan place. But since the establishment of the People's Republic in 1949, Guangzhou has lost out to nearby neighbor Hong Kong. The city is now trying to reposition itself as a bridgehead for foreign trade in China, while paving the way towards global importance for the rest of the country's cities. Guo and Liu identify one of the main challenges of this task as building an increasing resistance to the negative influences of globalization on the path towards becoming a global city.

Part Two examines the cultural expression of the rural-urban migration taking place in China (the largest anywhere in the world). This is done in two of the papers through the medium of cinema. Ana M. Moya Pellitero's 'Repairing the Rural-Urban Continuum: Cinema as Witness' examines the work of the Fifth- and Sixth-Generation film directors such as Zhang Yimou, Chen Kaige, Jia Zhang-ke, and Wang Xiaoshuai. These filmmakers established their reputations by depicting the rural-urban dichotomy that has existed in China since the economic reforms of 1978. Moya Pellitero asserts that until the end of the imperial system in 1911, China was a single hybrid continuum that was neither urban nor rural, and that its civilization was based on a complex web of relationships and hierarchies where individuals could be urban in their political and religious outlook but rural in their bond to the land and their place of origin. In contemporary China, particularly since the economic reforms, the traditional urban-rural continuum has come under attack, a phenomenon that has been in explored in films such as Chen Kaige's *King of the Children* and Zhang Yimou *Shanghai Triad*, as well as Jia Zhang-ke's *Platform* (which forms part of his trilogy *Rèn Xiāo yáo*) and Wang Xiaoshuai's *So Close to Paradise*, all of which are examined here.

The second chapter that takes cinema as its point of departure is 'Revisiting Hong Kong: Fruit Chan's "Little Cheung"' by Tsung-yi Michelle Huang. In it, Hong Kong's postcolonial condition is examined by initially drawing on a number of commentators, namely Rey Chow, who sees Hong Kong's return to China as marking the beginning of another era of colonization rather than putting an end to one, and Ackbar Abbas, who argues that the 1984 Sino-British Joint Declaration has played a crucial role in the historical development of the territory's postcolonial consciousness by shaping how Hong Kong people define their own identity. Huang's own analysis, which is subtle and astute, seeks to clarify the interaction between postcolonial writing and the urban space of the global city by examining the cultural representation of the postcolonial consciousness rather than the political structures of postcoloniality itself. She makes telling use of Fruit Chan's film *Little Cheung*, which follows the life of a nine-year-old boy from the winter of 1996 through to the summer of 1997 (and the handover of Hong Kong). According to Huang, this deceptively simple device, generally regarded as the director's 'national' allegory, enabled him to constitute a local identity in response to the political impact of the handover.

Part Two contains one final chapter, and this deals with a portrayal of Shanghai in literature: 'Sensual, But No Clue of Politics: Shanghai's *Longtang* Houses' by Lena Scheen. Ever since Shanghai was opened up to foreign investment in 1984, and particularly since the Pudong area was established as a Special Economic Zone in 1990, the city has been undergoing an explosive process of urbanization. Scheen sees large-scale urban renewal not only transforming the physical appearance of the built environment (through new architecture, etc.) but also transforming the way in which people live in that environment, with profound effects on citizens' daily and inner lives. In identifying an increasing sense of nostalgia for Shanghai's semi-colonial past, Scheen's paper focuses on Wang Anyi's novel *The Song of Everlasting Sorrow* as one of the most representative examples of this new 'Shanghai nostalgia'. This novel centers on the life of a woman living in Shanghai's traditional *longtang* (or alleyway houses) rather than the glamorous Western architecture of the Bund. Its depiction of everyday life for middle-class Shanghainese should not be understood as any kind of negative response to the city's recent transformations; rather, Scheen sees it as a way of celebrating (and negotiating) the modernization process.

Part Three returns to the architectural-urbanistic point of departure of the book, with analyses of Hong Kong and Shanghai. Non Arkaraprasertkul's chapter 'Urbanization and Housing: Socio-Spatial

Conflicts over Urban Space in Contemporary Shanghai' seeks to make sense of the process of urbanization in China in a broader sense, and makes use of an understanding of such a process in a focused case study of local communities in Shanghai. Its discussion of the theoretical frameworks of urbanization takes into account various disciplines including history, geography, architecture, sociology, and anthropology, and tries to shed some light on the conflicts and tensions over urban space brought about by the sort of transformations that have been seen in Shanghai in recent years. It begins with the practical problems of housing in present-day Shanghai, for which the *lilong* (alleyway house[1]) has simply failed to deliver. While these old houses may help the city maintain its connection with the past, most people do not want to live in them because they are old and inconvenient and because there are better options in modern accommodation. Arkaraprasertkul is right to point out that what makes the *lilong* worth preserving is not just the house itself (although this is not unimportant) but rather the dynamism of the community that it forms a part of. This paper reflects an ongoing research that raises as many questions as it answers, including whether enough has been done in the study of *lilong* houses (and neighborhoods) to even understand the nature of the questions posed.

These chapters all represent different levels of academic expertise, and this has been a deliberate decision on the part of the editor. Any perception of unevenness that may result is regretted, but please try to be indulgent: the value of these different perspectives should, hopefully, outweigh any disjunction between the levels of ability in expressing them. This book, as has already been mentioned, has an architectural and urbanistic point of departure, but it is still very much a multi-disciplinary endeavor. This multi-disciplinary approach has been followed in an attempt to mitigate the occasional one-sidedness of the architectural-urbanistic views that tend to take a too rigidly architectonic stance. By placing these analyses alongside the perspectives of other disciplines, we can get a better understanding of what is going on in the cities of rapidly urbanizing China. Having said that, the book's final chapter – 'It Makes a Village: Hong Kong's Podium Shopping Malls as Global Villages' by Jonathan D. Solomon – makes copious use of the medium that architects are most comfortable in expressing themselves: the drawing. As a result, it is a much shorter chapter than some of the others, but this is because so much of its analysis is contained within these drawings.

Solomon points out that, despite its long colonial history, Hong Kong bears almost no physical trace of its past. The city has always been willing to replace buildings and urban fabric with the accouterments of globalism. He finds it unsurprising that links between the local and the global networks should exist in Hong Kong; what is surprising, however, is the fact that these should be found in the shopping mall – that most iconic of the spaces of globalization. It is this most conspicuously global of urban typologies that ultimately provides Hong Kong with its functional infrastructure for connecting between global and local communities. Solomon's analysis centers on two specific shopping malls: IFC Mall and Elements Mall, each of which has a different character. He argues that instead of being symbolic links to the territory's past and providing a basis for collective memory, these shopping malls provide functional links that bring diverse cultures into propinquity. That this should be achieved by a building typology that is widely considered to be fundamentally anti-urban is remarkable, and is indeed probably a unique characteristic of Hong Kong's urbanism.

The reader must understand that allowing an architect to express his work in this way – the combination of text and drawing – is all part and parcel of the multi-disciplinary ethos that informs the entire book. And even though the natural medium of communication for an architect is not often the written word (although there are some notable exceptions: Le Corbusier, Koolhaas, et al.), academics will perhaps be less familiar with the drawing as a mode of scholarly communication. The attempt to make scholars more aware of what is going on in one another's disciplines is one of the key aims of this book, and it is hoped that with this richer awareness we will be better able to try and make sense of what is happening in China today as its cities and people experience the most massive wave of urbanization in history.

Globalization is not necessarily Westernization

China's rise as a global economic and political power is seen by the Institute for International Economics and the Center for Strategic and International Studies as being 'one of the transformative events of our time'.[2] China has been called the workshop of the world, not because it is home to the world's cheapest workforce (Southeast Asian and African workers get paid significantly less) but because it sits in a relatively stable part of the globe and offers reliable and capable workers who are kept in line by strictly enforced government discipline. This discipline is something that often causes unease in the West, but we must not forget that it is only one aspect of a regime that has managed to lift more people out of poverty in the last thirty years than any other regime in history – communist or capitalist. Hundreds of millions of people have seen their lives vastly improved thanks to China's industrialization and the agricultural and economic reforms that have accompanied it.

One seemingly inevitable outcome of industrialization is urbanization: workers tend to migrate to centers of manufacturing, but it could just as easily be argued that industrialization was the product of urbanization (although the more balanced view would be to suggest that they enjoy a symbiotic relationship). Then there is the question of the wider pattern into which all of this industrialization and urbanization fits into – i.e. modernization. Peter G. Rowe has been examining the cities of East Asia for many years, and he poses the question: how well do cities in East Asia conform to modernization as it is understood elsewhere in the world, particularly in the West? And to what extent does it describe a regional modernity that is '... different in kind, as well as degree, from other modern cities?'[3]

He then quite cleverly answers this by equating any understanding of these views as being a question of perspective. Modernization, in Rowe's view, is 'commonly understood through an ensemble of interrelated characteristics. Chief among them is industrialization, or the conversion of raw materials into marketable manufactured products and sources of power and propulsion, along with tertiary functions to deal with the mass distribution and information transactions involved'.[4] In other words, it was often defined by a combination of processes including 'industrialization, urbanization, labour diversification, social mobility and, as a result, substantially improved material standards of living'.[5]

The perspectives offered by the papers in this book may well afford new insights into what is happening in three different cities in China: Shanghai, Hong Kong, and Guangzhou. These three different cities all contain different responses to urbanization and the globalization that is propelling it. They also have three different sets of problems: Shanghai has to deal with the sheer scale of its physical size; Hong Kong is trying to come to terms with its reintegration into a country that has undergone massive changes over the last century and a half; while Guangzhou, traditionally the international conduit for China's trade, is having to play catch-up in a rapidly changing world.

All three of these cities have one thing in common: they were all influenced to a greater or lesser degree by colonialism, particularly in the nineteenth and early twentieth centuries (with Hong Kong remaining a British colony until as late as 1997). Whether as a colony or a treaty port, these cities were what this editor has referred to elsewhere as the 'interface of empire'[6] – the place where Western colonial and imperial ambitions (and later the Japanese) were brought to bear on a fragile and crumbling Chinese imperial system.

In the colonial era, to modernize meant to Westernize – i.e. adopt Western modes of dress, customs, language, laws, moral outlook, etc. Peter G. Rowe reminds us that this is not necessarily a case of

Westernization *per se*; rather, it is more a question of there being only '... a comparatively limited number of ways of accomplishing something efficiently, with the result that things begin to look much the same'.[7] To give an analogy from the motor industry: motor cars are increasingly beginning to resemble one another because they are all designed with the same aerodynamic principles in mind. Rowe's point that 'the similarity in modern building design between one place and the other need not mean that one culture is being converted to another' is a valid one. His notion that modern architectural expression, which began in the West and can be profitably deployed elsewhere, 'represents, in effect, an expansion of local cultural identity in a manner that suits the social, economic and material transformations taking place'.[8] In other words, globalization is not necessarily Westernization.

While this thesis is convincing, there is a downside – something which Rowe himself also mentions, although not in a negative way. He sees another of the developments of modernism as being 'the technological advancement of building materials and mechanical systems' which bring with it 'an independence from local climate and other geographical circumstances, as well as from local building materials, all of which formerly shaped local architectural expressions quite strongly'[9]. This was, of course, the concern of architects like Team Ten and the later Critical Regionalists, who sought to raise valid concerns about the monolith of High Modernism.

Before the advent of air conditioning, factors such as local climate and traditional building methods were taken into account, resulting in environmentally responsible and often extremely elegant styles of architecture. The Singapore black-and-white bungalow is a perfect example of this hybrid style: a subtle mix of the then globally ascendant neoclassicism with a thorough understanding of indigenous Malay building techniques (i.e. raising the house on stilts, making use of overhanging eves and open verandas, etc.). This resulted in a comfortable and indeed attractive home, creating an architectural style that has since become an architectural icon.

China is currently embracing experimental architecture in an effort to bolster its image abroad. It did this with the venues for the Summer Olympic Games in Beijing in 2008 and with other ambitious projects such as the CCTV complex. These all tend to be designed by big-name foreign architects, but does this mean that the Chinese are Westernizing? Peter G. Rowe is correct to point out that '... spectators in the future might be forgiven for labelling this form of hypermodernism as a Chinese style'.[10] The fact that most of these projects' architects are actually Westerners would make this a little unlikely, but Rowe does raise a valid point in that we are now at a stage where we have to ask ourselves what is actually Western and what is Chinese? Is it a Chinese building simply because it was built in China? Would it be Chinese if it were designed by a Chinese architect but built in New York? And what if equal numbers of Westerners and Chinese collaborated on the design team? And what about the places that these designers have been educated in? If they are Chinese or Asian or African for that matter but have been educated in the West and then go on to borrow selectively and cleverly from the West, as the Chinese have been doing, then it is not a simple matter of labelling them one thing or another. These new designers are creating – like the builders of the colonial era's black-and-white bungalows in Singapore – a new kind of hybrid, one that has every potential to be as successful as its colonial predecessor.

Capitalism with Chinese characteristics

As we have seen, urbanization is playing a vital role in China's recent and remarkable resurgence. It is estimated that more than 200 million people have moved from rural areas into China's cities in recent years.[11] These people are taking part in what is the largest mass migration in human history, sparked by Deng Xiaoping's 'Open Door' economic reforms that began in 1978. This 'second revolution' turned China into the world's workshop and enabled the country to move into the footlights on the world stage. A carefully controlled capitalist enterprise, which goes under the rubric of 'capitalism with Chinese characteristics', has enabled China to overtake Japan as the world's second-largest economy (which it did in August 2010). Some commentators even see the country as potentially toppling the United States from its number one position within 20 years. (Although America's economy is still three times that of China, if China manages to sustain a growth rate of 9 percent per annum this could well be a possibility.)

This miraculous economic growth also has its downsides, which are particularly apparent in China's cities. The country has a population five times that of the United States, yet its per capita income is on a par with countries like Algeria, El Salvador, and Albania (i.e. approximately $ 3,600 per annum, while in the United States it is approximately $ 46,000). Despite this, China has become the world's largest market for passenger vehicles, which reflects an interesting new stage in the country's economic development in that it no longer relies on the export of cheap toys and clothes which first earned it the nickname 'workshop of the world'. Instead, it has begun to turn to domestic demand in an effort to boost production and encourage Chinese people to buy products that are made in the country. While this may seem like a step in the right direction, it is having some unfortunate side effects such as the environmental impact of the increase in steel and cement production as well as an increase in demand for power which is still primarily fuelled by coal (China surpassed the United States as the world's largest emitter of greenhouse gases in 2006).

The changes that this rapid economic development have caused have often been painful, even for those who have seemed to benefit – those with good jobs in the country's manufacturing sector. The Chinese government introduced a minimum wage in 2004, yet such moves – promising as they are – do not go far enough to alleviate the problems associated with the country's rapid economic growth, as witnessed by the increase in strike activity in recent years. The government's apparent reluctance to repress these strikes is seen as a turning point in a country known for having little tolerance for labor militancy. This newfound tolerance is yet another sign of China's increasing economic maturity. Concern for workers' rights and the gradual increases in wages that have resulted from it are signs that China is leaving behind the old era of low-wage capitalism.

In the early 1980s, Deng Xiaoping famously dismissed any potential problems regarding future inequality with the memorable phrase 'some people have to get rich first'. Yet what about those who have been left behind by this economic miracle? Or those who have been imperfectly able to partake in it? This is one of the most important sub-themes of this book: the 'floating population' of millions of migrants to China's cities, victims of the restrictive *hukou* registration system. These people simply disappear when the economy takes a downturn. Of course they haven't disappeared, they have just returned home, which does nothing to solve their problems – in fact it exacerbates them, as there's nothing for them to go home to. A number of the chapters in this book concentrate specifically on the plight of people who are very far from being members of the new global elite – whether Filipina maids in Hong Kong or the *lilong* dwellers of Shanghai – people who are increasingly excluded from parts of the city that have been set aside to cater to the needs of what Leslie Sklair refers to as the transnational capitalist class.

Aspects of urbanization in China

China has anything from 100 to 160 cities with one million or more inhabitants (America, by comparison, has nine, while Eastern and Western Europe combined have 36).[12] Peter G. Rowe points out that China is '... well on its way to becoming a predominantly urban nation by about 2035, before going on to stabilize, with a 60 per cent proportion of urban dwellers, probably around 2050'.[13]

During the last four decades of the twentieth century the world experienced unprecedented urban growth, most of it the result of migration from rural areas. In 1950, approximately 30 percent of the world's population lived in cities (a mere two percentage points under China's current figure). In fact, for most of the second half of the twentieth century, China's pace of urbanization lagged behind the rest of the world, so is it any wonder that it is now trying to catch up? However, according to the IIEC and CSIS, China's current pace of urbanization is unparalleled in history. The estimate is that China's urban population ballooned by 200 million within the space of a decade.[14]

One of the most important challenges facing China's government in the future will be the lessening of the income gap between urban and rural areas. One other area of inequality that has long existed in China is that which exists between the coastal region, which is developed, and inland areas, which are not. This gap has continued to increase in recent years. The infrastructure that is being created in order for the country to compete globally is also causing the displacement of populations, forcing them to make way for new roads, airports, dams, and factories. According to a 2005 report, the Chinese Academy of Social Sciences estimates that up to 40 million peasants have been forced off their land to make way for these infrastructure projects, with an additional two million being displaced every year.[15] These millions become part of China's 'floating population', flocking into urban areas in search of new means of livelihood. Vast migrant-worker 'towns' are springing up on the edges of major cities, engendering potential environmental, health, and safety issues as well as poverty and rising levels of dissatisfaction with the way the country is being run. According to the IIEC and CSIS, China's National Population and Family Planning Commission estimated the number of internal migrants to be 53.5 million in 1995 and well over 140 million by 2004.[16] In fact, migrant workers account for approximately 20 percent of China's working-age population (i.e. those between 15 and 64 years old).[17]

Chinese leaders have begun to take cognisance of the fact that such inequalities between urban and rural areas and within cities themselves could, if they are allowed to increase unabated, lead to political instability. In an effort to circumvent this, they have begun to implement policies designed to accelerate both the pace of farm income growth and the economic development of interior provinces that have been left behind in the rush to a market economy.

This book on some of the aspects of urbanization in China has, as has been pointed out earlier, a distinctly architectural-urbanistic point of view. Whereas architects often tend to concentrate exclusively on buildings (though the better ones do tend to take other factors into account), urbanists are better at seeing the spaces in between them not just as empty space but as the nexus of connections that link buildings to one another, which of course enables them to function. A popular area like Xintiandi in Shanghai, for example, is full of people going there to have fun; but they don't go there to see the buildings, they go there because of what goes on *in* them. And then there is the public spaces formed in between these buildings. Spaces between buildings function very much like the space between the spokes of a wheel: the wheel's integrity depends as much on the spaces between them as on the material the spokes are made of. However, none of this – neither the buildings nor the spaces – would be anything without the people who inhabit them. And that is one of the themes that unites all of the papers in this book, because these contributors, from different disciplines and at different stages in their academic or professional careers, have all bent their focus to the cities of China in an attempt to understand what life is like for the people who call them home.

Notes

1 N.B. *Lilong* is the Chinese term for the Shanghai alleyway house and is also the one that is more generally used; *longtang* is the word that is used in Shanghai itself.
2 IIEC and CSIS, *China: The Balance Sheet*, p. ix.
3 Peter G. Rowe, *East Asia Modern: Shaping the Contemporary City*, p. 9.
4 Ibid., p. 11.
5 Ibid., p. 12.
6 Gregory Bracken, 'The Interface of Empire', conference paper at the International Forum on Urbanism, Tsinghua University, Beijing, 2006.
7 Peter G. Rowe, *East Asia Modern: Shaping the Contemporary City*, p. 145.
8 Ibid., pp. 144-145.
9 Ibid., p. 17.
10 Ibid., p. 139.
11 IIEC and CSIS, *China: The Balance Sheet*, p. 31.
12 Ted C. Fishman, *China, Inc.*, p. 7.
13 Peter G. Rowe, *East Asia Modern: Shaping the Contemporary City*, p. 24.
14 IIEC and CSIS, *China: The Balance Sheet*, p. 31.
15 Cited in IIEC and CSIS, *China: The Balance Sheet*, p. 41.
16 Cited in IIEC and CSIS, *China: The Balance Sheet*, p. 46.
17 IIEC and CSIS, *China: The Balance Sheet*, p. 46.

GLOBAL AMBITIONS

2 Towards an Understanding of Architectural Iconicity in Global Perspective[1]

Leslie Sklair

Abstract
Despite the fact that architecture and the built environment confront all of us in our daily lives, they have received relatively little attention in discussions of globalization, capitalism, or postcolonialism. Certain types of architecture can be hegemonic in a class sense, serving specific class interests alongside their recognized aesthetic qualities. Until the middle of the twentieth century, this idea was discussed mainly in terms of monumentality and political power. However, in recent decades, with the spread of the culture-ideology of consumerism around the world, notably in the cities of the postcolonial newly independent countries of East Asia, iconic architecture is becoming increasingly important in understanding how capitalist globalization works.

Introduction

The relationships between the forces of globalization, capitalism, and postcolonialism that are at work in the architecture of the cities of East Asia today have received relatively little scholarly attention. This chapter rests on the general idea that certain types of architecture can be hegemonic in a class sense, just like other art forms (particularly literature and the plastic arts), and that certain buildings and spaces can and do serve certain specific class interests alongside their recognized use or aesthetic qualities.

This paper can be seen as a point on the trajectory of investigations I have been undertaking into the transnational capitalist class and the networks of global capitalism. The argument that certain types of architecture can be hegemonic in the class sense and that certain buildings can serve specific class interests is argued convincingly by Bentmann and Muller (1992) in their book on the villa as an example of hegemonic architecture. Their brilliant study examines how the villa, largely associated with the great Renaissance architect Andrea Palladio, faithfully reproduced the class structures and divisions of northern Italy in the sixteenth century. It also, of course, went on to become an immensely popular architectural typology and was widely imitated throughout the rest of Europe and then, via the Western European empires, propagated worldwide.

The construction of Hilton hotels in what would come to be known as the Third World after 1945, provides a more recent example of this phenomenon. As Conrad Hilton himself once said, his hotels were literally 'a little America' for upper middle-class travellers, a 'space of modern luxury and technological desire ... [signifying the] new and powerful presence of the United States' or, more accurately, its dominant class, in the post-war world (Wharton 2001: 2). Between 1949 and 1966, Hilton built hotels in San Juan, Istanbul, Mexico City, Havana, Port of Spain, Tehran, Hong Kong, Athens, Tunis, Tel Aviv, Cairo, Barbados, and Bridgetown. The Istanbul Hilton is a typical example: it was built in the International Style (with lavish use of transparent glass revealing a mini-mall in its spacious atrium) and is located on one of the city's best sites. It also illustrates a classic postcolonial theme that will reappear in this narrative in that it was claimed that the process of fitting out the hotel had helped to reinvent the ancient Turkish art of tile-making. Wharton comments: 'Whether these tiles were modified or reinvented, they were deployed as a sign of the Other within a dominant aesthetic of American Modernity' (ibid.: 26).

Coterminous with the public relations industry that disseminates them, city symbols (like the Sydney Opera House) and national symbols (like government buildings in Chandigarh and Brasilia or the Three Gorges Dam in China, and of course the skyscrapers that have emerged on the skylines of so many cities) all reinforce processes of global image-creation that can be mobilized in the interests of the powerful. As we shall see shortly, the Petronas Towers in Kuala Lumpur, Beautiful Indonesia in Miniature in Jakarta, and the República de los Ninõs in Buenos Aires all use architecture to reconstruct history and to create new national identities as well as to boost the all-important tourist industry. All of this is being done in order to consolidate the power of the local and transnational elites. In the era of globalization, some of these processes have evolved in surprising ways.

Globalization, at least as a sociological concept, has always been too frail to sustain the theoretical and substantive burdens loaded onto it. It needs to be deconstructed. In order to do this I will distinguish three different modes of globalization: generic, capitalist, and alternative globalizations. Globalization, at least in its generic sense, is all too often confused with the dominant type that actually exists, namely capitalist globalization. In previous publications (Sklair 2001, 2002), I have argued that capitalist globalization is driven by a transnational capitalist class, which consists of four main factions: 1) those who own and/or control major transnational corporations and their local affiliates (the corporate faction); 2) globalizing politicians and bureaucrats (the state faction); 3) globalizing professionals (the technical faction); and 4) elites that consist of merchants, the media, and advertising (the consumerist faction). Architecture and urban design provide plenty of examples.

Generic globalization and capitalist globalization

The basic premise of my argument is straightforward: generic globalization offers almost unlimited emancipatory potential for life on earth, whereas capitalist globalization subverts this potential in the selfish interests of the transnational capitalist class. Please note that I define generic globalization in terms of four phenomena, listed in increasing order of significance, that have emerged since the middle of the twentieth century:

1. The electronic revolution, notably transformations in the technological base and global scope of the electronic mass media and most of the material infrastructure of the world today;
2. New forms of cosmopolitanism;
3. Postcolonialisms;[2]
4. The creation of transnational social spaces.

These four phenomena are the defining characteristics of globalization in a generic sense. The concept of postcolonialism is used here in its widest possible interpretation. While also acknowledging its complexities (as well as those of the closely related concept of Orientalism),[3] I am, however, trying to avoid becoming embroiled in the abstract debates that surround them. Each category clearly offers, at least in principle, tremendous emancipatory potential over a wide range of economic, political, and social issues. However, as capitalism began to globalize in the second half of the twentieth century, the emancipatory potential of generic globalization began to be systematically undermined (see Sklair 2009). While the impact of the electronic revolution and new forms of cosmopolitanism are discussed briefly below, the main focus in this paper is on iconic architecture in the context of postcolonialisms and transnational social spaces.

Iconic architecture I define in terms of the fame of a particular building or space, which can come about through a distinctive aesthetic and symbolic significance. Buildings and the architects who design them can achieve iconic status on a number of levels – locally, nationally, regionally, or globally (see Sklair 2005, 2006). Historically, iconic architecture tended to be driven by state and/or religious elites, while in the age of capitalist globalization (defined initially in terms of the electronic revolution), those in control of capitalist globalization – the transnational capitalist class – have become increasingly implicated in the production of iconic architecture, particularly with respect to their own narrow and specific class interests. As Vale argues in his study of power and identity embedded in the design of parliament buildings in the Third World in the second half of the twentieth century (often the realm of quixotic and grandiose gestures): 'grand symbolic state buildings need to be understood in terms of the political and cultural contexts that helped to bring them into being' (2008: 3). He goes on to demonstrate that, despite the stated aim of postcolonial state architecture to create a national identity, what really happens is a reinforcing of existing hierarchies. These existing hierarchies – led by (in my terms) the emerging state and corporate factions of the transnational capitalist class – become ever more connected with the multifarious world of capitalist globalization. As a result, iconic architecture – old and new – tends to become ever more consumerist. This is apparent in a city like Shanghai, where the city authorities, in an effort to show the city's global credentials, have been building the hardware of the global city – the skyscrapers, hotels, and office buildings – often at the expense of those who used to call the city home. The people who lived in the low-rise *lilong* have been shunted aside to make way for this new transnational capitalist class. The picture in Shanghai is further complicated by the existence of a 'floating population' of internal Chinese immigrants who have come in search of a better life but who find themselves trapped in what amount to ghettoes and are unable to benefit from the new wealth the city is generating (see Campanella 2008, Ren 2011). This is a topic that is examined by Ana Moya Pellitero in her chapter in this book.

Architecture operates hegemonically in terms of the four defining characteristics of generic globalization in the abstract, and capitalist globalization in the concrete, with significance for the study of postcolonialisms. First, there can be no doubt that the electronic revolution has transformed the practice as well as the reception of architecture in the era of capitalist globalization. A very clear statement of the former can be found in Tombesi's research (2001), where the overwhelming evidence of the creation of a new international division of labor in architecture is presented. While architects have always worked 'abroad', since the 1990s, digital technology has facilitated qualitatively new relationships between design offices in the First World and low-cost, local architectural labor occupying low-cost office space in the Third World, both in terms of the design process and the operation of architectural markets. In the US, the percentage of architecture firms transferring drawings electronically rose from 35 percent in 1996 to 83 percent in 1999 (ibid.: 173). Not only does digital technology make it possible to build previously unbuildable designs – the move from self-same to self-similar building components that computer-generated drafting has enabled has seen the proliferation of odd or even extravagantly shaped buildings, which is something that would not have been possible without the advances in computer-drafting technology. Designs can also be transmitted across the globe almost instantaneously, vastly speeding up the design and construction processes.

In a case study of how these developments have impacted Indian architecture, Tombesi et al. (2003) shows that this has benefitted the globalizing-commercial segments as opposed to the domestic-traditional segments of the industry. With the rise of consumerism and demand for luxury homes, office blocks, and five-star hotels, in the 1990s 'fully computerised new firms rose to industry leadership as exclusive purveyors in India of the latest in fashionable architectural imagery worldwide'.[4] Thus, as generic globalization opens up architectural and developmental possibilities, capitalist globalization provides the framework for the transnational capitalist class to exploit these in its own class interests in new markets.

Considering this book's focus on China, it might be instructive to take a look at the impact these new technologies are having on that country's cities, where we have seen unprecedented transformations at the city level as well as in the nature of architectural labor. The number of architects in China in the late 1990s was ten percent of that of the number in the US but, according to one estimate, they designed five times the volume of projects (in millions of square meters) while earning only one-tenth of the design fee per job. In Shenzhen's Special Economic Zone, extraordinary records have been set, such as five designers working for one night using two computers to produce the design for a 300-unit single-family housing development, and one architect working for seven days to produce a 30-storey concrete residential high-rise. Most of these high-rises are built off the shelf and are only distinguishable from one another by the distinctive 'hats' that top them or their facade variations, usually based on 'architectural recipes' and often lifted directly from foreign publications and domestic competition entries (Chung et al. 2001). This system remains highly dependent on foreign architectural firms, although government regulations require all foreign firms to work with domestic joint-venture partners on Chinese projects.

Where Shenzhen has led, the rest of China has followed, and over the last twenty years this model has transformed the skylines of many of the country's cities (see Cartier 2002, Campanella 2008, Ren 2011). New forms of cosmopolitanism can also be easily identified in the field of architecture in the person of globally iconic architects (also known, somewhat whimsically, as 'starchitects'). The majority of contemporary architectural icons in the Third World have been designed by starchitects, who usually come from the First World. Many of them are in demand to build spectacular buildings, often in an ill-advised attempt to put some city 'on the map'. This is particularly the case in China, but the Gulf States and some former Soviet Republics also seem to have a similar penchant for this type of iconic building, seeing it as some kind of magic wand that will ensure economic growth and cultural development.

Few are the architects from the Third World, even those who have produced iconic work, that have completed projects in the First World. There are many whose work is universally admired, for example Luis Barragan in Mexico, Oscar Niemeyer and Paolo Mendes da Rocha in Brazil, and the Baghdad-born Zaha Hadid – all winners of the Pritzker Prize, the architectural equivalent of the Nobel Prize. Other names include Carlos Villanueva from Venezuela, Charles Correa from India, Hassan Fathy from Egypt, and Ken Yeang from Malaysia, whose recently completed National Library in Singapore has raised his signature bioclimatic style to the level of an icon. It is an immensely popular building, despite having replaced an already popular predecessor (which was knocked down with typical Singaporean pragmatism to make way for a new road). The work of these architects is generally considered to be more 'local' (i.e. regional) than 'global' (modernist) – a contentious distinction to which I now turn.

Postcolonial understandings of architecture and transnational social spaces

My argument assumes that there has been a gradual shift in capitalist hegemony between the pre-global era (in my formulation, approximately up to the 1960s and the advent of the electronic revolution) and the era of capitalist globalization. In the pre-global era, capitalist hegemony legitimated itself using claims to cultural superiority by colonialists/imperialists, which produced a form of racist Orientalism. For architecture, this is expressed in many ways, for example in the idea of the tropical vernacular, the poorly and/or quaintly designed buildings that were built for the threatening tropical climate, as well as the bastardized classicism that sought to emulate the elegant Palladian buildings of colonial power and governance. In the present era of capitalist globalization, ideological hegemony is based more on the claims to cultural superiority of a transnational capitalist class, which has produced a form of consumerist postcolonialism that is expressed in terms of a hybridity that is being used as a marketing tool in architecture. As we shall see below, this hybridity favors particular materials and design forms, and it is also almost always used in the direction of capitalist consumerism. As Vale (2008: 60) observed in his study of postcolonial parliament buildings: 'part of the national identity of some developing countries has come to be defined according to the dictates and tastes of Western consumers'.

The literature on postcolonialisms and architecture since around the 1920s can be seen as the most important branch in one of the most fundamental debates in the history of architecture: namely the contrast between what can be called international modernism and architectural regionalism, although these are not the only terms in which it can be portrayed.[5] Briefly, international modernism refers to buildings characterized by thin curtain walls as opposed to the massive load-bearing walls which preceded them, regularity as opposed to symmetry, and the use of new materials such as glass, steel, and reinforced concrete (as opposed to stone and earth). There also tended to be very little decoration, if any. Despite the original radical intentions of most of its founders, international modernism resulted in the monotonous tower blocks and glass and steel skyscrapers that dominate the skylines of most cities on earth, usually executed, it has to be said, by less-skilled imitators than the talented generators of this style, notably Ludwig Mies van der Rohe or Le Corbusier.

Architectural regionalism, on the other hand, is based on the idea that the vernacular – namely buildings using local methods and materials for small-scale, site-specific projects – should be the guiding principle for architecture. The upper-class El Pedregal gated estate in Mexico City by Luis Barragan would be a good example of architectural regionalism that is 'a major revision of the International Style, an icon of Mexican cultural identity yet still intensely personal, poetic, and mysterious' (Eggener 1999: 179). It is interesting that this project was marketed in Mexico by making references to that other icon of architectural modernism, Frank Lloyd Wright's Fallingwater.

The history and theory of postcolonial understandings of architecture, before and after the end of formal colonial rule, revolve around these idealized tropes of international modernism and architectural regionalism, the dominant metaphor being the imposition of First World versions of international modernism on Third World communities, whose needs would perhaps be better served by versions of architectural regionalism. The reality is, unsurprisingly, somewhat different.

In the decades before and after the end of formal colonial rule in Africa and Asia, there is ample evidence to suggest that reactions to international modernism and architectural regionalism by indigenous and colonial architects in the actual and nominal colonies and in the imperial powers spanned a wide spectrum (see Crinson 2003). In Latin America, of course, formal colonial rule ended much earlier, in the first decades of the nineteenth century, but the same also holds true for architects there. In the first half of the twentieth century, many European architects, fleeing persecution in their homelands, took international modernism with them when they fled. The Russian emigré Gregori Warchavchik built the first modernist house in South America, the Casa Modernista (Sao Paulo, 1928), and the German Eric Mendelsohn, who arrived in Palestine in 1934, helped create the image of Tel Aviv as a modernist city. And, of course, two of the greatest architects of the period – Le Corbusier and Frank Lloyd Wright – both travelled outside of their home countries. Wright's influence mainly bore fruit in Mexico (as in Barragan's El Pedregal estate) and Japan, while Le Corbusier's work was even more widespread, with projects throughout Europe, North Africa, Latin America, and even, in the 1950s, as part of the team that developed Chandigarh, the capital of the Punjab in a newly independent India. (The irony of a Swiss-French architect building in the erstwhile British colony must have played no small factor in the Punjabi government's decision to hire him.) Those they have influenced are to be found all over the world; international modernist buildings with regional vernacular characteristics and/or regional vernacular buildings with international modernist characteristics were built everywhere.[6]

The importance of the postcolonial understanding of architecture is vital in any attempt to understand the background of what is going on in China's cities today, especially for the former treaty ports like Shanghai and Guangzhou. China is, of course, an even more interesting and complicated case in this regard because it was never actually colonized. All the Western powers ever managed to achieve was a series of toeholds along the Chinese coast and some penetration of the country's rivers. Treaty ports such as Shanghai, Fuzhou, and Guangzhou and a scattering of colonies like Hong Kong and Macau were expected to force open the rest of the country to international trade. The strategic importance of these cities can still be seen today in that this is where the massive wave of urbanization is heading – to cities like Shanghai, Hong Kong, and Guangzhou, the three cities examined in this book.

What is clear is that whether we see international modernist buildings with regional vernacular characteristics or regional vernacular buildings with international modernist characteristics, the identity of the architect still matters and, no less importantly, the identity of the architect (indeed any artist) is a social construct. This raises the key question of representation, an issue constructively problematized but not resolved by the subaltern studies project[7] – a project that has particular resonance for the architecture and postcolonialism debate. In a devastating critique of what he labels 'postcolonial celebrities', in particular those occupying comfortable university chairs in the First World,

Araeen argues that continuing Western cultural domination 'does not necessarily manifest in suppressing other cultures, or artistic forms of other cultures, but denying other cultures, or peoples from other cultures, their subject positions in modernism' (2002: 4). Those postcolonials who are used in an essentially Orientalist manner to represent the Other in architecture – Barragan for Mexicanness, Niemeyer for Brazilianness, Correa for Indianness, Fathy for Arabness, and so on – are denied their subject status in modernism as they are celebrated for their bogus regional exoticism. In a convincing critique of Critical Regionalism and its Western theorists, Eggener points out that: 'it is ironic that writers discussing the places where these [regionalist] designs appeared so often emphasized one architect's interpretation of the region over all others: Tadao Ando for Japan, Oscar Niemeyer for Brazil, Charles Correa for India, Luis Barragon for Mexico. In other words, a single correct regional style was implied or imposed, sometimes from inside, more often from outside' (2007: 399). Prakash speaks of 'Identity Production in Postcolonial Indian Architecture: Re-Covering What We Never Had':

> When one talks of an Indian architect, or of an architect from the 'non-Western' world, it seems necessary to deal with the question of identity. While discussing Western architects one can get away with dealing with supposedly universal architectural issues like aesthetics and technology, but it seems necessary that in discussing the work of an architect from India the issue of identity be specifically raised in addition to, or in dialogue with, issues more directly aesthetic or architectural. Architects of the West do not specifically make Western buildings. Architects of the non-West are expected to. Even architects of the West working in the non-West in one way or another find themselves obliged to deal with the issue of non-Western identity.[8]

Brazil, which is often considered the first country to create a national style of modernist architecture, appears to be something of a special case – though in Turkey (Bozdogan 2001) and Indonesia (Kusno 2000), there were also strong early state-sponsored modernist movements that came into creative contact with traditional regionalist forces. However, only in Brazil was a whole new national capital city built along modernist lines (though Canberra is a partial exception). The story of Brasilia revolves around President Kubitschek, who provided the political will, and the eminent Brazilian architects Lúcio Costa (actually born in France), who created the master plan, and the communist Oscar Niemeyer, who designed most of the buildings, as well as Le Corbusier and the Soviet Constructivists, who provided the inspiration.

The president promoted Brasilia, located deep in the interior of this vast country, as a motor of regional economic development, as a hub of a new communications revolution for national integration. He wanted the architects to create a material embodiment of the blueprint for the socialist utopia. In the middle of the twentieth century, Brasilia's planners were calling it 'the capital of the twenty-first century',[9] a much sought-after title, and one that Shanghai has set its sights on in recent decades. As Holston convincingly argues, the intentions of each of these parties were not always realized. The architectural context in which all this was taking place was a vibrant modernist movement that began in the 1940s and which took the so-called 'Brazilian Style' to international prominence, thanks to a wildly successful exhibition and book under the same title – 'Brazil Built' – at the Museum of Modern Art in New York in 1943. Deckker (2001), in her definitive history of the movement, shows that the 'Brazilian Style' had as much political as aesthetic significance, being seen by some in Brazil as a symbol of American imperialism but by others as Brazil's true path to modernization and development. Holton, in his book on Brasilia, expresses this in the following terms: 'an architectural sign [the appearance of a building, for example] may remain constant while its denoted meanings shift dramatically with changes in use, context, and intention' (1989: 97; see also Vale 2008: 137-44).

Figure 2.1 *Niemeyer's Congress buildings in Brasilia: a site of multiple meanings*

Photo: Leslie Sklair

The main lessons of this case for the postcolonial understandings of architecture and urban planning are firstly, that the end results of such a project (and probably even single buildings) are highly unpredictable over time with respect to aesthetics, politics, use, and reception; and secondly, that the categories of international modernism and architectural regionalism often pose as many questions as they answer.

There is (sometimes literally) a concrete representation of generic globalization to be found in the creation of what has been termed transnational social spaces – notably skyscrapers, globally branded shopping malls, theme parks, waterfront developments, and transportation nodes – spaces that, despite their regional characteristics, could be almost anywhere in the world (see, for example, Abaza 2001, Marshall 2003, King 2004). This is something that is examined in Jonathan D. Solomon's chapter in this book. These articulations of transnational social spaces are routinely referred to as the 'icons of modernity' and, as we have seen, the ways in which dominant classes in postcolonial societies appropriate symbols of modernity (and tradition) is fundamental to understanding the role of architecture in class society. A study of how the Chinese state enters the global market through the heritage industry describes how preservation is presented locally by the example of the clean new Shanghai Museum on Renmin Square which until recently found itself surrounded by dirty streets. As Abbas points out: 'suddenly you realize that the museum does not think of itself as being part of a local space at all, but as a part of a virtual global cultural network' (2000: 782) – and as a result excluding, we might add, the subaltern local Other (see also Arkaraprasertkul 2008). Ren (2011: chapter 4) usefully discusses this in terms of the Chinese words *Chai* (demolition) and *Bao* (preservation). This exclusion is not uncommon, as Edensor (1998: chapter 5) shows for the Taj Mahal and Wharton (2001: chapter 4) for the 'forceful Modernity' of the Hilton Hotel in Tel Aviv which diverts attention from the Arab slums to the east, as its prime site looks out to the west and the sea.

Abbas argues that it is not in transnational states but in re-imagined cities that we find transnational social spaces (and this is happening all over the world). In the late 1990s, 13 of the 30 largest architect-developer firms working in Asia were based in the US, Australia, or the UK. 'This leads inevitably to a collection of architectural projects that are remarkably the same in cities such as Tokyo, Shanghai, Singapore and Jakarta' (Marshall 2003: 2). However, all of these megaprojects will have partners on the ground – not just architects but also engineers, real estate agents, bankers, lawyers, and support staff – out of which new local affiliates of the transnational capitalist class will emerge as part of transnational urban growth coalitions. Kuala Lumpur, and what has been dubbed Malaysia's Multimedia Super Corridor, provides a potent example. The Multimedia Super Corridor (with no less a figure than Bill Gates on its International Advisory Panel) is an extension of Kuala Lumpur, spanning the Petronas Towers, formerly the world's tallest buildings, Cyberjaya, the world's first fully smart city, and Putrajaya, the first multimedia paperless seat of government, all the way to Kuala Lumpur International Airport, the biggest airport in the region. This 'carefully articulated "hybrid" Multimedia Super Corridor landscape ... embraces not only the economic magnetism of modern global-city architecture but also the repackaged symbolisms of tradition and culture that reifies the national integrity of the country', complete with the strategic placement of new mosques (Boey 2002: 207).

While this immense project has stalled somewhat in recent years, the rhetoric and some spectacular architecture remain. Nevertheless, the iconic buildings of the Multimedia Super Corridor obscure the lives and living conditions of the poor (see Bunnell 2004), frequently hidden from the tourist gaze, as in the case of Shanghai and Tel Aviv. Kusno (2000) forcefully makes the same point for Jakarta, and indeed this appears to be true for most if not all globalizing cities, and not just those in the Third World – it is a condition of existence of transnational social spaces from above. On the surface, this appears to turn the earlier critique of capitalism – private affluence and public squalor – on its head. Through the culture-ideology of consumerism, which seems to promise the fruits of capitalist globalization to all (fortified by platitudes like 'the rising tide lifts all boats'), transnational social spaces from above create apparent public affluence through iconic architecture. This is achieved through an appropriation of modernist iconicity with regionalist characteristics that prevailing postcolonial modes of representation translate into a language that sits comfortably with the culture-ideology of consumerism inherent in capitalist globalization.

Three main audiences are targeted by those who run such globalizing cities. First and most directly, these spaces and buildings seek to attract the national and international tourist trade, an important component of which is business tourism (trade shows, conferences, sports events, etc.), which we see highlighted in Jacob Dreyer's chapter as well as Xiangmin Guo and Changtao Liu's chapter. The second audience is the local urban upper-middle class, whose numbers have increased rapidly over the last few decades in most cities. And the third, and only indirectly, is the local working class who are encouraged to participate by looking at and taking occasional outings in their new, gleaming city centers, public buildings, and suburban shopping malls, all of which are promoted as sources of civic and national pride, even in the poorest countries (see Abaza 2001, Ren 2011).

The construction of the Petronas Towers in Kuala Lumpur is a case in point. Malaysia is a 'moderate' Islamic state and provides a good, if convoluted, example of how such issues are typically addressed under conditions of capitalist globalization. The architect, Cesar Pelli, was born in Argentina in 1926 and moved to the United States in 1964. Pelli had attracted international attention with his World Financial Center in Battery Park, New York (1981) and in Canary Wharf in London (1986), so it was no great surprise when he won the international competition for the Petronas Towers in 1991. The project was the centerpiece of then President Mahathir's Wawasan 2020 (which

Figure 2.2 *Petronas Towers, Kuala Lumpur*

Photo: Gregory Bracken

translates as 'Vision 2020') and was based on two 88-storey towers that were 451.9 meters high, with a skybridge between them on the 41st and 42nd floors. Petronas Towers is owned and largely tenanted by the consortium led by Petronas, the state petroleum company, as part of the Kuala Lumpur City Center masterplan. The architect reported that: 'It was never specified that the towers should become the tallest buildings in the world, just that they be beautiful' (Pelli et al. 1997: 66), though the fact that the tallest building in the world would be located (for a short time at least) in Kuala Lumpur was certainly appealing to the Malaysian client.[10] Pelli & Associates won, apparently, not only because their 'proposal met the desire for a uniquely Malaysian design' (ibid.: 66) but because meeting this desire also solved a problem in international modernist skyscraper design. In Pelli's own words: 'Linking the Petronas Towers to Kuala Lumpur and Malaysia required rethinking the character of the traditional skyscraper to unburden it of American or European connotations. ... [the] shape of the towers has its origin in Islamic tradition, in which geometric patterns assume greater symbolic importance than in Western culture' (ibid.: 68).

Where, then, does this 'uniquely Malaysian design' come from? At one level, as noted above, it comes from the Islamic geometry of the floor plan, but at another, deeper level it comes from the break with modernist tradition embodied in the symmetrical arrangement of the towers and what this means for the space between them. Pelli explains: 'Through Frank Lloyd Wright, many architects have been influenced by Lao Tzu's teaching that the reality of a hollow object is in the void and not the walls that define it ... This quality of the building is not derived from Malaysian tradition. But because it appears for the first time in Kuala Lumpur, it will be forever identified with its place' (ibid.: 70). Just as the Eiffel Tower, whose structure and form were not French in origin, became synonymous with Paris, Petronas Towers will become synonymous with Kuala Lumpur, as indeed it has. This is clearly a rationale that is open to many types and layers of interpretation. Suffice it to say here that, at one level and for some professionals and ideologues, it painlessly reconciles international modernism and architectural regionalism in a conciliatory postcolonial direction. It is also worth noting that the ground floor of the Petronas Towers complex has become one of the most iconic shopping malls in Asia and that, as Pelli had predicted, it has become a first-class marketing symbol for Kuala Lumpur and for the country of Malaysia as a whole, despite its purported 'break with modernism'.

Perhaps the most extraordinary example of this phenomenon is taking place in Shanghai under the banner of the 'One City, Nine Towns' plan. To provide appropriate accommodation for its newly prosperous upper middle class and expatriates, numbering around half a million, the Urban Planning Institute in Shanghai has begun to create a series of satellite communities,

> each inspired by a country that played a pivotal role in the colonial and commercial history of the city ... China is slowly coming to terms with its semi-colonial past and has been inviting foreign investment back into Shanghai. Now, a scheme is underway to mark the impact of colonialism – not in the city centre but out in the suburbs.[11]

As of the summer of 2009, this vast project envisages a Dutch town in Gaoqiao which has gabled canal houses, windmills, and drawbridges as well as facsimiles of well-known Dutch landmarks such as the Scheepvaartmuseum (which contains a Chinese restaurant) and Drakensteyn (which overlooks the marina). A British-themed Thames Town has been completed in the city of Songjiang (the one city of the 'One City, Nine Towns' plan), this is replete with Tudor, Georgian, and Victorian-style buildings, as well as a gothic church, which acts as the backdrop for photographs taken by newlyweds. There are plans to attract a Scottish whiskey retailer as well as shops selling English Premier League souvenirs, both of which are hugely popular in Asia.

The other towns in this ambitious plan include Anting, which has a German theme and was designed by Albert Speer (the son of Hitler's architect). Anting also has another German connection in that it is home to a Volkswagen plant (while the motoring theme is carried still further by the fact that the town is also home to Shanghai's new Formula 1 race track). The plan also includes two Euro-American towns in Buzhen and Zhoupu, a Spanish town in Fengcheng, and a Canadian one in Fengjing. Luodian is Nordic, while Pujiang is Italian. And lastly, there is Zhujiajiao, the only town to have a style based on a native Chinese model: the water town. However ridiculous all of these may seem, in comparison with the haphazard high-rise development of Pudong in Shanghai, some Chinese architects have tended to take a more benign view of the 'One City, Nine Towns' plan.[12]

Not all transnational social spaces have been created anew in the era of capitalist globalization. Indeed, one of the most prominent types of transnational social space is the postcolonial rebranding of ancient monuments as prime tourist and consumerist sites (Vale 1999). Tourism at ancient monuments has of course existed for centuries, significantly boosted by the invention of photography in 1839, and has accelerated spectacularly since the growth of the Internet. The Taj Mahal is a paradigm example. As Pal (1989: 194) demonstrates: 'The best-known symbol of Indian civilization is essentially a creation of Western enthusiasm', though its contemporary significance for internal tourism in India is also growing rapidly. This and the consumerist significance of the Taj, as well as the prime importance of agents' commissions in the local tourist economy, is brought out by Edensor's ethnographic study showing that tourist paths around the Taj focused on 'realizing anticipated consumption ... the next stop is invariably a craft emporium' (1998: 109). It comes as little surprise to learn that the Indian Department of Tourism called in the US National Parks Service for help with its development plans for the site in the 1990s.

Let me bring this necessarily incomplete discussion to a close with reference to one of the most successfully iconic transnational social spaces of the global age in the eyes of the public and urban boosters (events which give a city's urban ambitions an edge), if not architects: namely the Disneyland phenomenon. Feierstein (in *H&W*) tells the fascinating story of the Peronist building projects in Argentina (1945-55). Evita's unique contribution was República de los Ninõs, a city scaled to the height of ten-year olds, with copies of the British Houses of Parliament, a gothic Palace of Justice, a Venetian Ducal Palace-style bank, and a Palace of Culture (whose exterior was modelled on the Taj Mahal and interior on the Alhambra). It has had a chequered history. After the Peronista period it gradually decayed, and it was only in 2001 (the 50th anniversary of the death of Evita) that its commercial and ideological potential was realized and renovations began to rebrand it as a tourist attraction in Buenos Aires. Legend has it – and current websites tell us – that it inspired Walt Disney! The first Disneyland opened in California in 1955.

In 1966, a military coup brought General Suharto to power in Indonesia, proclaiming a New Order for the nation. The general's most famous architectural expression became the Beautiful Indonesia in Miniature Park (known as Mini) which opened outside Jakarta in 1980 (Kusno 2000: 74-79). Apparently, Mrs Suharto was inspired by a visit to Disneyland and took it upon herself to create this more complete and more perfect version of it in Indonesia. The centerpiece of Mini was a large lake with islands to represent the whole country, surrounded by replicas of ancient monuments and religious buildings, a 1,000-room hotel, and, of course, shopping malls. Each of Indonesia's twenty-six provinces was represented by displays of 'genuine customary architectural styles'. For example, Borobudur, the most famous ancient monument in Indonesia, is according to the locals best seen at Mini rather than at the actual confusing and inconvenient ruins (Pemberton 1994). 'What has been crucial in this process are the replica of tradition and not the tradition itself' (Kusno 2000: 79). This is true for all three cases – in Buenos Aires, Jakarta, and actual Disneylands – and for many more, for example, the modernization of traditional neighborhoods in Shanghai and Beijing (Ren 2011). In the era of capitalist globalization, the transnational capitalist class, led either by corporations or by the globalizing state faction (and usually both), appropriates existing iconic monuments or builds new ones in the interests of the culture-ideology of consumerism.

Postcolonial understandings of iconic architecture help to explain why the struggle between modernism and traditional culture is almost always resolved in the interests of capitalist consumerism. Nevertheless, the incisive comment by the Chinese artist Zhang Huan on the hybrid Jin Mao Tower in Shanghai, built by the US architects Skidmore, Owings, and Merrill in the 1990s, suggests that there are many challenges to the friendly relationships between iconic architecture and postcolonialisms still to come.

I have discussed here only the transnational social spaces as seen from above, and usually imposed with little genuine democratic process.

Figure 2.3 *Jin Mao Tower, Shanghai*

Photo: Gregory Bracken

Figure 2.4 *Zhang Huan, Donkey (2005), Saatchi Gallery London Exhibition 2008*

'Farm animal humping the famous Jin Mao tower ... Zhang's icon of modernization gets a literal ... shafting from the beast of burden "proletariat" ' (from the exhibition website)

Photo: Leslie Sklair

Transnational social spaces seen from below are also important, such as those that migrant communities create in globalizing cities (for example the Filipino community's meeting places around Statue Square in Hong Kong – something that is examined in Jonathan D. Solomon's chapter – and which can be found in some Chinatowns as well), not to mention the virtual communities of migrants all over the world. Alas, they fall outside the scope of this all-too-brief paper.

Notes

1 This chapter is a revised version of a chapter due to appear in O.P. Dwivedi and M. Kich, eds. *Postcolonial Literature in the 21st Century* (Youngstown NY, forthcoming).
2 For further discussion of this point see the scholarly, albeit inconclusive, analysis in King (2004, especially chapter 3).
3 See, for example, the varied contributions to Nalbantoğlu & Wong, eds. (1997).
4 Tombesi et al. 'Routine production or symbolic analysis? India and the globalization of architectural services', *Journal of Architecture* 8: 83. And not just in India. See also, among many others, the case of the World Trade Center in Cairo, constructed by the wealthy Sawiras family: 'a success story, symbolizing the triumph of the new class of tycoons in Egypt' (Abaza 2001: 111).
5 See, for example, two wide-ranging collections: G.B. Nalbantoğlu and C.T. Wong, eds. *Postcolonial Space(s)* (New York: Princeton Architectural Press, 1997) and P. Herrie and E. Wegerhoff, eds. *Architecture and Identity* (Berlin: Lit Velag and Habitat-International, 2008), hereafter cited as *N&W* and *H&W*.
6 For Mozambique, see Sidaway & Power 1995; for Ghana, see *N&W*; for Uganda, see Olweny & Wadulo in *H&W*; for Turkey, see Nalbantoğlu in *N&W* and Bozdogan 2001;

for Israel, see Levin 1991 and Weizman 2007; for Argentina, see Feierstein in *H&W*; for Brazil, see Holston 1989, Deckker 2001, and Philippou and Lehmann, both in *H&W*; for Mexico, see Eggener 1999 and Herzog 1999; for Latin America in general, see Fraser 2000; for China, see Chung et al. 2001, Rowe & Kuan 2002, Broudehoux 2002, Lu & Li in *H&W*, Campanella 2008, and Ren 2011; for India, see Prakash in *N&W* and Tombesi et al. 2003; and Kalia 2006; for Indonesia, see Cairns in *N&W* and Kusno 2000; for Australia, see Lovanovska in *N&W* and Baker in *H&W*.

7 Citing literature for this is fraught with difficulty. The overview that I have found most useful is Currie (1996, chapter 5).

8 Prakash in *N&W*, p. 39; see also Kalia 2006 and Ren 2011. The latter has some interesting ideas on this issue in relation to China.

9 Cited in Holston 1989 (p. 85); see also Vale 2008 (chapter 4) and Fraser 2000 (chapter 3).

10 See King (2004: chapter 1).

11 From the website of Gregotti Associati, who won the contract to design Pujiang, the Italian town. However, the chief architect, Augusto Cagnardi, claims to have identified the same model in ancient Chinese cities.

12 See Bracken 2010, Lu & Li in *H&W*, Arkaraprasertkul 2008, and Campanella 2008.

3 Shanghai and the 2010 Expo

Staging the City

Jacob Dreyer

Abstract
A city is much more than buildings – it is a way of social relations, a way of understanding the world, a language, a rich bank of memories and images. Shanghai's authorities, in changing the buildings, are seeking to control the latter categories, shaping the personality of the city as it heads towards 'global city' ambitions. What, then, is the direction that it is going towards? What is the vision for the future of Shanghai, not in terms of buildings but in terms of the soul of the city? Is the city the product of our mutually imagined image of it? Rem Koolhaas wrote of Manhattan that it was 'delirious', wild with organic growth. Shanghai's growth in contrast is deliberate, purposeful, intentional, entirely planned. This chapter will explore issues in Shanghai's urbanism, addressing why architecture is the language in which the contemporary spirit of the city expresses itself best, how the city has tried to 'brand' itself, the conditions that have been made possible by the post-1984 economic situation. It will also address at length the World Expo, which took place in 2010. I will argue that downtown Shanghai is being crafted into a symbol of just how modern China is – and it is, there's some substance there – but the degree to which it is a managed image, with clear utility to the state of making it seem that way, is my subject. The narrative of the Expo seems to be precisely that redemption, or a 'better life', will come through infrastructural and economic change and the greater access to technology that it will provide, and not through political change (which at best is acknowledged as an unfortunate side effect). However, as writer Wang Anyi notes, 'There is something to be said for illusions. Though lacking substance, illusions can serve as the basis on which more substantive structures can be built'. In spite of the obsessive attempts on the part of the state to manage Shanghai's growth, the city remains a zone of explosive potentialities, and an exploration of the liberatory potential inherent in the urban form now emerging will conclude my discussion.

Introduction

Shanghai, 2010: large swathes of the city have been transformed for the International Expo. For the past 20 years, Shanghai's authorities have been altering the cityscape with ambitious infrastructure projects and showy buildings seeking to enhance the city's status both abroad and domestically. Simultaneously, the vast economic and cultural changes taking place in China, led by the vanguard city of Shanghai,[1] seem to be altering the nature of the social contract itself and the ways in which urban space is inhabited. The Expo is the latest incarnation of this process. It has not only entailed construction of a contemporary architecture theme park but also invaded the discourse of daily life in the city through omnipresent advertising and various changes vaguely described as "preparing for the Expo" that range from slum clearance to infrastructure construction to language education and a greater attention to petty crimes. The slogan of the Expo – 城市让生活更美好 or "Better City, Better Life" – seems to highlight the ways in which urban planning has been linked to the utopian nature of the landscape emerging in China. The municipal authorities in charge of the Expo are quite frank that they see their city as the essential terrain of the future and that they consider local developments to be of cardinal importance. Their website proclaims: 'The theme of the Exposition 2010 Shanghai is "Better City, Better Life"[2] The topic has its origin in the thousands of years of human civilization.' The Expo is both a symbol and the centerpiece of a narrative of localized urban progress. The discourse of universality used by the Expo would perhaps only be possible in Shanghai; other Chinese cities don't have the total commitment to the outside world that Shanghai has. Within the paradigm of the Expo, this discourse is actively being constructed. The stones of this edifice have been recuperated from the ruins of the cosmopolitan Shanghai of the 1930s via nostalgia; a memory of the city's past greatness pervades contemporary image-making. This base is fragile, though, for the history is problematic. Moreover, Shanghai is arguably more dynamic, cosmopolitan, and central to the global discourse than ever before, surpassing its former greatness even as it lives in the shadow thereof. The Expo fuses this legacy with a contemporaneity so fresh that it almost seems to be the future rather than the present. Pavilions to sustainability, urbanization, and the other banalities of the early 21st century abound, but in practice, there is no space for these solutions in Shanghai's present. The Expo is by definition unsustainable, as it will be largely dismantled after it is complete. The incredibly grandiose vision of the Expo reflects Shanghai's self-image as an upwardly mobile global city; the reality of it, while encouraging, helps us to identify the weak points in this discourse. The Expo is a lens through which we can understand developments in contemporary Shanghai more broadly.

Shanghai emerged from the crucible of colonial development, a paradigm that has renamed itself globalization today (the same handful of cities – London, New York, Paris, etc. – remain central to this process). The melange of different cultures under the sign of economic utility was the environment of the Shanghai that incubated Chinese modernity. The cosmopolitan environment of 1920s Shanghai – which was much more ethnically diverse than contemporary London or Paris – and the space of innovative Western technologies and lifestyles proved liberating for some, such as writer Lu Xun, who based himself there. The same environment motivated others such as the communist party, founded in a Shanghai alleyway in 1921, to find a new kind of liberation. Shanghai's colonial past is the dominant vernacular of the city center. Shanghai's past is today, as it was at the time, simultaneously liberating and horrifying, and the architectural relics it left behind have been better preserved than those in any other Chinese city: if in other cities the dynamic is straightforwardly modern versus ancient, Shanghai has already seen a utopian modernity emerge, only to fail. Perhaps ironically, this bittersweet legacy has been preserved, especially the spaces most marked by melancholy, such as the Jewish ghetto of Hongkou district, certain great mansions of the French Concession, and the buildings of the Bund. The colonial legacy extends beyond the built environment, as Shanghai today cultivates links with the outside world that echo its past glory. If most of China is 'new' today, Shanghai is better described as experiencing a renaissance, and the relations with capital and foreigners that were once a source of status and angst at the same time have re-emerged along similar lines. Shanghai cannot claim political centrality, and its claim to be China's first city is based on the openness to the outside world that is a remnant of colonialism. The dynamic created by colonialism remains a source of tension, creative and otherwise, in today's post-colonial Shanghai.

Shanghai has always been a central symbolic space within China;[3] if Beijing has long been identified as the space of tradition and the symbolic center of China, Shanghai has always been the symbolic outlier of China, a space fundamentally out of step with the rest of the country because it is ahead of it. To use Anne Querrien's terms, Shanghai "offers its own mode of space-time to those for whom the principles of a sovereign people and a nation state do not apply."[4] Though some have characterized the city as 'Westernizing', this doesn't quite make sense, as the changes taking place adopt neither the logic nor the form of any major Western city. It would be more sensible to say that, without necessarily coming closer to a Western model, Shanghai is escaping the confines of the Chinese model of urbanism, and in the process of doing so transforming that model – it is the avant-garde space of 'first tier' whose achievements are scrutinized with astonishment by planners in second- and third-tier cities. The authorities would like to control private space, but in practice have greater power over public space. Using mega-events like the recent Beijing Olympics or the Shanghai Expo, though, this distinction becomes blurred, as a communal effort is needed to secure the superficial benefits of the spectacularized event, while the infrastructural and legal legacy continues indefinitely.[5] The difference between the two events attests to the strengths and characters of the two different spaces: while the Olympics brought all of the massive power of the state to bear, the Expo found funds from a consortium of national and local authorities as well as corporate sponsors and even foreign governments. Shanghai's networks are its strength, even as Beijing's centralizing tendencies, apparently an opposite approach, served a similar objective in 2008.

In contemporary China, the most forceful language that the government can speak is the language of controlling urban space itself, and the space of Shanghai is itself symbolic of the future of China. Reshaping central Shanghai can be thus read as an attempt to reshape the imagined future, a self-conscious effort which touches upon sustainability, urbanization, diversity, etc.[6] The language of the Expo's buildings, though it is equally a language spoken by power to justify itself, is compelling, and seeks to appropriate the cultural space of optimism about the future for the state. Though the main audience for Shanghai's Expo is composed of the anticipated 70 million visitors, 95% of whom will be Chinese,[7] it has also been a display to the world of the opulence of a city that is striving towards becoming the capital city of a reality it has yet to define. This metropolis will not become the capital city of a place but rather of an epoch – as Paris in the nineteenth century – defining its time by reshaping it.[8] The Expo is both symbolic of and central to this process; in literally seeking to frame Shanghai as the urban space of the future, substantial revision of the past and present might be necessary. The economic function of this project is potentially long term. Shanghai has long pursued the strategy of creating a visible set of monuments that anticipate economic prosperity rather than inspiring it, as in Rem Koolhaas's narration of Manhattan.[9] In Shanghai, the skyline was constructed before the economic base that is normally reflected by a skyline came into existence – a testament to the unique role of the state in Chinese society, which has wished into existence a new economy while remaining in control of it in a way that differentiates it from Western capitalisms. Though Shanghai's size and economic significance is unmistakable, its role in a China full of enormous cities isn't purely functional; Wasserstrom describes its role as being 'as much symbol as physical city'.[10] In a country so vast that many cities seem to be merely warehouses for their huge numbers of inhabitants, Shanghai is a symbolic space, recuperating the legacy of its colonial history to stake a claim to be not China's capital but rather its definitive metropolis, the urban space that defines itself as 'city' and everywhere else as suburb.

A city is much more than buildings – it is a way of social relations, a way of understanding the world, a language, a rich bank of memories and images. As Lefebvre puts it, 'a space is not a thing but rather a set of relations among things.'[11] However, cities are often read or understood based on their spatial manifestations; architecture becomes the language of the contemporary because it is much more malleable to change. It somehow expresses more clearly the realities of power in the contemporary city; space 'socially appears as the intangible outcome of history, society, and culture, all of which are supposedly combined within it.'[12] Some cities build iconic buildings as civic symbols. For Leslie Sklair, 'iconicity in architecture is a resource in struggles for meaning and, by implication, power.'[13] Shanghai has built so many of these that a previously irrelevant zone, Pudong, to the east of the old center, has become a museum of them: these buildings are beautiful objects more meant for display than utility, and many remain vacant or useless in practical terms.[14] In the visual culture of the city, Lujiazui CBD seems to be the focal point of the city. However, it is less so in reality than in representation. After all, skylines are invisible to those who walk among them, and therefore are best placed on the other side of the river from the main life of the city, where they can be appreciated as a stunning view – views are meant to be viewed, not inhabited.[15]

Shanghai's authorities, with their frequent interventions, seem to be trying to assert control over the vast and relatively unregulated space of the city. The symbols that power has been scrambling to erect to itself have ramifications domestically as well as internationally; these buildings create an image of power and stability that is read differently by potential citizens and potential investors.[16] As the art historian Hubert Damisch suggests, 'in today's China, architecture functions as one of the most visible instruments ... of "modernization", ostensibly proving to the world and the Chinese masses that the Chinese can be "modern", that they know how to build and maintain very tall buildings.'[17] The message is more sophisticated than this, but it hints at the fact that, in contrast to a 'delirious' Manhattan, Shanghai has been constructed deliberately, centrally, with cool reason and extensive rationales, and without a clear or direct economic utility. What is the purpose of this construction?

'The Shanghai economic zone is the biggest subnational planning entity in the world, encompassing the metropolis and 5 adjoining provinces with an aggregate population almost as large as that of the US'.[18]

Greater Shanghai takes as its point of departure April 1990, the date that the Pudong Special Economic Zone was established, since which time Shanghai has been able to reassert its cosmopolitan identity. In this city, the normal markers of an urban identity are in flux. The structure of the city on a basic level has changed altogether, as questions such as 'Is there a subway system?', 'Where is the business district?', and 'What is the housing stock like?' have been given different answers. The language spoken on the streets has changed as well: the Shanghainese dialect is ever more marginal, supplanted by Mandarin, English, and the languages of the businessmen from all over the world who have transplanted themselves here. Even the ethnic composition has changed: many foreigners have immigrated here for work, but even more socially dramatic has been the influx of peasants from the countryside looking for work. Shanghai's changes, though, aren't equivalent to the ones in Western cities. Shanghai isn't being gentrified, it is itself gentrifying people – a factory that invites in these countryside people and rapidly transforms them into *wenming*,[19] or civilized/Westernized urbanites.[20] Or, as Eileen Chang puts it, 'the people of Shanghai have been distilled out of Chinese tradition by the pressures of modern life'.[21] These changes aren't taking place at random, though; as Kirby recently observed, 'In China ... the government is responsible at the end of the day for almost everything'.[22] The radical changes that ordinary people in China are going through may seem chaotic to them and in fact to those who unleashed them, but are in fact part of a highly ambitious plan to completely change the urban fabric, and in so doing, the fabric of everyday life itself. 'When the economic limits were taken off 30 years ago, did anybody imagine that there would be hundred-storey buildings in Shanghai and subway lines and cars everywhere? The process feels almost experimental,'[23] posited a moderator of a recent debate about these changes. An experiment, to be sure; in fact, for some who know the city, its very existence seems like one of the most inspiring experiments of the contemporary era. However, waiting in the background are those who, despite having set this experiment into motion, may conclude that, after all, every petri dish must be disinfected at some point.

The Shanghai Urban Planning Museum is surely one of the most eloquent testaments to the existence of the 'Better City, Better Life' narrative long before the Expo. It opened in 2000, two years before the Expo was announced. In this museum, the city itself is on display; the entire zone of the city limits is displayed in miniature in an auditorium lit by floodlights. The visitor may note the contrast between the muggy clamor of People's Park and the tranquil, unproblematic city on display; in fact, what is on display is not the actual city but rather its ideal form. An exhibit of the city in 2020 is also on display, a gesture only possible in a city where the future is seen as entirely malleable and subject to manipulation and quality control, entirely a 'product', to echo Lefebvre. The transformation of the city into a symbol enshrined in a museum can only be thought of as a canny attempt at branding. 'Branding is all about boiling down perceptions to their essentials. Nobody is more self-conscious than the brand stewards themselves about the artificiality of brand construction. A brand is no different from any other discursive construct ... to rise above the information clutter, a brand's DNA is crystallized into a few pithy campaign concepts.'[24] In Shanghai, these concepts are: futuristic skyline; enormous highways lit by neon; and now, the Expo. The production of space in the most literal and self-aware sense has a long history in China; a recent book about architectural innovation in contemporary Beijing tells us:

> In 1414 [Emperor] Yongle ... [travelled to Beijing] accompanied by a group of artists, poets, and painters, who were given the task of executing a series of views, accompanied by poetic descriptions. The 8 Views had no realistic intentions. Instead, the politically intelligent and careful objective was to compose an artificial image of the places that would legitimize Beijing as capital. Even the names of the views made no references to anything that is urban, or barren, or under construction, nothing at all recalling the dusty reality of the Beijing of that time.[25]

For most residents of Shanghai, these new buildings have no more presence in their daily lives than the luscious gardens of the 8 Views commissioned by Yongle did for the Beijingers of the time; nor are they any more accurate as samples of typical urban scenes. However, in a city where any building is liable to be torn down and replaced with a new one, the buildings that represent the future are somehow more telling than those that are presently undergoing demolition. These buildings are compelling if only because they symbolize the desires of a power strong enough to alter the cityscape at will; if they ostensibly symbolize government ministries or banks, they actually represent a violent, dominating force (a distinction that might seem semantic to those whose homes have been demolished by those same governmental and financial warlords). 'The element of repression in [the monument] and the element of exaltation could scarcely be disentangled; or perhaps it would be more accurate to say that the repressive element was metamorphosized into exaltation ... it replaces a brutal reality with a materially realized appearance,'[26] Lefebvre writes, in what could be a potently accurate summary of the situation in Shanghai.

In the Chinese political landscape that has emerged since 1989, the state has cynically claimed credit for the new prosperity and futuristic cities in order to postpone and foreclose upon political change. Opposition is dismissed less as unjustified and more as irrelevant in a cityscape changing so rapidly, as both domestic and foreign observers have suggested that democratic consensus-building is simply too slow and cumbersome to navigate such rapid changes.[27] Subtly posed in this formulation is another proposition, replacing politics as the sphere of potential social change by technology and the future, with their implicitly redemptive qualities. The debate about changing the urban fabric somehow aligns state power with civilized values/the future, and resistance to state power with peasantry/lack of education/malignant traditional values, exemplified by the burgeoning use of the term *wenming*. The narrative of the last 15 years and the Expo in particular seems precisely to be that liberation will come through economic change and the greater access to technology that it will provide, and not through political change, which at best is acknowledged as an unfortunate side effect. The Shanghai Expo authorities tell us that 'Our motto is: "Keeping in mind the next 60 years' development while preparing for the six months' Exposition,"'[28] as if the Expo (and of course, the modernity that would sprinkle into each resident's heart with it) will somehow transform the very texture of daily life in a magical way. Can we really take this modernity – which has clearly resulted in real changes to the lives of average citizens in stark, material terms – at face value?

城市让生活更美好 is the omnipresent slogan of the expo – seen on TV, on the subway, on billboards in the street, and near the statues of the blue mascot Haibao distributed all around Shanghai and the Sinosphere. The official English translation is 'better city, better life'; in Chinese, the phrase is literally: 'city, then life, becomes better'. The changes of the city are first labelled as improvements in themselves, and then we are told that they will actually make our lives more magical or better. In the space of Shanghai – long notorious among locals and foreigners as a space of intrigue, chaos, dazzling wealth, and abysmal slums – an antiseptic new hero has been seen presenting this slogan to the people, explicitly seeking to stay on message about Shanghai's 'real' character all the while. 'The blue colour represents many elements – such as the ocean, the future and technology – which are consistent with characteristics of the host city.'[29] This figure, selected in a competition that many locals insist must have been rigged, crystallizes the tediousness that Shanghai authorities seek to cultivate in escaping the seedy legacy which is in fact the city's greatest asset. Baudelaire felt that the creation of a cliché was the greatest objective of an artist,[30] and all those who are bored and not shocked by Haibao must acknowledge the artful nature that has inserted him into the urban fabric. The genius of Haibao is to successfully personify Shanghai not, as previously, as a Whore of the Orient, but as an inoffensive and even boring cartoon character. The model for city planners is somewhere between Manhattan and Singapore; but Manhattan was a spontaneous response to very different economic and social conditions, and Shanghai is and always has been infinitely more vibrant, diverse, and chaotic than Singapore. Those who love the city and Chinese culture can have no wish to see a great city model itself on the sterile and hyper-controlled ones that inspire so much admiration in those who wish to do what has proved impossible for 5,000 years – make China boring. Haibao points the way to a new mode of citizenship, one that invites diversity, sustainability, and anything else currently in fashion, while keeping close, homogenizing control over it all – a Shanghai melting pot with a lid firmly clamped over it.

'The current campaigns for the Expo play upon this Shanghainese notion that it is the centre of Chinese urban modernity,'[31] writes Gina Anne Russo, and that is exactly why it is a worthy topic of examination. Shanghai's growth is directed explicitly at becoming a great city, a world city, and the Expo is the centerpiece of that plan. The slightly feeble, stale feel of the project, which has not attracted as many people as anticipated, is hardly surprising. Shanghai is in fact a wonderful and astounding city, but the city on show is a bowdlcrized version of itself, with all of the charm removed. However, the framework of Shanghai's developments offers a clear context for what will be the greatest realization of it so far, as well as flagging the future hoped for by those in control. The Expo invites countries from all over the world to join under the umbrella of a benevolent Chinese state capitalism that welcomes everyone, provided that they don't embarrass the hosts.[32] The city has seen countless changes initiated in order to prepare for the Expo; the construction of large infrastructure projects (notably the expansion of the Metro), the re-education of peasants in order to confirm to new social standards vis-à-vis personal comportment, and a relentless cleaning-up campaign has taken place in order to show off the city in the light that it would prefer to be seen. Shanghai, somewhat like the Paris it was once compared to, has two competing versions of itself separated by a river; the West, called Puxi, shows off colonial buildings, while Pudong, to the east, shows the face of the future. The Expo, which centers on a bridge across the Huangpu river, will spread into both districts, recuperating the past with a gesture as retro as a World's Fair in a colonial architecture to match it even as it beckons towards the future, an uncharted zone that is being remade constantly. If Shanghai truly is the capital of the coming era, then perhaps it is precisely this new space that constitutes the great experiment taking place there – 'the pursuit of symbols of progress is at work.'[33] Shanghai's multiple identities are presumed to be a totality by the Expo, occupying as it does all of the different symbolic spaces of the city, old and new. The Expo will present

Shanghai as a unity, perhaps the largest urban space ever presented as such (Paris within Haussmann's periphery and Manhattan, the two most lucid models for such a project, are both dwarfed even by Shanghai within its city limits, to say nothing of its suburbs). The Expo, then, seeks to present a space even as it changes it for its own purposes, exposing as well as expositing, not to mention depositing, as the impact of the event, whether it will ultimately be judged a success or a failure, will no doubt shape the psychology of the city for years to come.[34] The metro lines built for the Expo, the China Pavilion (now to become a museum), and the central Expo grounds (now being converted into commercial space) will memorialize the Expo, implanting the DNA of the mega-event into the city's collective memory. The possibility also hovers that, hidden beneath the blaring, unsubtle rhetoric that the state has crafted to suit its own purposes, an inspiring urban form really is taking shape, due to (or despite) the machinations of planners. Surely, the real interest in Shanghai is not in the superficial forms of buildings that may be transient in any case, but in the shifting community that they are the shadow and echo of, the aspirations of a city that, though formless, may be more substantial than buildings that vanish within a few years.

As we quoted novelist Wang Anyi earlier, 'There is something to be said for illusions. Though lacking substance, illusions can serve as the basis on which more substantive structures can be built.'[35] Maybe the suspiciousness with which we, whether as residents of Shanghai or not, view these maneuvers must be tempered by our recognition that they are, after all, aspirations for a better life and symbols thereof that have helped to galvanize the greatest poverty-relief program in human history. The goal of the Expo is to create, for economic as well as symbolic reasons, a dream city which is never fully present, and invites the spectator to realize it himself. Jean Cocteau wrote in 1936: 'Nothing in Shanghai was in the least like the picture I had formed of it ... yet I am convinced that there exists a Shanghai corresponding to the city of our dreams, perhaps excelling it.'[36] Who could not be similarly inspired by this eccentric city that aspires, perhaps legitimately, to cast itself as the central actor in the history of our time? The city as structure waiting for our exploits exists, with an eerily ghostlike quality – these great buildings have not yet come into their destiny, thereby inviting our own intervention in the fiction they seek to convey, that 'Shanghai has a right to be called the cultural capital of a different era, the coming era ...'[37]

Notes

1 'Shanghai is central to China's "official imagination of modernity". Innovations are "culturally legitimate,"' according to King, *Spaces of Global Cultures: Architecture, Urbanism, Identity* (London, 2004), p. 125.

2 http://www.expo2010.cn/expo/expoenglish/ps/regulations/userobject1ai42658.html, accessed 15 May 2010.

3 'Shanghai and Beijing seem to have a similar urban resonance within China as do Paris, London and New York in their national contexts.' Peter Rowe, *Shanghai: Architecture and Urbanism for Modern China* (London, 2009), p. 21.

4 Anne Querrien, 'The Metropolis and the Capital,' *Zone ½* (1986), p. 220.

5 For example, the temporary car ban in Beijing has been extended indefinitely. http://www.china.org.cn/china/2010-03/15/content_19610542.htm, accessed 13 March 2010.

6 As in the Urban Planet pavilion. http://en.expo2010.cn/c/en_qy_tpl_275.htm, accessed 13 March 2010.

7 A figure that at this point seems impossibly optimistic: http://china.globaltimes.cn/society/2010-05/528554.html, accessed 13 March 2010.

8 This concept is hinted at in Hans Eijkelboom's book *Paris, New York, Shanghai* (New York, 2007), which plays precisely on Benjamin's concept of Paris as the capital city of the nineteenth century, in describing Shanghai's role for the twenty-first century.

9 Rem Koolhaas, *Delirious New York* (New York, 1977).

10 Jeffrey Wasserstrom, *Global Shanghai 1850-2010* (London, 2009), p. 13.

11 Henri Lefebvre, trans. Donald Nicholson, *The Production of Space* (London, 1991), p. 81.

12 Ibid., p. 93.

13 Leslie Sklair, 'Iconic Architecture and Capitalist Globalization,' *City: Analysis of Urban Trends, Culture, Theory, Policy, Action* Vol. 12, No. 3, 2008: 22-23.

14 Pudong's 'abrupt metamorphosis from farmland to financial capital' is described in Jay Pridmore, *Shanghai: the Architecture of China's Great Urban Center* (New York, 2008), p. 10.

15 'Such buildings were conceived from a bird's-eye view, but slighted the ground-level experience of the city and its buildings as perceived by citizens in the street.' http://harvardmagazine.com/extras/architecture-and-urbanism, accessed 15 May 2010.

16 'Much of the admiration for Shanghai is based on visual evidence. Just look at Shanghai's impressive and imposing skyline and the conclusion is obvious," writes Yasheng Huang in a chapter primarily about how Shanghai's skyline is, in fact, belied by a somewhat meager economic performance. Yasheng Huang, *Capitalism with Chinese Characteristics* (Cambridge, 2008), p. 177.

17 Hubert Damisch, *Skyline: The Narcissistic City* (Stanford, 2001), p. 84. His chapter from which this is taken hints at Westerners' ideas about Shanghai in its title, 'The scene of the life of the future'.

18 Mike Davis, *Planet of Slums* (London, 2006), p. 7.

19 '*Wenming* is difficult to define. Most dictionaries say it means 'civilized', but this definition carries as many problematic connotations in Chinese as it does in English. Leo Lee, in his book *Shanghai Modern*, traces the development of this word in modern Chinese. The term was originally borrowed from the Japanese, who used the same characters (pronounced differently of course) in the late nineteenth century to define behavior that was specifically "modern" and "Western," thus maintaining the same connotations as "civilized" in English.' http://www.thechinabeat.org/?cat=64, accessed 24 March 2010.

20 Recalling Virilio's citation of Vauban's military structures: 'A totality of mechanisms able to receive a defined form, ... to transform it and finally to return it in a more

appropriate form,' Paul Virilio, trans. Mark Polizzotti, *Speed and Politics* (Boston, 2006), p. 36.

21 Eileen Chang, *Lust, Caution And Other Stories* (London, 2007).

22 http://harvardmagazine.com/2010/03/changing-challenging-china, accessed 24 March 2010. The same article notes that 17 of the 31 regional party chiefs in China have a background in the media; image management has become management in a country where the substance is constantly in flux.

23 http://harvardmagazine.com/2010/03/changing-challenging-china?page=0,6, accessed 24 March 2010.

24 Jing Wang, *Brand New China* (Cambridge, MA, 2008), p. 136.

25 Claudio Greco, *Beijing: the New City* (Milan, 2008), p. 37.

26 Henri Lefebvre, trans. Donald Nicholson, *The Production of Space* (London, 1991), p. 220-221.

27 For example, Thomas Friedman of the New York Times recently editorialized, 'One-party autocracy certainly has its drawbacks. But when it is led by a reasonably enlightened group of people, as China is today, it can also have great advantages.' http://www.nytimes.com/2009/09/09/opinion/09friedman.html, accessed 5 April 2010.

28 http://english.sina.com/china/2010/0209/303830.html, accessed 22 March 2010.

29 http://www.japanfocus.org/-Jeff-Wasserstrom/2980, accessed 5 April 2010.

30 'Créer un poncif, c'est le génie. Je dois créer un poncif.' Charles Baudelaire, 'Fusée,' XIII, in *Oeuvres complètes*, ed. Claude Pichois (Paris, 1976), 1: 662.

31 www.thechinabeat.org/?cat=180, accessed 5 April 2010.

32 The Americans, perhaps aware that the elephant being slowly tugged out of the room is their own dwindling hegemony, resentfully refused to make an entry until the last minute, when they offered a hideous structure most resembling a Walmart – the truest expression of Sino-American cooperation so far. http://www.usapavilion2010.com/usapavilion2010/index.php, accessed 5 April 2010.

33 Peter Rowe, *Shanghai: Architecture and Urbanism for Modern China* (London, 2009), p. 34.

34 The only consolation for an architectural critic in contemporary Shanghai is the delicious certainty that sometime soon, perhaps within less than a decade, it will all be replaced by something else anyhow – most of the structures of the Expo, from the impressive offerings fielded by the United Kingdom or Romania to the hideous wrecks from the United States and North Korea, will be demolished after it is finished.

35 Wang Anyi, translated by Michael Berry & Susan Chan Egan, *The Song of Everlasting Sorrow* (New York, 2008), p. 202.

36 Jeffrey Wasserstrom, *Global Shanghai 1850-2010* (London, 2009), p. 136.

37 Ibid., p. 13.

4 Guangzhou's Special Path to Global City Status

Xiangmin Guo and Changtao Liu

Abstract

Guangzhou is a unique city in China with regard to its special role throughout modern history, beginning from the Qing Dynasty. Its uniqueness resides in the way it has engaged with the outside world – in a pendulum movement from passive to active engagement.

When it was first appointed as China's only trading port to the Western world during the Qing Dynasty, Guangzhou never expected to be part of the newly industrialized developed world. Up to then, its only mission had been to serve the Emperor, who had little interest in learning more about the Western nations and who moreover considered China to be the only global superpower of that era. However, this illusion was soon broken as colonizers swarmed into this oriental feudal empire. Guangzhou was forced to become one of the first treaty ports, and part of its land – known as Shamian – was ceded to foreigners. This can be seen as the first page in Guangzhou's history of opening up to the rest of the world.

Guangzhou maintained its status as leased territory for such a long time that, until 1949, when the People's Republic of China was established, it basically never changed. But after 1949, Guangzhou played a positive role in welcoming guests from the former Soviet Union and other communist countries at a time when the former Western colonizers withdrew their capital – and their generosity – from China. Lacking funds for construction, Guangzhou was forced to become involved with the outer world. For this reason, Guangzhou became the only city permitted to carry out import and export trading. A symbolic milestone was the first China Export Commodities Fair (also known as the Canton Fair) in 1957, which was seen at the time as the 'window of China'. When the Cultural Revolution finally came to an end in 1978, China entered a new period in its history in which all capable cities become equal competitors in attracting foreign commerce. With the disappearance of its special trading privileges,

Guangzhou lost its direction in these years. The focus of both domestic and international commercial interests had moved to new, hot development points such as Shenzhen, adjacent to Hong Kong, and Pudong in Shanghai.

Introduction

In the last two decades, the pace at which China has urbanized has been extraordinary: the urbanization level in the country has doubled from 25 percent in 1987 to roughly 50 percent in 2010. Presently, the most urbanized areas are distributed along the southeast coast of China and includes the Pearl River Delta cities, the Yangtze River Delta city group, and the Beijing Tang urban groups. In China's western regions, the Chengdu-Chongqing urban cluster is quietly rising. Urumqi, the western interior's most important city, is a city that is changing quickly to play a unique role in the mid-Asia region as a trading and financial center.

Without doubt, from a historical point of view, China's rapid growth in urbanization has been related to its policy of opening up to the outside world. However, throughout the history of China there have been many significant changes in political attitude towards foreign trade and globalization. These changes have had a major impact on the cities, which have experienced a high degree of opening up, and even on the entire process of China's urbanization. For this reason, it is meaningful to grasp the role of China's urbanization against the background of globalization.

China has a long and proud history of foreign trade. Guangzhou, which is located in the southwest of China, possesses a rich history of foreign trade that dates back to the Qin Dynasty. As the only city permitted to trade during most of China's dynasties, Guangzhou occupied a leading position among Chinese cities and contributed greatly to the economic development of ancient China. During almost a century of colonial rule, Guangzhou developed at a far faster pace than the other inland cities and mushroomed into a highly cosmopolitan city. Today, Guangzhou is still the bridgehead for foreign trade in China and continues to play an important role as a model for Chinese cities exploring the path towards global importance.

The First Opium War (1839-42) marked the beginning of Guangzhou's semi-colonization and semi-feudalization. The colonists brought two notable benefits to Guangzhou that accelerated the process of urban construction. First, the industrialization process in Guangzhou was accelerated: an industrial base developed rapidly, as did municipal infrastructure, with the agricultural civilization soon being replaced by an industrial civilization. Second, there was an appreciable expansion in the range of foreign trade, with trade routes increasing during the colonial era, most of which remain important for the development of Guangzhou to this day.

Guangzhou's path towards globalization during the colonial era objectively met its needs for city development for a long time. Guangzhou imported surplus commodities and exported raw materials passively. As a consequence, the management of imports and exports boomed in the city. After the foundation of the People's Republic of China in 1949, Guangzhou made great efforts to import labor-intensive industries, most of which were based on manual labor. This helped the city to rise to prominence once again within a short space of time.

Although Guangzhou has achieved great successes in its development as a city, it is not necessarily the best nor the only path to becoming a global city. Over the past thirty years, Guangzhou found itself steadily sinking to the bottom of the global value chain, with economic growth rates falling substantially in recent years. Everything indicates that Guangzhou has run into a dilemma in maintaining its development concepts. The old path of the colonial era is difficult to continue in the post-colonial era. As a model of the process of globalization for Chinese cities, Guangzhou has to find its own special path towards being a global city in the post-colonial era.

Globalizing the Chinese city in the post-colonial era

Recently, the Chinese city has experienced a development trajectory filled with pain and hardship. It has tried numerous paths during the course of its integration with the global economy.

China's trade with foreign countries started during the Qin Dynasty and reached a peak in the Song and Yuan Dynasties. It decreased in the Ming and Qing Dynasties because of the country's policy of seclusion. After the First Opium War, Guangzhou was forced open by the colonists and ruled by them for one century. Colonization forced colonial cities open without exception. Whether openness to foreign trade is a benefit or a handicap for the development of cities or countries is still being debated within economic circles. The orthodox school believes that foreign trade was the decisive factor behind the development of these backward cities. This school emphasizes the positive aspect, pointing out that developed countries' commodities, capital, and technologies can transform developing economies. At the other end of the spectrum is the radical school, which emphasises the negative: they believe that trade between developed and developing economies worsens trade conditions. The interests of developing economies are trampled upon by the trade methods adopted by developed countries, which lead to the inequality of international income distribution (Zhang Xiaohui 2009: 91). Regardless of which side is right in this debate, in Guangzhou's case, colonial rule actually seems to have enhanced its international trading activities.

Except for Guangzhou, Chinese cities were closed to foreign trade for most of the last two thousand years. In his famous tour of southern China in 1992, Deng Xiaoping encouraged people to 'be free from old ideas and unite together to move forward'. It was at this point that many Chinese cities began to re-examine their constrained development of the past and to set a new development target of 'constructing an international metropolis' through a new foreign policy. There were 75 cities advocating this target in 1997, and this number rose to 183 in 2004. These high numbers illustrate the urgent desire of Chinese cities to be international after the colonial oppression of a century. Viewed from another angle, this unrealistic target also reflects the confusion in Chinese cities about the best path of international development to take.

How will Chinese cities find the best way to internationalize in the post-colonial twenty-first century? This is a major challenge. Many cities are attempting to provide answers to this in their continuing exploration of the appropriate development path. Guangzhou, with its long history and myriad experiences as an open city, is a prime candidate for providing a valuable model for other Chinese cities.

Guangzhou's unique evolution process from colonial city to international city

Guangzhou is on China's southeast coast facing the sea to the east, south, and west. It was open to foreign trade over the last two thousand years thanks to its advantageous geographical location (Huang Qichen 2007: 150). The development of Guangzhou was closely interrelated with that of the world. So a closer look at Guangzhou's process of internationalization since the First Opium War should be helpful in providing lessons for Chinese cities in their quest to develop ties with the rest of the world.

'Passively open' Guangzhou: Ming Dynasty to Qing Dynasty

Guangzhou was open to the world in the two centuries between the beginning of the Ming Dynasty in 1644 to the eruption of First Opium War in 1839. This was the policy of the central government.

China was highly active in foreign trade during the Ming and Qing Dynasties. From the Yongle Emperor's third year (1405) to the Xuande

Emperor's eighth year (1433), the Ming Dynasty sent Zhenghe's huge fleet to the Great West Ocean (the Atlantic) to visit thirty countries in Asia and Africa (Shangchang 2007: 63). After that, however, foreign trade was severely restricted by the central government.The danger to China's south coast from the navies of Japan and Portugal during the Ming Dynasty, as well as the nuisance from the Dynasty's remaining confederates in coastal districts, who were beginning to throw off the shackles of imperial control, possibly caused the rulers to rethink their strategy of maintaining such a shipping fleet in the face of increasing costs and the internal inflation that the trade with Europe was causing. Seeing little profit in this trade, and thinking it a cause of insecurity in coastal districts, the central government saw little value in continuing it. As a result, the central authorities decided that Guangzhou was to be the only city permitted to engage in international trade (Table 4.1). In this period when the city was controlled by the central government and became a base for the regional economy, Guangzhou was referred to as a 'passively open' city.

Guangzhou was at its most powerful in the Ming and Qing Dynasties, which had a sound economic basis as their goal. As the only trading port, however, Guangzhou always braced itself for the possibility that it would be closed off from the outside world by the central government, which thought little of foreign trade and was sensitive to the risk of invasion from the sea. During the Ming Dynasty and at the beginning of the Qing Dynasty, the strictest rules were imposed on the city. Guangzhou's local government remained in favor of continuing trade with foreign countries despite the constraints imposed by the central government. It was clear that foreign trade was being conducted for the pure benefit of the central government. At the time, more goods were imported than exported, and these imported goods were rarely common household goods – most of them were luxury items like ivory and diamonds and were for government use. Six of the seven ocean trade routes starting from Guangzhou were managed by foreigners. As a

Table 4.1 *The external trade routes of Guangzhou in the Qing Dynasty*

Trade Routes	*Nationality of Operator*
Canton - Macau - Goa (India) - Lisbon (Portugal)	Portugal
Canton - Macau - Nagasaki (Japan)	Portugal
Canton - Macau - Macassar (Indonesia) - Timor (East Timor)	Portugal
Canton - Macau - Manlia (Philippines) - Acapulco (Mexico); Lima (Peru)	China
Canton - Macau - New York (America)	America
Canton - Macau - Кронштадт (Russia)	Russia
Canton - Macau - Port Jackson; Sydney (Australia)	United Kingdom

Figure 4.1 *The external trade routes of Guangzhou in the Qing Dynasty*

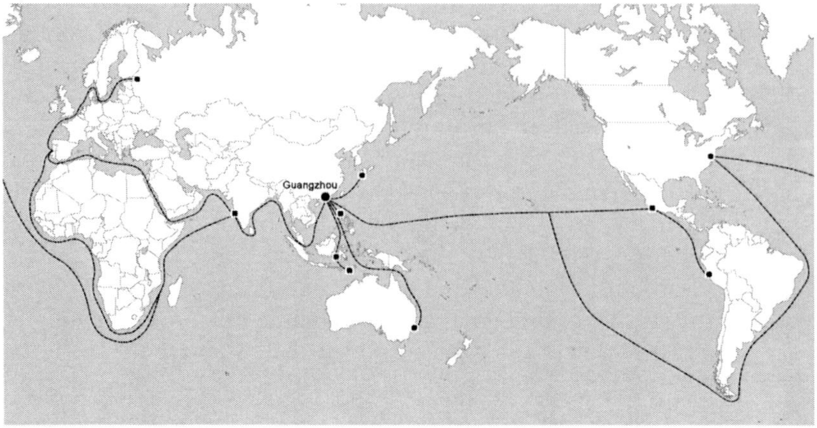

whole, the central government's foreign policy isolated China from the outside world at this time. According to Shang Chang, the 'Qing Dynasty's seclusion policy constructed a great isolating embankment which was an obstacle to the advanced development of Chinese society' (2007: 63).

Guangzhou's desire to be a global city was constrained at this time. Foreign trade was conducted following the strict orders of the central government and was not allowed to exceed what were considered to be the needs of a self-sufficient regional economy. The central government's attitude was negative for globalization. Guangzhou was like a city contained within an invisible embankment and kept isolated from the normal inter-city interactions that are so necessary for a city's normal development.

'Forced open' Guangzhou: Late Qing Dynasty to the Republic of China (before liberation)

The period from the outbreak of the First Opium War in 1839 to the formation of the People's Republic of China in 1949 was Guangzhou's colonial era. The comprehensive opening of Guangzhou to foreign trade was the decision of the colonists as well as the local government.

China and Britain's First Opium War marked the beginning of China's semi-colonization and semi-feudalization. The Qing government was forced to sign the Treaty of Nanjing at the point of a sword. Guangzhou, Xiamen, Fuzhou, Ningbo, and Shanghai were five cities that were opened up as trading ports. From that time, the central government lost control of Guangzhou and the embankment that had been constraining the city from becoming a global city collapsed. From then on, Guangzhou was controlled by Britain, America, and eventually Japan. The colonists colluded with the local government. Guangzhou was 'passively open' to the world at this time, as it was largely controlled by colonists.

Guangzhou became the portal and frontier for the opening up of the Chinese state to international markets. Globalization brought a number of benefits to Guangzhou. A large amount of foreign goods poured into the city in a short space of time. The value of goods imported and exported from Guangzhou was 10 percent of national value in 1867, 13.4 percent in 1894. 10.1 percent in 1926, and 21.41 percent in 1949 (Huang Qichen 2007: 156). Guangzhou was an international trade city and the main distribution center for the South China Sea. Colonists were responsible for banking and insurance as well as storage and entrepot facilities, among other things. Light industry also developed at a rapid pace. A number of foreign-owned factories were set up. Private capital and the local government invested heavily in these factories, which did a lot to facilitate the Westernization movement that was making itself felt in China at the time.

In terms of city construction, Guangzhou achieved great things, especially when compared to the interior and western Chinese cities which were still controlled by the central government. Guangzhou built the first paved roads and the first railway in China (at Yuehan). By the end of 1931, Guangzhou had about 40 paved roads and 1,000 motor vehicles (Huang Songhua 1998).

However, 'passively open' Guangzhou also experienced the negative influences of globalization along with these development opportunities. Traditional industries contracted or were destroyed, and handicraft industries declined each year. The city's handicraft industry made up 13 percent of the city's economy in the 1860s but had slumped to about 5 percent by the time of the Japanese invasion in 1937 (Huang Songhua 1998). Colonists also dumped goods on Guangzhou, thereby exacerbating the Great Depression being experienced by the world at the time.

The colonists forced Guangzhou into globalization, allowing the city to break the chains of the central government's restrictions to global development. Guangzhou returned to the world stage without constraints to its regional development. However, Guangzhou also suffered the negative influences of globalization without its 'embankment': the city was at the mercy of its colonists and was without the protection of the central government.

'Semi-actively open' Guangzhou: after the revolution, before the reform

From 1949 to 1980, the central government once again had control over all of China and its foreign policy. When the new People's Republic was founded in 1949, there was an urgent need for goods that were scarce after World War II. The central government appointed Guangzhou as south China's main trading port. But this was not a sign that the city would retain its former globalization path. As Xiao Yanming notes, 'Because of the political movement, "left" ideas, uncertainty of social economic construction, and the unfavourable international environment, the central government did not pay enough attention to the use of foreign capital' (2010: 43). The city's development rate was slow because it traded only with less-developed communist bloc countries. The harsh political situation rebuilt the 'embankment' surrounding Guangzhou, effectively putting constraints on the process of globalization. Local government had certain discretionary powers in a limited economic area, which was different from the 'passively open' age. Guangzhou was called a 'semi-open' city at this time, one whose economic endeavours were small scale and severely limited in scope; this policy, which saw a slight opening up of the city to some of the rest of the world was, however, strictly controlled by both central and local governments.

In an attempt to expand its trading partners and its investment capital, the local government of Guangzhou Province proposed to the central government a set of rules to attract investment by overseas Chinese and residents of Hong Kong. But support from the central government was not forthcoming, as the central authorities' focus was on the political movement (Xiao Mingyan 2010: 41). Guangzhou's effort to expand its foreign commercial ties involved globalization at a time when the nation was focused on rejecting cronyism. In 1957, Guangzhou made a major move to attract foreign capital by opening the Canton Fair, which was to be held every six months. The first fair attracted 1,223 foreign businessmen from 19 countries, thereby expanding the area with which the city conducted foreign trade. Guangzhou's local government understood clearly the role of the Canton Fair in Guangzhou's relations with the world. As Luo Qiuju remarks, 'Canton Fair was the only important window to the outside world at that early stage. It never stopped throughout the 1960s, overcoming the worsening of Sino-Soviet relations, natural disasters over three years, and the interference of the Culture Revolution' (2004: 31). By the time of the 107th Canton Fair in 2010, the fair had been visited by a total of 203,996 foreign businessmen from 212 countries and districts. The fact that the Canton Fair has continued for more than 50 years demonstrates the local government's determination to continue Guangzhou's development into a global city.

Although the Fair was a significant achievement, Guangzhou was only open to trade for certain partner countries due to political constraints. The city's development thus relied only on a few trading partners, which meant that the pace of development slowed. This new 'embankment' allowed only partial room for Guangzhou to globalize, making it increasingly distanced from other world cities.

'Actively open' Guangzhou: after the reform and before the Southeast Asian financial crisis

From the economic reforms of 1978 to the 1997 Southeast-Asian financial crisis, China underwent a period of reform and opening up. In Guangzhou itself, the policy of opening up was controlled by the local government.

During the turbulent ten years of the Cultural Revolution (1967-1977), the central government paid nearly all its attention to the political struggle, which meant that the state economy was seriously undermined. After the Cultural Revolution ended in 1978, the central government realized that political struggle alone could not solve the problem of poverty. Deng Xiaoping then gave his famous speech encouraging people to 'be free from old ideas and unite together to move forward' in 1992. The central government began to focus on the economy. Deng Xiaoping's speech marked the start of the central government's policy of granting economic autonomy to local governments. For the first time in its history, Guangzhou had absolute economic freedom and independence. Guangzhou became an 'actively open' city with a global economic policy controlled by the local government.

Due to its advantageous geographic position, Guangzhou became a major international port city. Up to 2009, Guangzhou port conducted trade with some 350 ports in around 80 countries (Economic Daily, 2009). The local government supported this trade through its policies: cheap labor and land were encouraged in order to attract foreign capital in the development of processing industries and import and export industries. The city developed rapidly. The value of its imports and exports was many times that of 1949 (Table 4.2). Guangzhou's local government tried hard to absorb foreign capital within its 'embankment'. However, in its zeal to develop, the city's industrial structure became increasingly deformed because it relied too heavily on the sort of downstream industries that no longer existed in the developed countries. As a result, Guangzhou's manufacturing base was at the lowest end of the global value chain. There was no independent research and development, no industrial or technological innovation. Moreover, Guangzhou relied excessively on the outside world: its dependence on foreign trade (the value of imports and exports as a percentage of

Table 4.2 *The value of imports and exports and the amount of cargo loaded and unloaded in Guangzhou*

Period	*Volume of Trade(100 million dollar)*
M & Q (1644-1842	5.15 (ounce of silver)
POC (1922)	0.348 (ounce of silver)
ROC (1949-1976)	134
PRC 2000	100
PRC 2006	530
PRC 2007	379
PRC 2008	429
PRC 2009	374

M & Q: Ming Dynasty & Qing Dynasty
ROC: Republic of China
PRC: People's Republic of China

economic growth) was 81 percent. In addition, an excess number of foreign factories constrained all motivation for future development. Attempts to reform the economic system and introduce new rules more in line with international standards did not go far enough; this was a lost opportunity for Guangzhou to engage in high-level international cooperation in trade. Liu Jianghua writes: 'the market-oriented economic system produced significant achievements in the 20 years of reform and opening up, but the system was heavily constrained by the revolution environment. The macroeconomic management system and microeconomic factories system were kept at a distance from the ordinary requirement of the market economic system' (2000: 14).

With the devolution of power from the central government to the local government Guangzhou was free to develop as a global city. Its development rate was faster than ever before. However, without adequate policies in place to tame and guide foreign trade and investment, the city's industrial structure developed in a distorted manner. The 1997 Southeast Asian financial crisis forced the city to reform its industrial system. Up to then, the city had very little in place in terms of financial supervision or factory supervision. But when much of the economy could not pay its debts during the financial crisis, the local government was forced to reform the system. It abandoned its 'government's infinite responsibility' policy, leading to the first failed factory in Guangzhou. Although the central government was able to put an end to the finance turbulence by using its foreign exchange reserves, Guangzhou implemented more far-reaching system reforms later on.

Guangzhou lacked direction in its development as a global city and was powerless against the negative influences of globalization once the central government's trade 'embankment' was removed.

Guangzhou's unique progress towards global-city status

Guangzhou's path to becoming a global city moved through four different stages: from 'passively open' to 'forced open', then 'semi-actively open' and finally 'actively open'.

Those four stages have some similarities as well as differences. Under the 'passively open' and 'semi-actively open' paths, the will of the central government and the political situation determined the degree of opening to the external world. The scope of the city's trading activity was narrow, which meant that the city was to a certain extent immune to the negative influences of globalization. However, on the negative side, it meant that the opportunities of globalization were neglected or squandered. The city's development lagged behind the rest of the world. In the 'forced open' and 'actively open' paths, the will of the local government determined the degree of opening to the external

Figure 4.2 *Guangzhou's path towards global-city status*

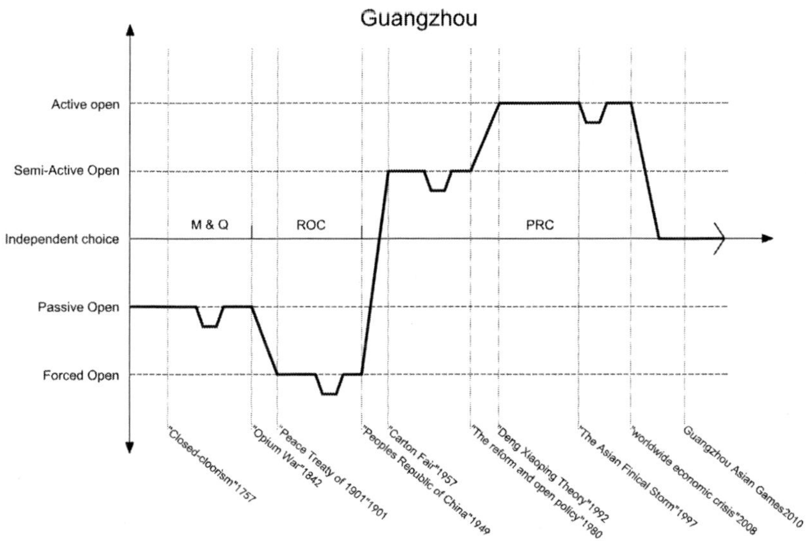

The vertical line represents the opening-up policy of Guangzhou; the horizontal axis represents Guangzhou's historical periods and great historical events. It is clear from the figure that Guangzhou's process of opening up has experienced great difficulties in its history. Many great historical events were closely connected with Guangzhou and acutely changed its development direction. In each historical period, there were many small events, but none of them played a decisive role.

world. The scope of the city's trading activity was broad, and Guangzhou received all the benefits of globalization. The city developed rapidly. However, the city was susceptible to the negative influences of globalization. It also lost personality and a certain degree of choice.

Throughout its history, Guangzhou has had an 'embankment' – sometimes visible and sometimes invisible – around it to protect it and hold it back from the outside world. This embankment sometimes isolated Guangzhou from the rest of the world, but it was destroyed by the influence of globalization, leaving Guangzhou unprotected. At present, most cities in China are choosing an 'actively open' model. But, as mentioned before, this is not necessarily the best path to becoming a global city. The impact of the 1997 and 2008 economic crises proves this point.

At the same time, we notice that central and local governments in China have contrasting ideas about which globalization path to choose because they assess the advantages and disadvantages of globalization differently. The central government tends to emphasize the unstable factors and negative influences of globalization and is inclined to follow a conservative path. So even in the 'actively open' model, the central government is always mindful of fluctuations in the business cycle. Local governments generally focus on the advantages and opportunities brought about by globalization, so it is inclined towards a global and open path.

According to the analysis above, we can construct a model for Chinese cities aspiring to become global cities. Such a model would involve the joint role of 'political power' (central government and local government) and 'economic power' (globalization and regionalization), with the relation of these four kinds of power determining the best path to becoming a global city.

Analyzing Guangzhou's path to becoming a global city

The challenge and difficulties in the era of globalization

The main challenge for Chinese cities is how to increase their resilience to the negative influences of globalization on the way to becoming a global city. In a highly globalized world, the greater the degree of openness, the less one is able to avert risk. This rule also applies to mainland China. At the time of the 1997 Southeast-Asian financial crisis, Guangzhou's dependence on foreign trade was low and it had a relatively closed financial system. This meant that the impact of the financial crisis was limited mostly to reform of the system rather than economic losses. At the same time, the international city of Hong Kong, close to Guangzhou, was harder hit by the crisis. In the 2008 financial

Figure 4.3 *GDP growth rates of Chinese cities*

	The growth rate of GDP of Guangzhou	*The number of non-coastal cites among top 20 GDP growth rate cities*
1994	18,83	9
1995	16,44	9
1996	12,45	10
1997	13,39	10
1998	13,13	8
1999	13,18	10
2000	13,35	8
2001	12,74	7
2002	13,24	5
2003	15	6
2004	12,8	6
2005	11,1	8
2006	14,7	6
2007	11,14	4
2008	12,5	4
2009	11,5	15

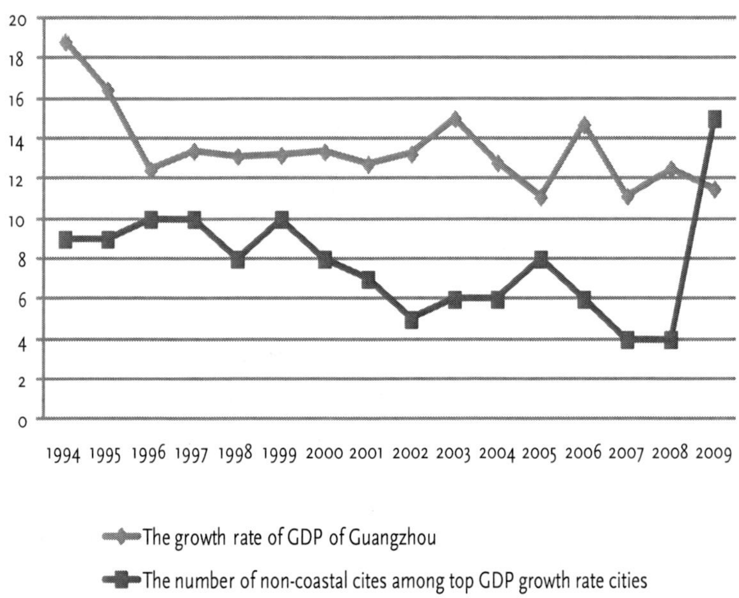

Between 1998 and 2008 the economic development of Guangzhou was seriously affected by economic crises. The recession of 2005 caused an increasing number of crises in Chinese enterprises. The damage caused by economic crises increases each year in line with the increase in openness. Moreover, during the same period, the speed of economic development in China's coastal cities was also affected.

crisis, however, Guangzhou's dependence on foreign trade was higher and concentrated on the West. By this time, China had joined the WTO and Guangzhou's financial system was integrated with international standards. Guangzhou was seriously influenced by the crisis. The West's trade demands diminished. The amount of trade commodities being loaded and unloaded in Guangzhou sharply declined. The financial system was seriously impacted. At the same time, China's interior and western cities thrived economically because of their low dependence on foreign trade.

The low resilience to risk was not only the result of Guangzhou's high dependence on foreign trade but also the result of a weak regional economy. As a result of the crisis, the port cluster around Bohai and the Yangtze Delta port cluster experienced rapid economic growth, while the Pearl River Delta port cluster to which Guangzhou belongs experienced a decline in growth. A comparison of these regional urban agglomerations shows that the development of cities in the Bohai and the Yangtze Delta was relatively stable with regard to one another, while the integrated economic activity of the 50 cities in the mountainous area of the Pearl River Delta (excluding the three big cities of Guangzhou, Shenzhen, and Zhuhai) was only one-tenth that of Guangzhou (South China Daily, 2003).

Clearly, the higher the degree of globalization, the more susceptible an economy is to its adverse impacts. Moreover, we can conclude that regionalization did not vanish in the globalization era; in fact, its function as a potential buffer against the negative influences of globalization is more and more important. In order to meet these challenges, the four kinds of power that determine the path towards becoming a global city need to be used in such a way as to find the most suitable path.

The limitations of the traditional path to becoming a global city

From the point of view of 'political power' and 'economic power', the four paths to becoming a global city need to be examined from a new perspective:

1. In the 'passively open' model, the policy of the central government was focused on displaying national strength and stopping the invasion of foreign enemies. The policy of opening or closing was influenced by politics. The city's development was based on regional 'self-sufficiency' without the desire for development.
2. In the 'forced open' model, the colonists collaborated with the local government. The purpose of opening up to the outside world was to make profits. The city's industrial structure developed abnormally, although the development was based on the global model.

3 In the 'semi-actively open' model, the central government was focused on political conflict and opened up certain areas according to the international situation. Urban development was based on regional cooperation in limited areas.
4 In the 'actively open' model, the local government's somewhat ill-considered focus on economic development was based on global aspirations. At the same time, the city lost its ability to resist the negative influences of globalization.

The characteristics shared by the four urban paths that Guangzhou has experienced were as follows:
1 The leading political power was excessively powerful in the four urban forms.
2 The two kinds of political power (central and local government) had different attitudes to globalization and regionalization.
3 The policies of the two kinds of political power with regard to globalization lacked flexibility.

This means that the traditional paths to becoming a global city are unstable and lack continuity because they lack political and economic flexibility. They easily swing from one extreme to another.

Guangzhou's coping strategy and its effects

The 1997 Southeast-Asian financial crisis and the 2008 financial crisis sounded the alarm for Guangzhou. The city has taken some important measures in recent years after realizing its mistakes on its path to becoming a global city. These measures include:
1 Expanding domestic demand and reducing the dependence on exporting. This would entail enriching the urban industrial structure and changing the single-industry structure caused by too much opening up. From the end of 1997, Guangzhou has supported manufacturing industries such as motorcars, boats, steel, petrochemicals, machinery, electronics, etc.
2 Strengthening regional cooperation. This involves rapidly developing regional traffic and other infrastructure (like highways, railways, airports), strengthening the cooperation of the Pearl River Delta city cluster, and supporting industry exchange with nearby cities.
3 Proposing a strategic new regional city known as Guangfo City. Guangzhou is 19 kilometers from Foshan, with 58% of its industry dedicated to services; Foshan's industry consists of 60% manufacturing. Together, these two cities could form a complementary industrial cluster: Guangfo City could then be poised to form an

almost perfect super-city for dealing with the challenges of globalization.

At the same time, Guangzhou has been marketing itself through 'great events': it hosted the Asian Games in 2010 in an effort to increase the city's influence, improve its international stature, and increase the level of its international cooperation. This was also intended to improve its competitiveness and its ability to avert the negative impact of globalization. At the same time, Guangzhou must strengthen its supervision over financial capital and tighten its assessment standards, which have traditionally offered almost no resistance to international capital.

A new path for the future of Guangzhou

Guangzhou's coping strategies and actions show the subtle changes in political and economic power in recent years.

From the point of view of political power, the central government has assigned more power to the local government, with the central government's influence decreasing and the local government's power increasing. For a city to be able to develop as a global city, the central government must apparently loosen its control, allowing local governments and numerous centers of regional importance to be empowered.

From the point of view of economic power, Chinese cities are tightening their assessment standards and introducing measures to protect their social and economic development from the negative influences of globalization. Urban development has less and less local influence in the face of globalization. More and more regions are proposing joint development. There has been a strong trend lately whereby external forces (international capital) are replaced by domestic forces (regional development) due to the emphasis on domestic consumption and the changes in China's development model.

The two kinds of political power are complementary, as are the two kinds of economic power. The local government's power increases while the central government's power decreases. Global economic power decreases while regional economic power increases. Globalization is the external condition of Guangzhou's development, not its default condition. Guangzhou is gradually examining the conception of globalization from the point of view of localization and regionalization, which is different from the traditional views.

There is, therefore, a fifth path to becoming a global city: the 'independent choice' model. This model involves choosing to introduce the advantages of globalization and the equilibrium between global development and regional development. This path would increase Guangzhou's competitive ability as well as its international influence.

Viewed from another perspective, political power is more like a power that protects and is independent of the economic activity of the 'embankment' city. Political power constructs an 'embankment' – high or low – around the city to resist negative influences and ensure the safety of the city. Globalization should not be treated as a great scourge, and the 'embankment' should not be constructed to keep out outside influences, which would only isolate the city from the outside world. The opposite attitude of receiving all international influences should also be given up. Instead of an 'embankment', a 'dam' that can open and close at will should be constructed around the city. The dam will introduce, resist, and maintain the strength of globalization. It will balance the interaction of globalization and regionalization. This model makes best use of the advantages of globalization and constrains the disadvantages.

We believe that in the future China, the 'independent-choice'-oriented 'dam city' model will be the best path to globalization.

CULTURAL EXPRESSION

5 Repairing the Rural-Urban Continuum

Cinema as Witness

Ana M. Moya Pellitero

Abstract

Until 1911, with the end of the Qing dynasty, China was a single hybrid continuum that was neither urban nor rural. Its civilization was based on a complex web of relationships and hierarchies. The individuals were urban in their political and religious apparatus and rural in their bonds to the land, nature, and place of origin. Chinese society was also based on a social structure of mobility. A large proportion of the population of most cities was non-native and rural. The rural population that temporarily lived in urban centers were mostly rural sojourners. Despite this mobility, native bonds were a principle of social organization. The territory was not organized as a concentric structure of urban centers, with one central city surrounded by secondary subordinated urban nuclei. Urban centers of small size and low centrality were positioned everywhere between larger centers of greater centrality (Skinner 1977: 258).

In contemporary China, the traditional urban-rural continuum does not exist anymore. Instead, an extreme social, economical, and environmental contrast exists between the modern global Chinese mega-cities and the undeveloped hinterland, with its poor and derelict rural environment. There is also a duality and disjunction between the bright, optimistic progress of central mega-cities and the bleak way of life in provincial towns, where factories are closing and employment is decreasing. The post-Mao period has transformed agriculture into family farming; therefore, villagers in poor conditions seek work elsewhere. Rural migration to small towns and global metropolises is controversial in China. In the 1980s, the government slogan was *li tu bu lixiang* (to leave the land but not to leave the rural areas). Towns have become attractors of economic activity. One of the main characteristics of the new post-socialist city is an increasing residential mobility and the growth of its suburbia. State authorities no longer have the power to prevent movement. Researchers agree that in the mid-1990s, migration affected approximately 80-100 million people (Stockman

1992: 65). Those that belong to this autonomous floating population are dislocated from their place of origin, with a lack of emotional affectivity to the space that receives them, and are spatially limited due to low incomes. In Chinese cities, there is a space of illegality and irregularity in the periphery of urban areas, where migrants are concentrated (Wu 2002: 90-119). Rural migrants are a floating population without any interest to settle in the city, always free to return to their villages. The suburbia is a temporary stop that becomes a space of transit, although it is not known to what extent this temporal situation will become permanent in the near future. Chinese cinema plays a key role in providing social criticism. It depicts the evolution and changes that China is suffering in its urban and rural context, and the life of the rural migrants in the city. This chapter will combine the theory with examples of the work of Zhang Yimou, Chen Kaige, Jia Zhang-ke, and Wang Xiaoshuai (Fifth- and Sixth-Generation moviemakers) that have depicted this rural-urban dichotomy, from the 1990s up to the present day.

Introduction

Since 1949, a constant concern in China has been to repair the classical Chinese structure of a rural-urban continuum on a political level and to recover the lost equilibrium between the countryside and the city. For Confucian values, rural life was a container of virtue while cities were centers of corruption. Urban centers in China were traditionally tied to rural values and the countryside via a rural social, administrative, religious, and political structure (Stockman, 2000: 47). With the influence of Western powers after the First Opium war (1839-42), cities, mainly those with a semi-colonial status, started losing the traditional Chinese equilibrium between the rural and the urban world. Port cities like Shanghai became isolated clusters of economic and financial trade. They were centers of modern life, Western values, and borrowed foreign culture, distanced from Chinese traditions. Cities in mainland China were still preserving a harmony within a rural-based society not corrupted by commerce, which was deemed to be inherently immoral under Confucian principles. Shanghai, together with other port cities, was attracting impoverished rural peasants searching for job opportunities, but the rural migrants were not fully integrated into city life because they were considered second-class citizens (Cohen 1993: 151-70).

Since 1949, and the establishment of the People's Republic of China, with its planned social economy, the goal has been to reduce the social and economic differences between the countryside and urban centers.

The countryside and its rural lifestyle were a symbol of Chinese identity in the face of foreign influences. From the 1950s onwards, the Chinese Communist Party promoted an anti-urban policy that eradicated the culture of urban modernity that cities like Shanghai represented. Cities were meant to be centers of production and not consumption. Cities and villages were inhabited by a working class, both industrial and rural. The Chinese Communist Party also wanted to narrow the gap between urban intellectuals and laboring peasants, erasing the distinction between mental and manual labor. Intellectuals were asked to give up their urban identity and were forced to migrate, at various times, to the countryside and adopt peasants' values. The state, in order to restrict uncontrolled migration, imposed mobility restrictions based on a household registration system, the *hukou*, which was enforced by a strict migration law introduced in 1958. This created a number of physical barriers as well as social injustices (Gar-on Ye & XueQiang 1990: 46).

Since 1978, with the shift from a planned to a free-market economy, the aim was once again to reduce the economic gap between rural and urban areas, privatizing business and allowing the construction of competitive industries in rural areas. The rural land that belonged to the commune was divided into individual plots and leased to farmers who could start investing money in their own productive business (Wilson 1996: 170). Farmers, in order to cover their responsibility for maintaining rural infrastructure and services, were forced to find extra income in rural-based industries, as well as in the rural towns and cities. The Chinese government was willing to allow this movement of millions of rural workers into urban areas because as cheap rural labor they could help make the Chinese economy more competitive. However, these rural migrants arrived in cities without any legal household registration (*hukou*); they had no permanent abode and were stigmatized for being perceived as an urban underclass (Friedmann 2005: 63). In the global era, the Communist *hukou* registration system has exacerbated these problems, problems that paradoxically date from the period of the semi-colonial port cities, a time when being seen to be a peasant had a distinctly pejorative connotation.

The social and physical situation of illegal rural migrants inside cities is turning into a damaging social problem. Rural migrants have created a social space outside of official planning that implies a transformation not only of the physical space of cities but also of society in general (Zhang 2001: 202-3). Rural migrants create illegally built structures as temporary housing, which are seen as threats to the public order. Clean-up campaigns only erase the physical traces of a territorial rural-urban inequality. A more painful social assimilation in urban areas implies a renunciation of their own identity and their native bonds of origin, so prized by Confucian values. This negation of a migrant's rural identity shows a failure in attaining a hybrid social rural-urban structure.

Even today for the many Chinese who have migrated to the cities, the countryside and the rural world still represent a bond to their place of origin and a link to their family and rural communities. For urban dwellers who lived through the Great Leap Forward and the Cultural Revolution (1966-76), the countryside has also marked their adulthood, as they had to learn from the peasantry and land and nature how to make personal sacrifices. Chinese society, passing through the Communist Mao regime to the post-Mao government and the shift to a market economy, has been a mobile population located between two worlds: the countryside and the city. From the 1980s onwards, this social structure of mobility has been depicted in a number of Chinese movies, which have provided social and political criticism. Chinese moviemakers from the Fifth and Sixth Generations have acted as witnesses to these unsettling migrations. Often through a portrayal of their own personal experiences, they provide valuable criticism of the social and spatial failures in attaining and repairing a Chinese rural-urban continuum.

Chinese cinema, intellectual criticism

The Modern period in Chinese cinema started in 1978, when the Beijing Film Academy was reopened after the Cultural Revolution. All students that graduated in the first promotion from the fifth class at the school's directing department were called the Fifth Generation. Their experience during the Cultural Revolution influenced the way they reflected on social issues and Chinese traditions together with their questioning of established values and meanings (including a search for cultural roots and a Chinese identity). Fifth-Generation films during the 1980s were characterized by the juxtaposition between the rural and the urban as well as between Chinese traditions and modernization (Cornelius & Haydn Smith 2002: 58). Fifth-Generation moviemakers were familiar with living in the rural world and being close to nature. Most of them were sent to the countryside as forced labor during the Cultural Revolution. These movie directors, forced to be in the countryside for years, have a personal knowledge of rural life, which is very valuable when they depict the Chinese rural landscape and the traditional life of the peasantry. Chen Kaige and Zhang Yimou, prominent moviemakers of this generation, spent part of their adulthood in the countryside, forced by the government to learn from the peasantry. In their movies, they capture their individual experiences, the crude reality of distant rural areas, showing the beauty of nature inside a life of restrictions. Their movies generally portray adverse social conditions, interpreted as criticism against governmental policies. The employment of ambiguity, symbols, and metaphors along with a sense of open interpretation provided a certain degree of protection from strict film censorship. They look into the cultural past in order to understand the present. At the same time they are inspired by the artistic Chinese landscape tradition to depict the beauty, solitude, and mysticism of nature in contrast to the dual nature of city life. Chen Kaige, in his movie *King of the Children* (1987), aims to capture his own personal experience when he was sent as 'intellectual youth' to work in a production brigade in the countryside in Yunnan province during the late 1960s and 1970s. The movie is the adaptation of a novel of a fellow brigade member, A. Cheng. Also during the repressive Cultural Revolution, Zhang Yimou was sent to work in farm fields with Chinese peasants after finishing high school. Later he was transferred to a textile factory in the city of Xianyang. His acclaimed movie *Shanghai Triad* (1995), which won the prize for Best Cinematography at the Cannes Film Festival in 1995, is a reinterpretation of the Li Xiao's novel *Gang Law*. The title of the movie in Chinese in *Yáo a yáo, yáo dào wàipó qiáo*, which translates as 'row, row, row the boat to grandma bridge', a traditional rural Chinese lullaby. The movie uses the excuse of the depiction of a narrative set in the Shanghai of the 1930s, to speak about the nostalgia of an idyllic rural way of life that is vanishing.

Sixth-Generation moviemakers, also known as the 'Urban Generation', were characterized by the use of underground filmmaking. Produced using DVD cameras, Chinese film was adapted to low budgets, which in turn allowed for the fast-paced shooting and independence from the Chinese studio system that characterized this generation. As a consequence of their freedom and independence, many of the Sixth-Generation movies have been banned. These movies clearly value the sensitive aspects of urban life in contemporary China, especially in the late 1990s and the first decade of the twenty-first century. These films deal with topics such as poverty, rising crime, the marginality of the rural migratory groups, and a sense of youth disorientation in Chinese cities and provincial towns resulting from the changes brought about by Deng Xiaoping's economic reforms (Cornelius & Haydn Smith 2002: 106). With great emphasis on social criticism, they concentrate their attention on youths' urban experience, especially that of rural migrants who move to urban areas, facing issues such as dislocation, lack of emotional affectivity, social urban constraints, nonattachment to the environment, and passive acceptance of events or aggressiveness, with the cities and towns as the main scenario of the social conflicts.

Moviemakers from the Sixth Generation concentrate on modern China's cultural transition, and their narratives always hinge on urban areas. Two of the most representative moviemakers of this generation, Jia Zhang-ke and Wang Xiaoshuai, use their own life experience as migrants and the places where they have grown up in rural towns and cities to develop their plots. Cities and rural towns become protagonists in their stories, which center on the uncertain life of young rural migrants.

Jia Zhang-ke, a leading figure of the Sixth Generation, was born in Fenyang, a county-level city in Shanxi Province. His experience of childhood and adolescence in this rural town during the 1970s and 1980s, before moving to Beijing to study cinema, has marked the topics of his film trilogy *Rèn Xiāo yáo* (which translates as 'free from all constraints'). The films in this trilogy are entitled *Xiao Wu* (1998), *Platform* (2000), and *Unknown Pleasures* (2002), and all three depict the socio-economic changes that have occurred in recent decades in his home province of Shanxi as well as his hometown Fenyang. They depict an autobiographical experience of his youth and early adulthood. *Platform*, which is set in the small town of Fenyang and depicts a period of social transition and economic and cultural reforms from the 1970s to the 1990s, had a tremendous impact in the inland rural areas, which were unprepared to receive the new open Western influences that were beginning to be felt along the coastal provinces and cities; here they tended to be seen as forces imposed from the outside.

The movie director Wang Xiaoshuai expresses his experience as a migrant in his films. He was born in Shanghai and moved to Guiyand with his family who were forced to work in the industrial 'third line of defense', which was intended to protect the country in the event of war with the Soviet Union. In 1979, he and his family moved to Wuhan and later, in 1981, to Beijing. The film *So Close to Paradise* (1998) – Wang's first major film production within the Chinese studio system – depicts the life of constraints of three young rural migrants that live in the city of Wuhan. The movie takes place in the 1980s.

Repairing a rural-urban continuum

After the First Opium War and the establishment of the treaty ports, Western imperialism and the semi-colonial control of the Western powers slowly transformed not only the port cities like Shanghai (which had been open to foreign trade since the 1842 Treaty of Nanking that ended the conflict) but also their hinterlands, and with it, the nature of the classical Chinese territorial structure. Chinese territory was, at that time, a rural-urban continuum that was subject to a national system of administration and law and organized into counties that combined both towns and cities within a large rural area (Stockman 2000: 47). The territory was not organized by one central city surrounded by secondary urban nuclei subordinated to the main capital center; instead, centers of small size and low centrality were positioned everywhere between larger centers of greater centrality (Skinner 1977: 258).

In China's territorial structure, there was also interaction between an urban administration and a predominantly rural society. Individuals were urban in their administrative and religious apparatus and rural in their bonds to the land, nature, and place of origin. The rural population temporarily living in urban centers was made up of mostly sojourners who moved to cities for professional reasons. Chinese society was, therefore, based on a social structure of mobility: the mobility of merchants to cities to exploit business opportunities (where they were treated as second-class citizens), or the mobility of students and state administrators around the country. The state examination system allowed many students to become scholars and serve the state administration in urban nuclei for a fixed period of time. All social categories other than peasants were urban; nevertheless, non-peasant social groups were more urban in their abode than in their residence (ibid: 265). The residence was permanent, located in the rural place of origin where the family lived and ancestors were buried. The abode, by contrast, was the temporary urban residence for a fixed period of time, which sometimes stretched on for decades due to the demands of governmental service or business activities.

Despite this mobility, the place of origin and one's family roots were essential components of Chinese identity. Native bonds were the guiding principle behind social organization. Sojourners were organized inside the city by place of origin through the existence of native-place associations. The local residential unit was the compatriot's temple (*hsiang-tzu*) that took care of its members (Skinner 1977: 539). Economic organizations such as guilds also developed as fraternal organizations that were based on the provenance of its members. Society was linked to a socially bound construct of local systems connected to the overall structure of territorial systems. In addition, native bonds were connected to the Confucian commitment to family obedience. Any young man who left to seek his fortune elsewhere was expected to return to his rural home for marriage, for mourning the death of a parent, and finally, in retiring to the locality where his ancestors were buried.

Shanghai, once it was opened to foreign trade, became an international financial metropolis and the most important commercial center in China. Unlike Beijing, Shanghai was a symbol of modernity. In literary descriptions it was characterized as being isolated from Chinese

Figure 5.1 *Migrant 'village'* (cun) *in Fangzhuang, Beijing (2001)*

Photo: Ana M. Moya Pellitero

traditions and cut off from China's past by being thrown into modernity (Yingjin 1996: 117). Compared with Beijing, Shanghai was seen by the Chinese as a corrupted and degenerate urban center because it was not a Chinese city, as it was neither an administrative nor a religious center. Commercial and financial operations for private gain were considered inherently immoral under Confucian principles and tolerated to the extent that they were deemed necessary for the demands of the city. In China, the market and the commercial activities surrounding trade were always held as government monopolies. This is why Shanghai became an isolated cluster, like other international port cities, in order not to contaminate the traditional Chinese urban-rural continuum of the hinterland. The break with the past and traditions was also connected to the image of 'Shanghai sojourners'. In the late nineteenth and early twentieth centuries, the population of Shanghai consisted mostly of people who had migrated from traditional neighboring provinces and who found themselves confronted with Western culture. In international Shanghai, Chinese migrants who arrived from the hinterland to find work were organized into native-place associations and provincial guilds, which defended and protected their members. Seen through a Westerner's eyes, the 'Shanghai sojourners, with their rural backgrounds, were discriminated against and treated as an underclass. They were referred to by the Western pejorative term "peasant" (*nong min*), which entailed backwardness' (Cohen 1993: 151-70). This Western vision that valued the urban way of life over the rural was in opposition to traditional Chinese culture which valued the rural over the urban. It was a cliché of imperial Confucianism that rural life fostered virtue while cities were centers of vice and corruption (Wright 1977: 34). The Chinese migrants arriving in Shanghai were aware that the modern city was a source of contamination and depravation, a place of sexual promiscuity and moral corruption, and a dangerous trap for the young and the innocent. In the article 'Youth and the Countryside', published in the Morning Post on 20-23 February 1919, Li Dazhao writes:

> Listen to me, young friends who are wandering in the city! You must know that there is abundant evil in the city, whereas there is abundant happiness in the country; that there is more darkness in urban life, yet more brightness in rural life; that urban life is almost meant for devils, whereas rural activities are all human activities; that urban air is filthy, while rural air is fresh. Why don't you hurry to pack your bags, pay your hotel bills, and return to your native soil? (quoted in Yingjin, 1996: 11).

The movie *Shanghai Triad* by Zhang Yimou is not a film nostalgically depicting the modernity of Shanghai in the 1930s, with the glamor of Westernized urban life bathed in corruption. Neither is it a historical film depicting and describing how this cosmopolitan city existed in the past. As Christine Boyer asserts, 'Zhang Yimou takes the glamorous nightlife of 1930s Shanghai and deliberately flattens and twists it. (...) From the outset he offers the spectator painted backdrops and reflected images' (Boyer 2002: 88-89). Zhang Yimou does not show panoramic cityscapes, aerial or street views. He shows an urban atmosphere always experienced by individuals through interiors and at night, inside luxurious nightclubs, sophisticated mansions, secret warehouses, and mysterious streets. The city disappears in reflections, glasses, and mirrors, with the artificial light giving shape to misty environments, smoky dance salons, and warmly decorated interiors.

In this movie, Zhang Yimou does not aim to compare the values and lifestyles of the modern city with those of the traditional countryside. He does not want simply to emphasize the positive qualities of the rural over the urban and the negative influence of urban life on the virtue and simplicity of the rural youth. In reality, Zhang Yimou wants to reveal how the urban modernization in China was interwoven with a rural patriarchal clan system (Chen 2000: 235). These patriarchal clan systems were based on the filial obedience of blood and geographical relationships based on paternal relationships, which was especially true of rural society (Biliang 2007: 59).

The movie depicts the life of a rural clan community in the modern city of Shanghai of the 1930s through the innocent eyes of a young boy from the countryside. A rural migrant arriving in Shanghai, Tang Shuisheng has been summoned by his uncle Liu to work as a personal servant for the mistress of a distant relative, also called Tang, who is a triad boss. All the members of the gang belong to the same native place of origin, and they offer him a job and protection in a city of prosperity and opportunity. He is expected, and required, to respond with loyalty and obedience. The story is narrated as a diary of his first seven days inside the clan. At a certain moment the triad boss flees to the countryside, together with his most loyal men, in order to hide from a rival gang. They settle on an almost uninhabited island. Zhang Yimou uses an unsophisticated and natural feeling in most of the scenes of the island, with high wild grasses and bamboo. There are only two structures on the island: two small huts that are reminiscent of the classical cottage retreats of the literati. These cottages in a natural setting were important retirement and rural exile refuges for politicians and scholars who found themselves temporarily out of office throughout Chinese history. In *Shanghai Triad*, the retreat into nature is only temporary. The movie shows how corruption and brutality, which have a negative impact on the harmonious and simple way of life on the island, does not have its origin in the modern city life or in Western lifestyles. Violence is generated among the members of the same rural community, and it affects the humanity of three blameless countryside characters – Shuisheng (the servant), Bijou (the mistress), and Ajiao (the island neighbor). At the end of the movie, Shuisheng discovers that all three are victims. He is not able to escape the power of a hierarchical system and is forced to return to a city that, despite being a symbol of modernity and Western influences, still contains close circles of rural and loyal relationship networks that limit personal freedom.

During the communist revolution, foreign imperialism was identified with central cities, and it was believed that essential roots of Chinese nationhood and Chinese communism were in the countryside, with the peasants (Stockman 2000: 51). Communist and national ideals aimed to recover the equilibrium and equity lost between the rural and the urban world. When the People's Republic was established in 1949, the government aimed to create an industrialization plan based on the Soviet model in the cities. Cities were expected to be 'producers' not 'consumers' and were to be inhabited by an industrial working class. Besides, one of the aims of Chinese communism was to bring urban areas and the countryside to the same level of development, re-establishing a new economic and cultural urban-rural continuum. To equalize the opportunities in the cities and the countryside, the Communist Party initiated a campaign of urbanization for rural areas. Education and medical services were expanded, together with the creation of cooperative farming. Properties were confiscated and religious and traditional patterns abolished. Mao's aim was also to eliminate urban-rural economic and social differences.

To achieve that goal, the state maintained total control over population flows. From the middle of the 1950s onwards, the system of population registration (*hukou*) limited mobility. The *hukou* system was a household registration record that identified Chinese citizens as resident of either an urban or a rural area. Migrant workers required many bureaucratic passes in order to travel and settle in other areas. It was the Party who had the power to mobilize the population if this was considered necessary. During the Great Leap Forward (1958-61), urban residents were temporarily sent to rural areas to help in programs of rapid agricultural development, rural urbanization, and industrialization. This urban population was forced to move to the fields and factories in the countryside to improve the cultural and economic transformation; at the same time they could develop an appreciation for the problems of the rural population. From 1958 onwards, peasants had to belong to People's Communes that were responsible for their own agricultural and industrial gains and production. They were also in charge of maintaining, repairing, or renewing irrigation systems, dams, and ditches. It is in this period that schools and medical care were provided free of charge. A later modification of the commune system in 1962, after the Great Leap Forward, restored the private plots and free peasant markets, obliging rural communes to carry the costs of schools and health care (Parish & King White 1978: 34). Factories and cooperatives in rural areas had to establish their own schools and provide education for their members, combining a half-work, half-study system. However, many children in rural areas were receiving little or no education. 'Rural' workers had to be members of a specific production team, a unit of a brigade that was a sub-unit of a commune. The distribution of gains was allotted according to work points (i.e. labor contributed to the collective), while students paid for their education out of the work and wages of their communes (Gardner 1971: 245). Conversely, there were benefits for those living in the cities. Urban workers, i.e. those with an urban *hukou*, had the right to state protection for housing, schools, healthcare, food, and clothes. Thus, despite the good will of political campaigns, the equality between the urban and the rural world was never achieved. There were, still, many advantages for the urban dweller and many scarcities for those living in rural areas.

During the Cultural Revolution (1966-76), educated urban youth were sent to the countryside to learn true socialist values. Unconsciously, the Confucianist ideal of nature as deliverance from corruption was present in Mao campaigns. Mao called the campaign *shangshan-*

xiaxiang ('up to the mountains and down to the countryside'). Some young urban visitors became teachers in rural schools. However, the peasantry felt that rural areas were a dumping ground for urban youths who failed to follow communist mandates in the city (Gardner 1971: 239). The ones that married peasants maintained their urban *hukou*, while their partner (and their child) had to continue to live in the countryside (Friedman 2005: 60). Families were divided because of different household registrations. Some of the youths who had been sent to the countryside died as a result of the difficult conditions, the lack of medical attention, the hostility of the rural cadres, and the low wages and general levels of poverty.

Chen Kaige, in his movie *King of the Children* (1987) – *Haizi wang* in Chinese – aimed to capture his own personal experience during the Cultural Revolution, a time when he was sent as an 'intellectual youth' to work in a production brigade in the Yunnan countryside during the late 1960s and 1970s. The movie is the adaptation of a novel with the same title (1984) of his fellow brigade member A. Cheng. It tells the story of a young man, Lao Gan, who belongs to a brigade of city youths in the forests of Yunnan. Despite the fact that he is barely educated, he is chosen as a talented person with a good temper to be sent as a

Figure 5.2 *Film still from* King of the Children *(1987)*

In the movie *King of the Children* (1987), Chen Kaige introduces the oxen to symbolize both the proletariat rural masses and the intellectual servants.

Photo: Xi'an Film Studio

teacher in the second cycle of a countryside school. The school occupies a prominent spot on a hill, surrounded by forests, where nothing changes except the constant passing of time. The movie is an allegory of the relation of the powerless proletariat rural masses, with the urban intellectuals who are at their service. The children in the movie symbolize the Chinese people, represented as powerless figures. Mao Tse-tung ended a speech on art and literature delivered in 1942 with a couplet from the writer and poet Lu Xun's *Zizhao* ('Self-mockery'), supplying his own politicized interpretation:

> This couplet from a poem by Lu Xun should be our motto: Fierce-browed, I coolly defy a thousand pointing fingers; Head-bowed, like a willing ox I serve the children. The 'thousand pointing fingers' are our enemies, and we will never yield to them, no matter how ferocious. The 'children' here symbolise the proletariat and the masses. All communists, all revolutionaries, all revolutionary literary and art works should learn from the example of Lu Xun and be the 'oxen' for the proletariat and the masses, bending their backs to the task until their dying day.[1]

The image of the urban intellectuals becoming oxen for the rural proletariat is associated, in the movie of Chen Kaige, with the allegory of the teachers and the children. The story focuses on Lao Gan's relationship with the young rural students and the pedagogic aim of the Communist Party of bringing two worlds together, where urban intellectuals must learn from peasants, who are in turn served by the urban intellectuals. The educational experiences of Lao Gan in the countryside seem to be unsuccessful. Nature and the rural life seem to cause stupor, lethargy, and boredom in the teacher. Lao Gan feels unfortunate; he does not think he is learning or doing anything useful. He is constantly counting the time passing. He feels the weight of the years, forced against his will to be in isolation and constantly dreaming of his return to the city. With a critical attitude, Lao Gan introduces changes in the communist learning methods of the rural school. Students were used to mechanically copying standardized communist texts from the blackboard not knowing their meaning or content. The rural students start learning with him the meaning of characters, writing freely their own thoughts. From the imposed abstract political slogans to concrete life experiences, Lao Gan teaches individuals, not the collective. He wants the students to learn to think for themselves, and 'to speak when they have something to say', because 'nature' and the 'rural life' are a source of knowledge and freedom. Lao Gan teaches the students a new character *niú shui* ('ox-water'). He explains to the students this new character: 'Oxen are stubborn animals, you can scold them and hit them, and they just blink at you. But there are times when oxen go wild – that is, when you piss. This is because oxen love salt.' The ox in this case is at the same time the proletarian rural masses and the intellectual servants. The pissing master is the Communist Party, which gives to peasants education and culture and to urban intellectuals a peasant working experience with the aim of transforming them into obedient and pleased masses.

Traumatic contrast between rural and urban life

With the open economic policies of Deng Xiaoping in the 1980s, the countryside was de-collectivized. The rural land that belonged to the commune was divided into individual plots and leased to farmers for fifteen to twenty-five years. The single-family farm of freehold ownership allowed peasants to invest labor and money in their own land, paying part of their gains in taxes to the government. However, this household-responsibility system failed because farms were dispersed, and the lack of capital and large-scale farming made investment impossible (Wilson 1996: 170). The government also gave farmers responsibility for improving rural management and maintaining infrastructure, but farmers did not have a powerful organization as they had during the commune period.

From the 1990s on, farmers started engaging in sideline activities, working for industries and enterprises in rural towns. These industries were cooperative local organizations (the collective property of local governments), run by party members and local investors. Rural towns and villages were able to establish productive industries for basic consumer goods like textile, paper, simple electronics, simple agricultural tools, bricks for house construction, and extraction industries like coal. When there were no jobs in the factories or when it was harvest time, workers returned to tending their crops. However, many farmers lived in miserable conditions. Many services formerly provided by the state now had to be paid for by the farmers themselves, including roads, wells, schools, and electricity networks, which required extra income. The poorest farmers asked the youngest family members to seek jobs elsewhere as 'surplus migratory labor' in rural industries in the rural towns and cities. The farms were left in the hands of women, children, and the elderly, making rural development hardly possible. Despite the fact that most of the land was not cultivated, many farmers still preferred to abandon it rather than transfer it to others through rent contracts because they valued property as a form of security (Chang & Kwok 1990: 149). As a result, there has been a gradual abandonment of agriculture as a way of life in favor of work in rural industries and cities.

With the abandonment of rural land and rural production, there is the danger of an unsustainable situation in the equilibrium between the supply and demand of primary goods and food. The number of migrant people in big urban conurbations is increasing, while the rural countryside is being abandoned. The communist ideal of equilibrium and the achievement of a rural-urban continuum between both worlds has not been accomplished. The actual Chinese political goal is economic growth concentrated in big manufacturing companies in urban conurbations and the international projection of their mega-cities on a global scale.

With the economic and political reforms of 1978, restrictions on social mobility changed slightly. The government slogan in the 1980s was *li tu bu li xiang* (to leave the land but not to leave the rural areas). The peasant workers (*mingong*) lived in rural areas and commuted to the rural towns for work, or migrated to cities as laborers without getting an urban *hukou*. There was a 'decentralized urban growth' (Lee 1992: 89-118). Towns and cities became centers of economic activity but not bases of residential expansion. Townships (*xiang*) had a rural *hukou*, and many farmers coming from other rural villages could work and live in them. However, since 1984 many former *xiang* became towns with urban status (*zhen*). The first reform in the household registration system made it possible for peasants to move into these small towns (*zhen*). In 2000, over 100 million rural residents were making their living in them (Stockman 2000: 59). In 2001, a second round of major reform regarding registration resulted in rural *hukou* residents being able to move to small cities and designated towns of less than 200,000 inhabitants if they had a stable job and a legal urban residence. However, many rural migrants still live in poor conditions, and in their desperation they enter cities illegally in search of jobs. They do not have any rights to social housing or healthcare. Rural migrants are considered to be a 'temporary' population known as *mang liu* (blind migrants). They are not officially registered in the cities and therefore have become known as the 'floating population'. These illegal rural migrants live without fixed abode, constantly travelling from place to place. Many of them do not stay permanently in the city; they are either 'cyclical' (returning home in cycles such as during harvest time) or 'repeat migrants' (they return to their native place, only to leave again at a later time) (Friedmann 2005: 65).

In the movie *Platform* (2000) – *Zhàntái* in Chinese, named after a popular song about waiting at a railway platform – Jia Zhang-ke depicts his own personal memories of the times and places of his youth in an epic chronological linearity. It narrates the important changes of a period of transition during the 1980s and 1990s, seen through the lives of a group of young boys and girls working at a cultural brigade cultural

Figure 5.3 *Film still from* Platform *(2000)*

Jia Zhang-ke in Platform (2000), shows how modern urban trends do not adapt to a frozen rural way of life.

Photo: Ana M. Moya Pellitero

troupe (*wengongtuan*) in Fenyang, the hometown of Jia Zhang-ke, which is in Shanxi province. The movie registers the details of the daily life of this young group as they discover their adulthood and search for new dreams whose generational rupture challenges established party restrictions. The young group is always on tour, moving through villages and rural towns, celebrating Mao's teachings in their musical representations. They strongly believe in the security and protection of the brigade under the mandates of the Communist Party. However, they are also influenced by new fashions (clothes from Guangzhou, foreign movies and hairstyles, music from Taiwan, or European literature). All of them have big dreams about leaving the rural town and moving to big modern cities because there they can find a better future. However, they are trapped in a rural network of poverty due to their rural *hukou* and the limited opportunities for youth in rural areas, while modernity always comes from the outside, from the big urban centers. Throughout the movie the young group talks about progress without being fully able to achieve it. The film encapsulates a feeling of anticipation for a new modern life (illegal songs, hairstyles, clothing, literature) and disappointment once this modern culture is integrated by the government and adapted inside a rural context and a rural society (McGrath 2007:

97). New urban trends and fashions do not adapt to a frozen rural way of life. Historical and cultural change is depicted inside trivial events, quotidian moments, inactivity, and boredom. There is an experience of melancholy in the young characters about a future that remains out of reach and a past that is lost. Changes occur slowly and unnoticeably; signs of change appear as a result of a slow process, blurring the details of how they happened. After the privatization of the entertainment business, the cultural brigade is bought by one of the comrades. They are forced to be competitive and to earn their own economic benefits, so they reinvent themselves as an 'all-star rock-and-breakdance electronic band'. They try to copy commercial pop culture and operate at the mercy of the market. These new songs and international go-go dances are not well accepted in the rural villages and towns where they tour. They feel marginalized in their own rural environment. They are constantly travelling, short of money. As 'repeat migrants', they always return to Fenyang after long periods of touring, while the rural hometown remains unchanged. The young group is constantly drifting around in the same poor rural environment. In the middle of the valley, their truck breaks down; a train passes along a viaduct and they run towards it but cannot reach it. It is an allegory of modernity, experienced as an absence. They experience a life in which all the hopes of youth are truncated by the limitations of freedom of movement. The countryside and nature are vast but prisonlike due to the rural *hukou* registration. At the same time, rural areas are unprepared to deal with the modernity and cultural reforms coming from urban centers.

Rural migrants, a hidden reality

Researchers agree that by about the mid-1990s, migration to cities in China affected approximately 80-100 million people (Stockman 1992: 65). At present, temporary residents without a formal urban household registration arrive in large numbers in the cities. Most of them are temporary workers, construction laborers, and housemaids. Chinese megacities (Shanghai, Beijing, Guangzhou, Shenzhen, Tianjin) are magnets for young rural migrants dreaming of a better future and opportunities. This population is unskilled, but they know there is enough work for everyone. However, what they do not know is that their illegal situation with a rural household registration makes them secondary citizens, without basic rights for needs such as health, social housing, or a normal salary. Migrants, because of their rural status, cannot obtain state-subsidized housing in the cities (*anju*). Cities like Shanghai or Hong Kong with semi-colonial networks and international projection are proud of their urban international status. At the same time, their citizens are also overconfident of their job opportunities and their city's international status on a global level. Other cities in China are competing to reach the same degree of international projection.

Meanwhile, being a rural migrant in these global metropolises entails backwardness and illiteracy; it means not having a stable life or equal opportunities. This 'floating population' in China is now considered to be a dangerous class (Friedmann 2005: 63). They barely mix with the urban population because they live on the fringes, on construction sites, or in factories. It is an 'invisible population' that gathers together in groups coming from the same place of origin. This Confucian tradition and principle of social organization still holds today, and it helps migrants to find a safe place in the urban social structure, despite their illegal condition. The state does not control the numbers of illegal rural migrants. The majority of them end up doing dangerous, dirty, and difficult jobs, in family enterprises, manufacturing industries, or as maids in middle-class households. They also move to the marginal trades of the informal and illegal economies. All of them are exploited and paid less than the minimum wage. Young migrant women are also at high risk of being sexually exploited and abused. Migrants are housed in cramped dormitories, squeezed into rooms with many others from the same place of origin because their limited monthly salaries are not enough to pay for individual rooms. Migrants also need to save money to support families in the countryside, one of the major reasons why they left home in the first place.

Rural migrants have created a social space outside of official planning that implies a transformation not only of the physical space of the cities but also of society in general (Zhang 2001: 202-3). The migrants create alternative spaces to live in using illegal structures like temporary housing, stores, restaurants, and street markets. Beijing or Shanghai periodically eradicate migrant enclaves and repatriate the population because these areas are considered a threat to the public order (due to poor living conditions, social disorder, and the deterioration of the urban environment). For important international gatherings and events, the government mobilizes clean-up campaigns, demolishing illegal structures. In the cities, illegal enclaves are called 'villages' (*cun*) and are preceded by the name of the province where the migrants come from. In Beijing there is a Henancun, Anhuicun, Zhejiangcun, and so forth. These villages are conglomerations of illegal dwellings located in peri-urban zones (Friedmann 2005: 70). The main government action against illegal enclaves and urban deterioration is urban development plans with a 'demolition-development' model. In the case of peri-urban villages around big metropolitan conurbations, the government changes the residents' registration household from rural to urban *hukou* in order to expel the rural migrant population living inside these chaotic, shanty, and spatially segregated areas. When this happens, the migrant rural population living in them automatically acquires a status of illegality, forcing them to relocate elsewhere and be in constant drift.

In his movie *So Close to Paradise* (1998), Wang Xiaoshuai shares his personal experience as a migrant. The movie is recorded in the city of Wuhan, where he lived for two years. With a nearly documentary style, he depicts the marginal reality of the rural population. It introduces the problem of the invisibility of rural migrants in cities. Processes of assimilation inside the city are painful, and in order to survive, the rural migrants have to cope with uncertainties and hide or renounce their own identity. The story is explained by a country boy, Dongzi, trying to make a living in the city in order to send money to his family. He lives with another rural migrant from the same village, Huangpi. The young boy works as a 'shoulder pole' for two yuan per day. Comradeship based on place of origin is important for mutual help. However, his fellow countryman leads a criminal life. The young boy does manual labor, but he cannot pay for his miserable room, while his friend, hiding his rural identity, deals with illegal businesses and makes money. The movie questions the survival mechanisms of the migrant, living in a small ramshackle apartment at the riverside, where there is no running water

Figure 5.4 *Film still from* So Close to Paradise *(1998)*

In his film *So Close to Paradise* (1998), Wang Xiaoshuai introduces the problem of the invisibility of rural migrants in cities.

Photo: Ana M. Moya Pellitero

or heating. Dongzi cannot earn enough money to make a normal living. The boy begins to doubt. He wishes to go back to his village where life is easier despite the misery. Both rural migrants fall in love with a Vietnamese bar-singer, who is a victim of sexual exploitation.

The rural floating population plays an indispensable role in providing cheap labor for China's rapid urbanization. However, this floating population becomes the most heavily exploited in contemporary Chinese society, as rural migrants are disliked because of their propensity for petty crimes, untidiness, and dirtiness, as well as their lack of education. The movie also shows the power of the judicial detention system, reorganized in the early 1990s, to quickly repatriate the rural floating population and migrant laborers whenever necessary in order to preserve 'urban beauty and neatness' (Xu 2007: 68). Because rural migrants cannot become legal residents – it is only through education that it is possible to legalize one's move to another part of the country – migrants need to hide and renounce their identities. As Tsung-yi Michelle Huang refers to in her chapter in this publication, rural migrants have an attitude of 'flexible cross-border identity'. The aim of the immigrants is to make the process of assimilation in big cities less painful by negating the basis of the Confucian social structure of veneration to native bonds. Only by negating their own identity is it possible to enjoy their own freedom in the city. Wang Xiaoshuai reveals in his film the cruel reality of a rural-urban divide that only disappears by erasing the signs of identity such us accents, attitudes, clothes, etc. Migrant survival in the cities is about hiding status and identity.

Conclusion

The main reason for the People's Republic's failure to repair the rural-urban continuum has been the impossibility of solving the educational, social, and economic inequality between rural areas and cities. Despite the efforts to attain an equitable, productive society, where villages and cities are inhabited by a working class, and despite the good intention of levelling out the differences between urban intellectuals and laboring peasants and overcoming the distinction between mental and manual labor, peasants during the period that Mao was in power suffered isolation and poverty. They were asked to be responsible for their own production and the maintenance of infrastructure, services and education, while urban citizens enjoyed the advantages of free education, services, healthcare, food, and clothes.

With the reform of the agricultural system and the move to a socialist market economy, farmers have seen an increase in their responsibilities and taxes, forcing them to migrate to maintain their families. The reform of the economic system since 1984 has emphasized the development of urban areas. Education has been a mechanism for levelling society, and even today, rural students that score highly in the national examinations for college entrance have access to legalized urban *hukou* and can thereby improve their social status in urban areas.

The even bigger problem of inequality between the rural and the urban worlds in China cannot be solved by erasing or hiding the problem. The government's aim is to create cities that are clean and tidy. Therefore, since the 1990s, the judicial detention system has repatriated the rural floating population and migrant laborers whenever necessary by applying a development plan in cities with a 'demolition-development' model in order to clean up illegal enclaves.

Since the 1980s, Chinese moviemakers have felt responsible for reflecting on Chinese society, especially its rural-urban inequalities. Fifth-Generation moviemakers, in attempting to avoid state censorship, have used the technique of open interpretation and allegory in their filmic narratives. In that way they could expound their critical vision and standpoint without restriction. Sixth-Generation moviemakers have been more direct in presenting their critical overview by using a documentary style and using digital cameras with low budgets that do not require government funding. Many of their films have been banned in China.

Nowadays, a New Documentary Movement is proliferating in digital form. This has taken a central role in Chinese audio-visual culture over the last two decades. The films are characterized by immediacy, spontaneity, and closer contact with the lived experience (Berry & Rofel 2010: 4). This New Documentary Movement is acquiring an important role in the struggle to survive outside the state system. The films that are emerging from this movement are low-budget, independent documentary films using digital cameras, and bring together larger numbers of young filmmakers, and are shown outside the official Chinese film system. These young moviemakers can make themselves heard by exposing social inequalities, approaching individual realities and sharing them through visual mass media and information and communication technologies. The digital video in China is offering evidence of social inequalities, mainly among migrants, allowing the voice of ordinary people to be heard. In this way it has succeeded in opening up a platform for social debate.

Note

1 'Talks at the Yenan Forum on Literature and Art', Mao Tse-tung on Literature and Art (Beijing: Foreign Languages Press, 1960: 39-40; quoted in Chow, 1993: 91).

6 Revisiting Hong Kong

Fruit Chan's 'Little Cheung'

Tsung-yi Michelle Huang

Abstract

This chapter uses Hong Kong director Fruit Chan's city film *Little Cheung* as a case study in order to tease out specific aspects of the postcolonial narrative of the global city. The central argument is that in the global city, the 'localness' in the postcolonial discourse can never be taken for granted but must be realized as a kind of 'construction'. As seen in the film, one of the formative logics of the postcolonial discourse is the naturalization of the global: when urban space replaces rural landscape as the site to anchor one's local consciousness, the spatial geographies of global cities have to be erased or rendered unseen. Therefore, in the film the population flow in the global city becomes naturalized, and another salient sign of the global city – the monumental buildings – is represented as local landmarks rather than a symbol of global capital. My analysis of *Little Cheung* intends to foreground the dilemma that East-Asian cities face. On the one hand, to represent the subalterns, postcolonial narratives have to be written, and only in that way can the 'local' be recognized. Chan's representation of back streets and alleyways as the central setting of the film is clear evidence of this point. Without such narratives, the subalterns of East-Asian cities will remain the invisible other, marginalized in the grand narrative of contemporary globalization. On the other hand, as seen in Hong Kong's case, to construct an 'authentic' local, the first task to tackle in the postcolonial writing is the spatial characteristics of global cities. If the postcolonial writing of the 'local' erases the global to such an extent that the representation of the local turns into a de-territorialized myth, the postcolonial narrative, which originally is meant to speak for the local, might at the same time unconsciously facilitate the operation of global metropolises, and hence become an ideological instrument undetected by city-users.

Hong Kong and its (post)coloniality

> A poet in Hong Kong is by the very nature of things distanced from all that grandiose and heroic voice. He is writing like a clown speaking on television, like a cab driver speaking in the front seat, or someone speaking directly to the inner life, or intimately to his friends.
>
> *Leung Ping-kwan*

> I would suggest instead that postcoloniality is the condition of the intelligentsia of global capitalism. The question, then, is not whether this global intelligentsia can (or should) return to national loyalties but whether, in recognition of its own class position in global capitalism, it can generate a thoroughgoing criticism of its own ideology and formulate practices of resistance against the system of which it is a product.
>
> *Arif Dirlik*

In the 1990s, Hong Kong and its postcolonial present have received much attention among cultural critics. Most of the interpretations suggest the indeterminacy of Hong Kong's postcolonial condition. For example, Rey Chow argues that Hong Kong's return to China simply marks the beginning of another era of colonization instead of putting an end to it: Hong Kong's handover should be understood as a transfer 'between colonizers', since the 'One Country, Two Systems' means anything but an informed choice by Hong Kong people.[1] Esther Yau also points out Hong Kongers' contradictory mindset and calls for a careful analysis of local people's changing relationship to China as well as the colonial government in different historical contexts (180-81). For Ackbar Abbas, Hong Kong's postcoloniality is a happening that took place well before 1997: 'the eventualities have arrived before the event' (1997b: 304). Specifically, Abbas argues that '[p]ostcoloniality begins, it has already begun, when subjects find themselves thinking and acting in a certain way; in other words, postcoloniality is a tactic and a practice, not a legal-political contract, or a historical accident' (1997a: 10).

To draw on Abbas's observation, I argue that in the historical development of Hong Kong's postcolonial consciousness the Sino-British Joint Declaration signed in 1984 plays a crucial role in shaping how Hong Kong people define their own identity. A powerful statement reasserting China's sovereignty, the declaration stamped China into the collective cultural and national imagination of the Hong Kong people.[2] Starting with this (working) definition, I hope to clarify the interaction between postcolonial writing and the urban space of the global city by closely examining the cultural representation of the postcolonial consciousness rather than the political structures of postcoloniality. As Abbas argues, '[c]ultural forms, too, can perhaps also be regarded as a rebus that projects a city's desires and fears, although it is likely to be a rebus of a particularly complex kind' (1997a: 1). By interpreting the cultural forms represented in Fruit Chan's film *Little Cheung* (2000), the following analysis aims to illustrate the complexity of addressing such postcolonial concerns as the local and the rural in the global city.

Little Cheung: a postcolonial narrative of a global city

Chan's postcolonial narrative relies on a surprisingly simple device: the story of a young boy, the Little Cheung of the title. In the film, we follow Cheung, a nine-year-old from the Portland Street area in Mong Kok, through a short period in his life (from winter 1996 through summer 1997) that happens to coincide with the Chinese takeover of Hong Kong. As a part-time delivery boy at his father's restaurant, Little Cheung's life centers on his family and neighbors. Among them are his grandmother, a former Cantonese opera singer; his father, a serious and hard-working restaurant owner; his mother, a regular at the neighborhood mahjong house; Armi, the Filipina maid that takes care of him; neighbors from all walks of life; and his new friend, Fan, an illegal immigrant from China. During the summer of 1997, we see Little Cheung occupying himself at school by learning Mandarin Chinese, playing with Tamagotchi (his virtual pet), delivering food for tips, and asking around about his disowned, disappeared older brother. In the city, aside from 'celebrating the handover', as Chan ironically puts it, every Hong Konger is concerned with the sickly Cantonese opera-singer Brother Cheung and his family scandal due to a heritage dispute. Before the summer comes to an end, Brother Cheung and grandma pass away, Armi leaves, and Fan is deported back to China.

Partly because *Little Cheung* uses Hong Kong's return to China as its setting, the film is generally regarded as the director's 'national' allegory, an effort to constitute a local identity in response to the political impact of 1997.[3] In this last episode of his '1997 Trilogy', Chan persistently tells a story of how the handover changes ordinary people's everyday life.[4] The colonial power pitted against the local is China. Throughout the film, Chan shows the audience how China stakes claims on Hong Kong with shots like the street banners saying 'Celebrate the Handover' or the school children's Mandarin Chinese and civics lessons.

In addition to the apparent political subtext, quite a few critics believe that the film presents a realistic account of street life and stakes out a distinctive Hong Kong identity. For example, Shelly Kraicer points out that '[i]n its focus on the family and the surrounding neighbourhood, the film recalls the classic family neo-realist dramas of an earlier Cantonese cinema'.[5] For Yiu-wai Chu, the film represents a 'seemingly pure local identity' (250). Such arguments raise the question of how to read beyond the self-evident 'national' allegory and identify the particularities of Hong Kong's postcolonial writing. At a time when such ideas as 'local' and 'authentic' have been problematized, when the desire to possess a 'pure local identity' has been debunked as a naïve nostalgic longing, and when 'glocalization' (or 'localized global') has been appropriated as a *cliché*, we have to ask whether Chan's film embodies a 'seemingly pure local identity' told from an 'indigenous perspective' (Chu: 238, 250). To be precise, how does Chan's artistic representation of the local help us comprehend the challenges in fashioning a national or cultural identity in an age characterized by global flows?

To elucidate the problems facing a postcolonial author in the age of globalization, it is essential to trace the tension between Chan's formulation of a local identity and the operating logic of the global city. Therefore, in what follows, the 'local reality' as seen in *Little Cheung* is examined in relation to the urban specificity of Hong Kong as a global city. In a sense, Chan is able to present an 'authentic' local identity because he pushes front and center the seemingly banal everyday life of a grassroots community. More importantly, such a representation of the local is made possible by reconfiguring the global space in the local through innovative filmic language and narrative strategies, which not only naturalize foreign laborers and illegal immigrants as neighbors and family but also displace the monumental space of the global city into the postcolonial place for Hong Kong's identity formation. That is, the artistic treatment of global city vistas in *Little Cheung* suggests the dilemma of Hong Kong's postcolonial writing: the attempt to compose a counternarrative against the backdrop of cultural hegemony may also unwittingly re-marginalize the other (foreign laborers and illegal immigrants) in the global city and in turn fall prey to the ideology of 'local-centrism'.

Front and center: the politics of representing the local

The representation of the mundane everyday life of a local community in the film maps out an intelligible and concrete image of Hong Kong, an insider's account of how people in Hong Kong perceive and experience commercial urban spaces on a daily basis. In terms of constructing an indigenous cultural identity, Chan's camera captures the local to counter the stock image of Hong Kong as ungrounded capitalist space. For a long time, Hong Kong has been defined negatively: it is 'a borrowed time and a borrowed place', 'a culture of disappearance', and the epitome of an 'off-ground economy'.[6] The economic miracle is explained by the theory of 'lack', a derogatory rationale that attributes Hong Kong's economic development to its colonized status of lacking political agency, which redirects the libidinal drive to commercialism.[7] At the very beginning of the film, Chan addresses the meanings of economic development and materialism from a banal, pedestrian perspective. As a smart, precocious kid, Little Cheung opens the film with such remarks:

> I understood a lot when I was nine. My father owned a restaurant to make money. The Filipino maid at home was here to make money. My mother played mahjong in the mahjong parlor for money. And Brother Cheung went on TV charity fund-raisers for money. I am no exception. So I have known since little that money is a dream for everyone. No wonder everyone on the street is especially enterprising.

The protagonist's idea of the entrepreneurial mentality suggests that the 'lack' theory might be problematic. As Chow argues, '[w]ith its coloniality, then, economics and commerce *are* Hong Kong's "origins" ' (1993: 187, emphasis original).

The essence of Chan's 'local' lies in the neighborhood he portrays. *Little Cheung* exemplifies a community in the big city. People in the community might come and go; yet for those who stay, it is still the anchor and center of everyday life. Nevertheless, as the story unfolds, we come to realize that the community that promises a sense of belonging and a comfort of being 'at home' is actually the same one that witnesses people leaving one after another (Little Cheung's brother, grandma, Armi, and Fan). The disintegration of the neighborhood points to the instability of 'home' or 'the local'. Such a fast-changing community (the dynamics between mutability and stability, negatively defined and concretely represented, disappearance and reappearance) has to be analyzed in relation to globalization: the chosen local underlines the complicated pattern of transmigration, social integration, and perilous equilibrium in a global city.

Chan's aesthetic choice of the local in the global city deserves careful discussion: what makes Mong Kok a better local setting than any rural area? Does this site adequately represent Hong Kong's localness? Geographically speaking, Hong Kong comprises Hong Kong Island, Kowloon, and outlying islands such as Lantau Island and Cheung Chau. From its early history as a major port and fishing post, Hong Kong still preserves traces of that past, particularly in the New Territories and Sai Kung. Even as they have become increasingly urbanized, Hong Kong is never a land without any rural areas. Chan's cinematic option, in fact, has to be put in the perspective of urban spatialization. As the character Fan says in the film, 'Little Cheung once told me that people living in the old Hong Kong buildings have a lot of stories. I believe him'. To put it another way, *Little Cheung* is literally Chan's Hong Kong story. This story, as well as the Hong Kong identity it constructs, relies more upon the old mansions than the grassroots fishing villages or offshore islands. As Chu argues, Hong Kong's postcoloniality has to be situated not only in the context of global capitalism but also within the space of the metropolis. Compared with other postcolonies, this highly developed global city cannot cling to a prominent aboriginal culture as its grassroots. Therefore, 'the imagination of the rural as the local has to be replaced by the city' (172).

The cultural imagination suggested by Chan's representation of Mong Kok as the authentic local further points to the changing role of the rural in contemporary global cities. On the one hand, Hong Kong's rurality is virtually compressed in the process of modernization and globalization (see how Disneyland and Chek Lap Kok airport have transformed Lantau Island). In terms of cultural identification, rurality is at the same time marginalized, and hence becomes the anonymous 'other'.[8] Deviating from the stereotypical Hong Kong, which has long been celebrated as the dazzling 'City of Glass' or the glamorous 'Pearl of the Orient', the true Hong Kong that Chan has in mind is not the fishing villages at the other end of the spectrum, but the old communities in the city. In the same vein as Kar-wai Wong's Chungking Mansion, Chan's anonymous apartment buildings and popular local restaurants have, in the eyes of the insiders, become the authentic Hong Kong.[9]

The point of understanding Chan's alternative choice of local is not to argue for the 'authentic rural' as a site of postcolonial resistance or naively romanticize the outlying islands and fishing villages for their presumed innocent 'origins' that would keep commercialization and globalization at bay. Rather, the film's representation of 'rurality in the city' testifies to the fact that neither the 'rural' nor the 'urban' is something pure or homogenous. In other words, Chan's film provides a micro-personal account that sheds light on the relational understanding of the country and the city in the global age proposed by urban theorists. For example, Neil Brenner and Roger Keil suggest a Lefebvrian way to reconsider the urban society and the rural: for Lefebvre, 'the world city has emerged not because certain types of places have become control centers for the global economy, but rather because a generalized process of worldwide urbanization is now unfolding ... Lefebvre argues against the notion that there could, under contemporary conditions, be a rural alternative to global urbanization ... Lefebvre insists that *there is no "outside" to the world city. We all reside in it ...*' (358, emphasis added). Michael Woods, inspired by Doreen Massey's relational reading of space, also observes a trend of rethinking the urban/rural dynamics. He argues that in the accounts of global cities written by Friedmann (1986) and Sassen (1991; 1996), urbanity is the precondition of global cities for the operation and reproduction of globalization, the emphasis on the urbanity suggesting 'the exclusion of the "rural" as part of an undifferentiated "other" beyond the global city' (491). However, 'recent writings have emphasized the microprocesses involved in global city formation and redescribed the global city as a heterogeneous assemblage. In Chan's *Little Cheung*, I argue, the transformation of the old mansions, the 'rurality in the city', into the archetypal home of Hong Kong residents, exemplifies the global city as a 'heterogeneous assemblage' as well as the way in which Hong Kong's identity politics are deeply entwined with the metropolis itself.

Family and friends: the naturalization of global people flows

The rundown buildings situated in the old community cannot function as the bedrock of Hong Kong's local reality without Chan's powerful portrayal of the inhabitants of the space – the neighborhood centering around the sundry natives and those who join them from outside. These two groups of culturally underrepresented people serve as the subaltern figures in Chan's postcolonial writing. The former includes Uncle Guong of the newsstand at the street corner, the twin old-timers of the funeral store, Uncle Hoi, his gangster son David, and the strumpet sister, who dotes on Little Cheung.[10] They are members rooted in the community, utilized to foreground the local landscape. The Filipina maid Armi and the illegal immigrant Fan belong to the latter group of underrepresented people. They dramatize global people flow – the illegal immigrants and the transnational laborers, one of the intricate variables pertaining to globalization.

A careful interpretation of the filmic images and functions of these two types of subaltern characters helps us understand how Chan's postcolonial discourse understates globalization to invent a seemingly unvarnished account of Hong Kong's localness. First of all, the foreign domestic workers and illegal immigrants – the underclass brought about by capital flows – are appropriated on account of the director's deep concern with telling a story about local Hong Kong people. To make the postcolonial narrative of the global city 'authentic', Armi and Fan are transformed into a family member and a good neighbor, respectively. In this way, they are not only elements of the hybrid global city but also part of the local community. The process of naturalizing those who are brought into the local by global flows partly accounts for Armi's role as a surrogate mother, who takes care of Little Cheung. After being punished by his father, for example, Little Cheung turns to the maid rather than to his mother for comfort. The scene that shows Little Cheung crying bitterly, reluctant to let the maid leave after his grandmother passes away, also suggests his attachment to Armi. In the ensuing shots – a flashback to the past before Armi leaves – we see her skilfully cooking in the tiny kitchen and preparing food for Little Cheung, accentuating the child's sense of loss. The intimacy between Little Cheung and the maid further hints at an absent mother-by-blood, who spends more of her time in the mahjong house than with her child. These details, which accumulate through force of repetition, illustrate the Filipina maid's maternal function.

Like Armi, Fan as an illegal immigrant is naturalized as a next-door girl in Chan's postcolonial narrative. From Little Cheung's point of view, Fan is a neighborhood girl who simply shows up at his doorway, seemingly from nowhere, to take up a delivery job and earn tips just as if they were playing games together. Presented through Little Cheung's limited viewpoint, Fan is not a 'little snake' but a girl with a business sense almost as keen as his, though somewhat weirder: 'Our activities on the street are strange. But Fan is stranger than I am. She doesn't go to school, but tries to wash dishes like adults do'. At first, Little Cheung has no idea why one day Fan suddenly flees from two policemen. Cheung tails Fan but surprisingly never inquires into why she is hiding from the police: 'I followed her. When she found me, I didn't remember a thing. I just smiled at her. She smiled back'. For Little Cheung, even though he later comes to realize that Fan is an unregistered citizen, she is still his 'business partner' as well as a playmate, an identity drastically different from 'the little snake' his father has in mind.

As Esther M.K. Cheung notes, the micro-histories of Hong Kong tend to naturalize the history of colonization by 'invoking familial and natal images such as "parents", "offspring" and "birth"' (572).[11] Under the façade of a simple rhetorical kinship system (Britain and China as Hong Kong's parents), the quintessential violence of colonialism unfolds: 'Natal tropes such as "birth" and parental "passion" naturalise and implicitly endorse British imperial history' (572). Following this logic, we should by no means sentimentalize the maternal image of the Filipina maid and the playmate image of the illegal immigrant. The characterization of such a 'mother-figure' and the 'girl next door' does enable Filipina maids and unregistered children, who are deprived of adequate cultural representation, to seemingly acquire a positive image and cast away their destined role of the invisible 'other' in the city. However, it is exactly through the images of a loving family and a good friend that the people flow of the Filipina domestic servants or the illegal immigrants in a global city is rationalized to fit into the film's postcolonial paradigm of constructing a local community.[12] I would hasten to add that my attempt here is not to pose a simplified, romanticized account of justice, arguing how domestic laborers and illegal immigrants have been helpless victims exploited by global capital.[13] At issue is how the naturalization of domestic laborers and illegal immigrants may well write off the power struggles brought about by the international division of labor in accordance to either gender or nationality, or by the concentration of capital. Namely, if we tend to see transnational domestic laborers as the mother-earth and illegal immigrants as the playmate, we may also come to accept these identities as something given and thereby lose the critical distance needed to identify the problems of uneven development engendered by globalization.

Armi and Fan serve not only as a surrogate mother and a good friend but also as mirror images, the antithesis of native Hong Kongers. In other words, they are representatives of the outsider, who witness the construction of a local identity. For example, Chan uses Armi's otherness to highlight the key figure of the film, the eminent Cantonese Opera actor, Brother Cheung.[14] Near the beginning of the film, one shot offers an interesting global/local montage of Hong Kong culture: Brother Cheung's performance on TV is juxtaposed in a scene with Armi, the maid singing in her room. The lyrics of the song convey a sense of philosophical/religious optimism: 'Don't worry about life's failures. Tomorrow is the rest of your life. The sun will shine for you and light your path. Such is our life in this world'. Although the Filipina maid is placed side by side with Brother Cheung in this scene to suggest unity, she is seen only in silhouette. Rather than her physical presence, the political implications of the song against Brother Cheung's performance seem to dominate the scene. Later in another scene, the director again implicitly addresses Brother Cheung's seemingly unintelligible peculiarity as an icon of native Hong Kong culture through Armi's perspective. In this sequence of shots, Armi is making a phone call in her own room, presumably trying to tell someone at home about the phenomenal Brother Cheung:

> They are so crazy about this opera singer. It is all over the place. You know, on TV, magazines ... Hong Kong people call this guy Little Cheung, Brother Cheung, all sorts of names. He is really a super star. Very popular. You know when he dies he will get more attention than Deng Xiaoping died ... It is more fun than soap opera.

The Filipina maid's confusion is not so much a sign of her naiveté[15] but rather a marker that highlights the localness of Brother Cheung and Cantonese Opera, as is witnessed by the persona of a cultural outsider whose course of life is intimately attached to Hong Kong's living space. If this part had been articulated by any of the native people in the film, the director's attempt to construct an indigenous identity, when circumscribed by a tour-guide language and vocabulary of political reference, would precariously turn into a superficial self-indulgence of the native. Interestingly, the crane shot Chan uses in this scene to show Armi in a tiny compartmentalized room produces a sense of ambivalence: while the maid occupies a privileged space as a cultural observer, the camera's eye simultaneously suggests her confined and subordinate position of speaking.[16]

The gaze of Fan, the illegal immigrant in the neighborhood, has a similar significance as Armi's in a scene where the exasperated father punishes Little Cheung.[17] Like Armi, as an outsider who knows nothing about Brother Cheung, Fan witnesses the construction of a local identity.[18] Immediately after Little Cheung is found by his father after disappearing for a few days, he is stripped of his pants and forced to stand on a rock at the storefront. Little Cheung begins singing one of Brother Cheung's tunes, which he has learned by heart. He sings a few lines before discovering that Fan is staring at him, whereupon he turns around to Fan, which is to say, to the gaze of the camera and the audience. Subsequently, his father warns him not to see Fan anymore, claiming she is a good-for-nothing little snake. Little Cheung refuses to stop singing. The gist of the song is a blind beggar lamenting over his upbringing. Despite the fact that his mother has forsaken the family, his father wants him to keep his parents' love in mind instead of bearing a grudge against his mother. Accompanied by Little Cheung's song, the lens gradually pans to, and then fixes on, a close-up of Little Cheung's face, followed by a close-up of his buttocks, where the scars left by his father's whipping are still visible. Little Cheung starts to urinate as he sings along, and suddenly it begins raining heavily. With the pouring rain, the song terminates abruptly in the lament, 'Only god knows my true pain'.

The images and narratives of this climactic episode, in fact, work out an intricate postcolonial allegory, which brings home one of the most important themes of the entire film. On the surface, Little Cheung translates an embarrassing penalty into a spectacle (Ka-fai Yau: 557), thus demonstrating his resistance against his father's authority. More significantly, as Ka-fai Yau notes, it is through such cinematic arrangements that Little Cheung, a nine-year-old Mong Kok boy, merges with Brother Cheung, a once-dazzling Cantonese Opera star. What Little Cheung is singing is the very tune sung by Brother Cheung on TV in the opening shot. This scene thus not only allows Little Cheung to be connected with his grandmother's oral history but also elevates him to a cultural inheritor. That is, Little Cheung's impromptu 'performance' foregrounds the formation of a new postcolonial Hong Kong subject (558). The interwoven relationship between the music and the theme can be explained in two ways. The lyrics of the song artistically articulate the thematic betrayal by one's family, the blind beggar telling the unspeakable pain of being abandoned by one's own mother.[19] In a textual sense, the betrayal points to Fan and the twin old-timers of the casket shop, who disclose Little Cheung's hiding place and expose him to his father's humiliating punishment. On a symbolic level, if Little Cheung represents the new Hong Kong subject after 1997, as Yau asserts, his performance of Brother Cheung's song reveals the ambiguity of Hong Kong's postcolonial history. Indeed, if Hong Kong is the blind beggar, who is the mother that leaves the child behind? Is it China, the motherland that ceded Hong Kong to Britain after the first Opium War, or is it Britain, the colonizer that returned Hong Kong to Chinese sovereignty at the end of the lease? Both options lead to a plethora of complicated questions instead of offering a comforting closure. Perhaps the core of Hong Kong's postcolonial ambiguity lies in the problem of not being able to 'name the enemy' nor deny the historical reality and experience of being a colony.

In this climactic scene, with the depiction of Little Cheung's response to his father's punishment, the director successfully constructs an imaginative identity characterized by the local's resistance against hegemonic rule. Little Cheung's singing, a performance that defies both his father's authority and the onlookers' gaze, could be as powerful as Rabelais' 'laughter', both of which challenge authority. Nonetheless, this postcolonial writing is far removed from a grand narrative; rather, it is something interrupted, something that has eventually flowed away (the urine and the rain). Here the body politics, registered by the boy's pissing and the exposure of his penis, has a double meaning. On the one hand, it is a raw moment of vulgarity, emphasizing the grassroots culture. As Achille Mbembe observes, the word 'vulgar', etymologically, has associations with the crowd (129).[20] Matthew Arnold also points out that 'vulgar' implies a bird's-eye view from the stance of a 'high' culture, a perspective that despises the money-seeking and cultureless horde.[21] On the other hand, set against the sublime generated through the formulation of a cultural identity, excretion transcribes both an irony and a despondency, implying the gloom and doom of Chan's postcolonial writing, a narrative footnoted by the lamentation that 'only god knows my true pain' and the 'obscene sublime' in the torrential rain.[22]

This sublime cultural nationalism written against the local neighborhood of Mong Kok is seen through Armi's and Fan's gaze: they are the sympathetic others who direct the audience's attention to Brother Cheung and Little Cheung, the local heroes of the film. The images and functions of Armi and Fan suggest that Chan's cultural mapping of the local actually incorporates a fundamental rationale, which presumably *naturalizes* the global cities' uneven development propensity for the sake of asserting the primacy of the localness.

You are what you see: global monumental space and postcolonial identity formation

If the population flow in the global city becomes naturalized in the film, another salient sign of the global city, the monumental space, is displaced into Hong Kong's postcolonial identity imagination and hence converted into an invisible symbol in Chan's postcolonial self-writing. The episode that precisely signifies this transformation of spatial symbols is the scene where Little Cheung and Fan tour Kowloon, stopping by the Tsim Sha Tsui Promenade to look at Hong Kong Island. Little Cheung, after being punished by his father, runs away from home and disappears for a couple of days. One day he stealthily sends someone to find Fan, who is doing dishes as usual. What follows is a cut where Little Cheung and Fan, along with Fan's younger sister, go for a bicycle ride. On their way from Mong Kok to Kowloon, Little Cheung, as a local, assumes the role of a tour guide, saying, 'This is Kowloon City. There is a lot to eat and a lot of airplanes'. The happy trio arrives at the Promenade, greeted by the seascape of the Victoria Harbour, and faces the myriad of skyscrapers on Hong Kong Island across from them. Little Cheung resumes his tour-guide role and tells Fan, 'That's the peak, that's Bank of China. This is Central State Square, the tallest building in Hong Kong'. Fan retorts, 'My teacher says the Bank of China is the tallest'. The pair is caught in a standoff until they see the HMS Tamar, whereupon Fan happily remarks, 'I know. It will belong to People's Liberation Army'. Little Cheung goes on to introduce the Convention and Exhibition Center, but Fan replies with a smiling face, 'Hong Kong will belong to us when Chairman Jiang comes'. Little Cheung disputes this claim, 'It's already ours!' Afterwards, the two kids verbally joust for three rounds. Their tournament concludes with Fan's exclamation to the sea, half mock-prayer, half shout, 'Hong Kong is ours!'

With an episode of no more than a few minutes, Chan successfully presents the handover in a fairly direct way. The political intention of this dialogue is self-evident. The director assumes the role of a ventriloquist, articulating the '97-Complex' and specifying what is at stake – i.e. the question of to whom Hong Kong should belong. The 'innocent kids' speak about what the adults are afraid to say. More importantly, China is not presented as a pure ideological symbol; rather, here it assumes the form of a bank, the nexus of capital flow. The argument between the two kids may appear to be mere child's talk, yet a closer look exposes that what this 'child's talk' underwrites is an unchallenged assumption: skyscrapers are what define Hong Kong. Ironically, these monumental buildings that have shaped and still shape Hong Kong's identity are less a unique feature of the city than a basic feature Hong Kong shares with other global metropolises. In other words, these landmarks of the city are marked by their function as linkage in the network of global capital flows. Regardless of the director's arduous attempt to concentrate on constructing Hong Kong's local icons, this climactic scene seems to betray his intention and confirms the fact that Hong Kong's identity cannot be defined at the grassroots: skyscrapers, despite their globality, play a key role in pinning down Hong Kongness in Chan's postcolonial narrative. Like the naturalized foreign laborers and illegal immigrants, the landmark buildings in Central are transformed and re-coded as an integral part of the local identity. Indeed, in the film the decrepit community in Mong Kok and the glittering skyscrapers in Central ultimately compete against each other, both claiming themselves to be the inimitable authentic Hong Kong. This complexity might be something that Chan's story, one that focuses on Brother Cheung and the local restaurant, desires to conceal but never succeeds.

The spatial form upon which the political significance of this scene is constructed helps us grasp the entangled relationship between Hong Kong as a global city and its attempt to formulate a viable identity for itself. The meanings of the skyscrapers in Hong Kong should be interpreted beyond a mere background against which the 97-Complex is written. To put it another way, if Chan presents the local neighborhood in Mong Kok as the authentic Hong Kong, why doesn't he let the kids argue over the ownership of Hong Kong right in front of the restaurant run by Little Cheung's father? Evidently, the dramatic impact yielded by this quarrel scene has everything to do with the spatial background it is situated in. The skyline of Victoria Harbour has always been a metropolitan spectacle to put Hong Kong under the spotlight, a garish advertisement for 'The Pearl of the Orient'. We could say that the skyscrapers, which shimmer with the neon signs of transnational corporations, endow Hong Kong as a global city with a most lurid and powerful sign. On top of this, these skyscrapers often become a global sublime to foster a collective will.[23] For example, in Fan's mind, Hong Kong is not the anonymous back-street corners in which she lives or works, but the transnational skyscrapers fixed in front of her eyes from across the harbor. This kind of imagination registers less a misconception of an illegal immigrant, who presumably does not have a full picture of Hong Kong, than a common group consciousness shared among Hong Kong residents. According to the result of a questionnaire that attempted to determine how residents saw their city, Hong Kong residents rate the top five tourist sites in the following order: the Hong Kong Shanghai Bank, the Convention and Exhibition Center, the Bank of China, the Legislative Council Building and Victoria Harbour.[24] Except for the British Legislative Council Building, the rest of these scenes show us architecture built by global capital for the purpose of flexible accumulation. Paradoxically, these monumental spatial expressions that ordinary city-users (legal or not) identify with actually reduce the amount of living space available in everyday life.[25]

In the film, Fan and Little Cheung argue over whether the Bank of China or the Hong Kong Shanghai Bank (standing at the head of Statue Square) is the tallest building in Hong Kong. These two world-renowned edifices help us appreciate the significance of monumental space, the concrete-and-steel of global capital, in a postcolonial paradigm. The Hong Kong Shanghai Bank, designed by British architect Norman Foster, and the adjacent Bank of China by I.M. Pei can be seen as two political totems magically erected by Hong Kong's former colonizer and by China. Owning the highest building in Hong Kong, the Beijing regime, with a legible and controllable panoramic view, not only demonstrates its upper hand over Britain but also reminds Hong Kong residents, the British government, and all the international forces of China's sovereignty over Hong Kong since 1997. However, we cannot ignore the fact that in terms of its practical function, this bamboo-shaped 72-story skyscraper prophesies that China is about to thrive in the new global economy. The Bank of China, just like the Hong Kong Shanghai Bank and all the other financial towers in the world, will continue to be the material site in which global capital accumulates, operates, and circulates. In this vein, Fan and Little Cheung's shouts not only allegorize the political antagonism between national hegemony and local consciousness, they also reveal the fact that, apart from local communities and nation-state apparatuses, global capital has continually played a crucial role in Hong Kong's identity politics.

Conclusion

With this investigation into the production of local identity in *Little Cheung*, I hope to illustrate that in the global city, the 'localness' in the postcolonial discourse can never be taken for granted but must be realized as a kind of 'construction'. As seen in the film, one of the crucial formative logics is the naturalization of the global. When the rural imagination is replaced by cities, which have become the space to anchor local identity, the spatial geographies of global cities have to be erased or rendered unseen. Such an analysis of *Little Cheung* foregrounds the dilemma a postcolonial global city might face. On the one hand, to represent the subalterns, postcolonial narratives have to be written and only in that way can the 'local' be recognized. Chan's back streets and alleys are clear evidence of this point. But for such a narrative to exist, those among the underclass of the global city will need to remain the invisible other buried beneath the grand narrative of contemporary globalization. On the other hand, to construct an 'authentic' local, the first task for the postcolonial writer to manage is the spatial characteristics of global cities. If one's writing of the local dogmatically clings to postcolonial discourse, the 'local' may turn out to be a de-territorialized myth, which dissociates the Mong Kok restaurant in Chan's film from the flows of global capital. If that is the case, a postcolonial narrative, which originally is meant to speak for the local, might at the same time unconsciously facilitate the operation of global metropolises, and hence become an ideological instrument undetected by city-users. My interpretation of Fruit Chan's film as a case study therefore addresses the internal tensions inscribed in Hong Kong. Neither the identity politics of the postcolonial discourse nor the monumental space of the global cities are sufficient ground to ground an analysis of postcolonial global cities. More research has to be conducted to bring to light the complicated interaction between postcoloniality and globalization.

Notes

1 See Rey Chow (1992, 1998).
2 See http://www.info.gov.hk/trans/jd/jd2.htm.
3 See Ka-fai Yau and Laikwan Pang.
4 Chan's '1997 Trilogy' includes *Made in Hong Kong, The Longest Summer,* and *Little Cheung.*
5 See http://www.chinesecinemas.org/littlecheung.html.
6 For example, Frank Welsh's book is entitled, *A Borrowed Place: The History of Hong Kong.* Jean Chesneaux uses 'off-ground economy' to define Hong Kong, and Abbas (1997a) argues that Hong Kong culture is dominated by 'the politics of disappearance'.
7 Hong Kong's economic success is also appropriated as an easy label to legitimize its image of 'cultural wasteland'. See Rey Chow (1993) for the theory of 'lack'.
8 For a detailed discussion of the rural areas in Hong Kong, see Esther M. K. Cheung and James Hayes.
9 For Kar-wai Wong, Chungking Mansion in Tsim Sha Tsui best articulates Hong Kong's urban space, see Tsung-yi Michelle Huang (2000).
10 Ka-fai Yau has contended that one of the distinctive features of Chan's films is that, culturally speaking, his selections of themes and characters bring to light 'the under-represented' (543).
11 The transformation of Hong Kong's colonial history demonstrates 'Roland Barthes's idea of how a myth is constructed by transforming history into nature, through the process of naturalization' (Cheung: 572).

12 For an insightful analysis of how domestic laborers stake a claim on Hong Kong's public space, see Lisa Law.

13 See Katherine Gibson, Lisa Law, and Deirdre McKay.

14 Chan says the film is dedicated to Brother Cheung. The last shot of the film shows 'To our beloved Brother Cheung'. Besides, the mirroring shots of Brother Cheung's performance on TV that start and end the film again demonstrate the importance of Brother Cheung as a cultural icon.

15 She is characterized as practical, smart, and talented.

16 In addition to the Filipina maids, there are foreign laborers working in the restaurant run by David and Uncle Hoi such as the guy nicknamed 'Curry Boy'. Unlike Armi, they are more like 'extras' in the film, without a story of their own. The scene where two resentful foreign laborers come to David to vent their vengeance illustrates again the strategy of representing the local by highlighting the otherness of the outsiders. David sends his gangsters to take care of the workers. They come back to report what the Indians want: 'They complained that we know no loyalty and commitment'. David talks back in contempt: 'What do these Indians know about Chinese loyalty?'

17 Her immediate reaction to Cheung's physical punishment is not presented in this film. Yet, after that scene, Fan has become the omniscient narrator in the film, who tells the story of Little Cheung's life after his grandmother has passed away and the Filipina maid left. Fan's gaze thus becomes identical with the camera's eyes, through which the director shows the audience the local life-world of Hong Kong.

18 Fan once asks Cheung's grandma who Brother Cheung is.

19 For the theme of betrayal in the film, see Ka-fai Yau, p. 559.

20 'Vulgus', the Latin root of the word 'vulgarity', refers to the crowd. For a detailed account of vulgarity and crowd, see Achille Mbembe.

21 For Arnold's interpretation of vulgarity, see *Culture and Anarchy and Other Writings*.

22 Chan explained in an interview that the vulgarity as seen in the scene of making David 'the vampire tea' with a used tampon is mainly for dramatic effects. (http://www.newactionfilms.com/littlecheung/director.htm). Yet, if we consider the vulgar scene in the context of constructing a local identity, vulgarity is less a vehicle for poetic justice than an aesthetic strategy to highlight the grassroots and the folk culture.

23 For the forms, functions and meanings of monumental buildings, see Henri Lefebvre, pp. 143, 221-22.

24 See Ka Yee Janice Wong.

25 See the first chapter of my book, *Walking Between Slums and Skyscrapers*.

7 Sensual, but No Clue of Politics

Shanghai's Longtang Houses

Lena Scheen

Abstract

Since Shanghai's Pudong area became one of China's Special Economic Zones in April 1990, a huge transformation has swept across the entire city, transforming it into a global metropolis of gleaming skyscrapers. Accompanying this process of destruction and renewal has been a growing sense of nostalgia for the city's colonial past (1842-1949), the period in which Shanghai was celebrated as the Paris of the East. Shanghai's makeover is thus different from Beijing's: whereas for Beijing residents, urban transformation stands for China entering the new world of globalization, for Shanghai residents it stands for the revival of the old Shanghai in its heyday, as much as for the building of a new city. The typical Shanghai 'lane houses' (*longtang*) – built in the colonial period and characterized by a mixture of Chinese and Western architecture – have become one of the main symbols of this period. Accordingly, lane houses recurrently feature in contemporary Chinese fiction set in Shanghai. The influential novel *Song of Everlasting Sorrow: A Novel of Shanghai* by Wang Anyi is exemplary in this respect. In the first chapters, lane houses are brought to life by meticulous description and personification: the houses are 'sensual', 'a little self-centered', they 'dream' and 'gossip', and 'have no clue of politics'. This paper will discuss possible symbolic meanings of the prominent presence of lane houses in *Song of Everlasting Sorrow*, and how this type of architecture features not just in the novel's setting but as a protagonist in its own right.

Introduction

There is a popular story in Shanghai about a Chinese delegation on a visit to Berlin in 1997. The then mayor of Berlin boasted about the scale and speed of Berlin's construction work. Li Ruihuan, chairman of the National Committee of the Chinese People's Political Consultative

Conference (CPPCC), responded that in Shanghai it went probably 20 or 25 times faster, after which the mayor corrected himself saying that Shanghai was the number one construction site in the world. 'The mayor's words evoked a burst of hearty laughter.'[1]

Chairman Li's words were no exaggeration. Ever since the city has been allowed to open up to foreign investment (1984), but particularly since the Pudong area was established as a Special Economic Zone (1990), Shanghai has been going through an explosive process of urbanization, turning the city into a landscape of dusty trenches, towering cranes and skeletons of skyscrapers. Until 1984, the tallest building of Shanghai was still the 83.8-meter-tall Park Hotel from 1934 and only five buildings exceeded twenty floors.[2] In 2002, however, Shanghai had nearly double the number of skyscrapers of New York: 4,916 tall buildings, of which 2,800 were over 18 storeys high.[3] Between 1990 and 2005, 38 million square meters of old buildings were demolished in the ten central districts.[4] Hence, ten years after the Chinese delegation visited Berlin, the journalist Howard W. French wrote in the International Herald Tribune:

> The reason you must come to Shanghai now, if cities remotely interest you, is that the work here not only constitutes one of the world's great urban transformations, it also involves one of history's great disappearing acts. An old city of organic communities, with intimate, walk-up buildings and extraordinarily rich street life, is being replaced, almost in the blink of an eye, by a new city of expensive high-rises, underground parking garages, and lifestyles based on sheltered, closed-door individualism.[5]

As French points out, large-scale urban renewal does not only transform the physical appearance of our built environment – i.e. new architecture – it also transforms the way we live in this environment, having profound effects on citizens' daily and inner lives.

One could define Shanghai's transformation as a manifestation of modernity as described by Marshall Berman (1982: 6): a condition where 'all that is solid melts into air', and where people have to 'struggle to make themselves at home in a constantly changing world'. Or, to put it in the words of critic and curator Hou Hanru, 'Shanghai as the center of urban metamorphoses in the 1990s is of course the very central space in which the city inhabitants, for the sake of survival, have to renegotiate the relationship with their constantly shifting urban environment [...] and artists are of course among the most sensitive to the effects [of] all these brutal changes'.[6] Indeed, Shanghai shows a variety of artistic responses and cultural expressions to what is arguably a process of overall disruption in both individual and collective experience.

In this chapter, I will discuss one of those responses: a cultural trend referred to as 'Shanghai nostalgia' 上海怀旧 – i.e. a growing sense of nostalgia for the city's semi-colonial past as a treaty port (1842-1943). Since the mid-1990s, colonial Shanghai has become a favorite subject in 'high' as well as popular culture. After being presented as the epitome of evil in the Maoist era, this earlier period of Western-style urban modernity is now reasserting itself. Along with historians, literary writers have started to rewrite the colonial history of the city.[7] One only has to enter one of Shanghai's many bookstores to find special sections with several bookcases full of the city's history, of which a majority is exclusively about the 1930s, on subjects varying from coffee culture and fashion to jazz; others deal with the city's history during a large part of the nineteenth and/or twentieth century.

I will focus on one of the most representative examples of 'Shanghai nostalgia': the novel *The Song of Everlasting Sorrow* (2003) by the influential author Wang Anyi that was listed at the very top of China's Ten Most Influential Books of the 1990s.[8] Shu-mei Shih (2001: ix), for example, sees the novel as a prime example of what she calls 'a colonial nostalgia not by the colonisers but by the ex-colonised':

> No text better captures this nostalgia for semi-colonial Shanghai than Wang Anyi's widely acclaimed novel *Song of Everlasting Sorrow*, replete with a celebration of capitalist bourgeois sensibilities and lifestyle and a categorical negation of the intervening years.

Riding the wave of Shanghai nostalgia, the novel has been adapted in various forms of popular culture: from a film (directed by Stanley Kwan), a television miniseries (directed by Ding Hei), a stage play (written by Zhao Yaomin and directed by Su Leci), and a teleplay novelization (by Jiang Liping) to even an illustrated teleplay novelization (illustrated by Weng Ziyang). The author Wang Anyi acknowledges that 'right timing' was an important factor of the novel's big success: 'the novel's popularity is simply because it is about this city, so I should thank Shanghai'. But she also explains how it actually backfired on her. In an interview she remarks on the many adaptations: 'what I like most about the novel, is exactly what people didn't like and changed, while what I don't like about it is what made it most popular'.[9]

The Song of Everlasting Sorrow follows the adventures of Wang Qiyao, a Shanghai woman, from the time when she participated in a Miss Shanghai contest in 1946 until her tragic death in 1986. Even though the novel only portrays the very end of the colonial period in part I, its spirit lingers on in the postcolonial city of parts II and III that both serve as counterpoints to the first part. Or in the narrator's own words:

'the legend of Wang Qiyao is Shanghai's dream of glory. The glory and the dream might be old, but the lustre will shine through for another half century'.[10]

As Non Arkaraprasertkul points out in his chapter in this book, the two forms of colonial legacy in Shanghai are the 'sophisticated architecture', such as the iconic Western-style architecture on the Bund, and the 'run-down *lilong*' houses that are characterized by their mixture of Chinese and Western architecture. *The Song of Everlasting Sorrow* is set in the latter, depicting the everyday life of middle-class Shanghainese in a *longtang* 弄堂 (the Shanghai locals' term for *lilong* 里弄) neighborhood.[11] In my reading of the novel, I will discuss how the *longtang* houses are brought to life by meticulous descriptions that almost turn them into actual 'human characters', and that make this novel an intriguing case study for literary scholars, urban historians, and architects alike.

Reminiscent of the backstreet setting in the movie *Little Cheung*, as discussed by Tsung-yi Michelle Huang's chapter in this book, the *longtang* are presented as an enclosed space where an 'authentic' Shanghai lifestyle of the common people has survived despite political turmoil and capitalist globalization. Without going into the problematic ambiguity of the term 'local identity', it is important to note that in the local discourse, 'Shanghai identity' is never opposed to the city's colonial history but merely intertwined with it. The first and foremost image of Shanghai is to be 'cosmopolitan', i.e. the idea that its culture is characterized by an openness to (if not 'a mixture of') other cultures. In this chapter, I will explore the local meaning of *The Song of Everlasting Sorrow*'s prominent setting in a *longtang* neighborhood: a unique housing typology, the experience of its residents, and Shanghai history, all made one through the literary imagination.

Shanghai nostalgia

> Shanghai is a very modernized city now. But there are times when I feel depressed when I come across people and architecture that have become less and less refined. The city used to move me in a lot of ways, but nowadays, a sense of hollowness takes over me instead. I hear people talking about hooking up the track, to re-connect the historical flow of the present with the 1950s or even the 1930s, erasing the cultural void that occurred in between. Yet, I tend to believe that a void in history is irreparable and virtues that are lost are regrettably lost.
>
> *Stanley Kwan, director of the movie adaptation* Everlasting Regret

Every Shanghainese will proudly tell you that if you haven't been to the Bund, you haven't been to Shanghai. Along this boulevard, beautifully preserved Art Deco and neoclassical buildings have been regarded as symbols of Shanghai for over a hundred years. In its grandeur, the Bund is most redolent of early twentieth-century colonial Shanghai, when the cosmopolitan metropolis was world famous as a financial and cultural center, known by such colorful nicknames as the 'Whore of Asia', the 'Paris of the East', the 'Pearl of the Orient', and 'Paradise for Adventurers'.

Every day, people from all over China flock to the Bund to stroll along the river with their lovers, friends, or family members and take pictures – mainly of the *other* side of the Huangpu river, though, the Pudong area, with its futuristic skyline, all flickering neon-lit glass-and-steel skyscrapers. The so-called New Bund – with the historical Bund on the west and ultramodern Pudong on the east – reveals the citizens' paradoxical rejoicing in Shanghai's new global image and, simultaneously, their growing sense of nostalgia for the city's colonial past.[12]

In a society of such rapid and drastic change, nostalgia for a past period is a common reaction in both the individual and the collective consciousness, asserting a sense of stability. In the case of Shanghai, nostalgia has become a cultural practice that enables its residents to generate meaning in the present through selective visions of the past. It should not, thus, be seen as an exclusively negative response to the city's transformation, but also as a way of celebrating – or at least negotiating – the modernization process. Or as Dai Jinhua (1997: 145) argues in 'Imagined Nostalgia' 想像怀旧, an article which has become something of a classic:

> The modernization of the 1990s, or the globalizing burst of progress, causes people to panic, as if they are teetering on the edge of the abyss. The wave of nostalgia brings new representations of history, making history the 'presence in absentia' that emits a ray of hope on the Chinese people's confused and frenzied reality.

In addition, it is the ongoing commercialization and the global city's homogenizing space that scholars identify as important sources of Shanghai's nostalgic mood.[13] After being suppressed in the Maoist period, commercialism is now experiencing a renaissance, since China is back in the global arena of capitalism, with Shanghai in the vanguard. As Robert Goldman and Stephen Papson (1996: 115) put it:

> Capitalism and commodification have bred the conditions for nostalgia. The maelstrom of capital disrupts and displaces

> traditional structures of family, community, and religion that previously buffered – even if in oppressive and mystifying ways – the experience of rapid social change.

In the 1990s, vigorous discussions took place among the Chinese intelligentsia on the social and spiritual emptiness that was felt to lie at the heart of the 'money society'. Wang Xiaoming (2003: 284), for example, states in his 'A Manifesto for Cultural Studies':

> In the 1990s, reform seemed merely to mean the creation of an economic system whose only standard would be profit. All it now aimed for was efficiency, competition and wealth, and all it promised was improvement of material welfare. Nothing else – not political democracy, environmental care, ethical norms, cultural education – lay within its scope.

In 1994, a group of intellectuals working in the humanities published a series of articles in *Reading* 读书, condemning the increasing commercialization of culture and life and 'the crisis in literature and in the humanistic spirit' it caused.[14] The authors came from Shanghai, 'logically enough', as Wang Hui (2003: 59) claims, 'since Shanghai is the biggest consumer center in China and its intellectuals were shocked earlier and more deeply than their counterparts in Beijing'.[15]

However, paradoxically, it is precisely the past period of full-blown capitalism that Shanghai is yearning for. For the emerging global consumer culture – whether celebrated or condemned – is highly reminiscent of the city's previous period of cosmopolitanism and consumerism. By linking the 1990s to the years before 1949, Shanghai seems to want to erase a good forty years of upheaval and revolution and resume the rapid modernization process that ended so abruptly in the 1950s.[16] For this reason, Shanghai's makeover is different from other Chinese cities such as Beijing: where for Beijing residents the city's transformation primarily stands for China entering the new world of globalization while gradually forgetting its past, for Shanghai residents the transformation stands for the revival of the semi-colonial city as it is collectively remembered.

Preservation as place promotion

> *Longtang* was a product of Shanghai and belongs to the Shanghai people. As the city is now undergoing a large-scale reconstruction, the *longtang* of relatively good quality will be conserved and equipped with modern amenities; those of very poor condition

will be demolished and those in-between will be reformed in different ways, such as preserving their appearance while making them suitable for modern living. In this period of great development and drastic change, it is meaningful and important to recall and discuss the relations between the Shanghai *longtang*, Shanghai people and Shanghai culture.

Luo Xiaowei (1997), Professor in Architectural History and Theory

Just as the Parisians experienced during the Haussmann period, when a city was transformed over a decade and – on top of that – under an authoritarian regime, its citizens are sometimes reduced to bewildered spectators. Baron Haussmann (1809-1891) was hired by Napoleon III in 1852 to rebuild Paris from a medieval city of densely crowded quarters with narrow alleyways into a modern city with wide avenues and boulevards, expansive gardens, and parks. The project took only eighteen years (1852-1870) and was fiercely criticized by many contemporaries but is nowadays mostly praised for the achievement of transforming the city into a model of modern urban planning.

The striking similarities with Shanghai's transformation are worth noticing. Apart from the short time-span and the comparable urban planning, the involvement of the central government has side effects that are often overlooked. Both the French and Chinese governments used renewal projects to enforce their power: for example, Haussmann's preference for broad streets over small alleys was said to be motivated by a desire to have better control over the Paris citizenry. Interestingly, the Shanghai government has similar motivations for not condemning Shanghai nostalgia for its remembrance of imperialism and the country's humiliation by foreign powers but including it instead in their urban renewal plans, of which the 'One City, Nine Towns' plan, as discussed by Leslie Sklair in his chapter in this book, is a perfect example. In their work on advertising strategies, Goldman and Papson (1996: 115) show how 'advertisers turn nostalgia into a talisman to ward off fear of constant upheaval'. Indeed, 'we want to revive 1930s Shanghai' is a slogan often used by local officials, referring to cultural, economic, and urban developments.[17] By reviving this period, Shanghai distinguishes itself from other Chinese cities and constructs an exotic identity so as to be able to compete with global cities such as New York, London, and Tokyo. As Jacob Dreyer put it, 'a memory of the city's past greatness pervades contemporary image-making' (see Dreyer's chapter in this book). As market-oriented reform 'not only generates entrepreneurial activities *within* the city but also creates the entrepreneurial agency *of* the city', as pointed out by Fulong Wu (2009: 136), 'Shanghai nostalgia' has in fact become one of the key selling points in the practice of 'city branding'.[18]

Accordingly, the municipal government is showing an increasing interest in the preservation of buildings from the colonial period.[19] While preservation of old buildings might seem a way to 'slow things down – to preserve some almost erased concept of civility and respect for otherness in the midst of chaos', this is not the case in Shanghai, argues Ackbar Abbas (2000: 783): 'preservation and heritage do not act as brakes against development; in some strange way, they further a developmental agenda'. It is not a matter of 'back to the future' but 'forward to the past', as Abbas also famously stated. It is also in that spirit that we should read the boastful statement on Shanghai's World Expo website 'the wide-scaled preservation of spectacular old buildings in the Shanghai Expo is the first of its kind in the history of Expo park construction since 1851'.[20]

Before the 1990s, the Shanghainese showed very little interest in the city's old buildings. However, when the city-renewal process started, people became suddenly conscious of the local meaning of colonial buildings that have now become symbols of Shanghai's cosmopolitan identity. So the underlying social and economic strategy of the city government seems to use the past as symbolic capital to make Shanghai attractive to foreign investors and the tourist industry on the one hand, and on the other hand, to bring to a standstill the rising civil protest against large-scale demolition. Therefore, the city's heritage list does not only include famous public buildings like those on the Bund but also residential areas such as the traditional Shanghai *longtang*.

Longtang (also known as *nongtang, lilong,* or 'alleyway housing'), are the typical Shanghai houses that appeared in the semi-colonial period, 'a robust and popular housing typology born out of economic necessity yet managing to produce an effect of beauty', as Bracken (2010) justly typifies them:

> It survived and thrived despite floods of refugees, the Japanese occupation, World War II, the horrors of campaigns such as the Hundred Flowers, the Great Leap Forward and the Cultural Revolution, only to find that it is with the influx of money that occurred since the reform era that has seen the typology really begin to suffer.

In his work *Lilong Dwellings in Shanghai*, Shen Hua (1993) defines five subtypes of *longtang* houses: the old-style *shikumen* (老式石库门, 'stone gate houses', built in the 1870s-1910s), late *shikumen* (后期石库门, 1910s-1920s), new-style *lilong* (新式里弄, 1910s-1940s), garden *lilong* (花园里弄, 1920s-1940s), and the apartment *lilong* (公寓里弄 1930s-1940s). The late *shikumen* were less spaciously built than the old-style *shikumen* due to the increasing spatial constraints in the rapidly growing city. Whereas the *shikumen* 'are believed to derive from a more native dwelling concept and value system', as Chunlan Zhao (2004: 49) observes, the new-style *lilong* 'is believed to have its origin in western dwelling culture brought in by foreign sojourners and welcomed by locals'. The garden *lilong* ('urban villas') and apartment *lilong* were the more luxurious types with modern facilities. Roughly speaking, the lower-middle classes lived in the *shikumen*, the middle class in the new-style *lilong*, the upper-middle class in the apartment *lilong*, and the upper class and extremely rich in the garden *lilong*.

After years of large-scale demolition, the government suddenly started propagating these houses as representatives of a unique 'Shanghai culture', as expressed in the above quote by professor Luo Xiaowei that was recently republished on the World Expo website. Likewise, foreign visitors could spend one day with a family in a 'traditional Shanghai *longtang* neighborhood' for 100 yuan, which included 'taking part in Shanghai *longtang* games (hoop rolling, shuttle-cock kicking, billiards and rubber band skipping).' As the Shanghai Daily reported: 'These families will be natural "pavilions" outside the Expo site, directly showcasing Shanghai culture'.[21]

According to Wang Anshi, the head of the Shanghai Municipal Heritage Department, the government has set a list with '12.18 million m^2 of residential buildings built before 1949, of which 1.47 million m^2 are garden *lilong*, 1.19 million m^2 are apartment *lilong*, 3.35 million m^2 are new-style *lilong*, and 6.17 million m^2 are old-style and late *lilong*.' They are restored and/or rebuilt into tourist complexes, of which the Xintiandi project is the most well-known example (as mentioned in Non Arkaraprasertkul's chapter in this book), as well as modernized residential complexes. A recent example is the Jianyeli project, where an old neighborhood will be restored into a luxury residential community with 51 *shikumen*, 62 apartments, and more than 4,000 square meters of retail space. The selected American architect Portman remarks: 'We will make it a residential community, not a tourist attraction, we want to be as true to the existing architecture as possible. But only inside, we have to recognize that this is the twenty-first century, and we're doing the inside in such a way that anybody living there will have everything they need'.[22]

By 'inside', Portman is referring of course to modern facilities and sanitation, but what about the *way* people used to live in these *shikumen*? As Wang Anyi says in an interview: 'you could say a *longtang* is a certain type of architecture, but what it actually is, is a way of life'.[23] No matter how truthfully Portman will restore the architecture of these unique houses, it will indeed just be the outside that resembles its origin. As Bracken (2009: 81) puts it: 'In Shanghai today, without the extended family and the tradition of social and community life it entailed, what future can there really be for the alleyway house?' And this is exactly what Wang Anyi's novel under discussion is about: a disappearing way of life.

The *longtang*'s song of everlasting sorrow

> Looked down upon from the highest point in the city, Shanghai's *longtang* – her vast neighborhoods inside enclosed alleys – are a magnificent sight. The *longtang* are the backdrop of this city. Streets and buildings emerge around them in series of dots and lines, like the subtle brushstrokes that bring life to the empty expanses of white paper in a traditional Chinese landscape painting. As day turns into night and the city lights up, these dots and lines begin to glimmer. However, underneath the glitter lies an immense blanket of darkness – these are the *longtang* of Shanghai.[24]

Thus opens the novel *The Song of Everlasting Sorrow* by Wang Anyi, whose original cover tellingly features a picture of a *longtang*. The story follows the adventures of Wang Qiyao, whose life reflects Shanghai's turbulent history. Even though the timeframe of the three parts of *The Song of Everlasting Sorrow* corresponds to the political periods of pre-Mao, Mao, and post-Mao, it is not a historical novel in the strict sense. By depicting the daily lives and 'trivial' experiences of ordinary people in the cramped spaces of *longtang* neighborhoods, Wang Anyi reveals the untold stories of the city, or what Zhang Xudong (2008: 201) calls 'the natural history (*Naturgeschichte*)' in the aesthetic sense of Benjamin and Adorno. 'Something is flowing in the *longtang*', as the narrator tells us, 'it has nothing to do with things like "history", not even "unofficial history": we can call it gossip (7)'. In other words, Wang Anyi rewrites the history of Shanghai, not by simply narrating everyday life of the common people but by revealing its citizens' endless gossip hidden under the *longtang*'s 'immense blanket of darkness':

> Only in gossip can the true heart of this city be found. No matter how gorgeous and splendid the city may look on the outside, its heart is vulgar. The heart is born of gossip, and gossip is born of the Shanghai *longtang*. Magnificent tales of the Far East can be heard all over this Paris of the Orient; but peel away the outer shell and you will discover that gossip lies at its core. (10)

As if she is just one of the diverse elements that constitute a *longtang* neighborhood, Wang Anyi only introduces Wang Qiyao after four

Figure 7.1 *Cover of* The Song of Everlasting Sorrow *by Wang Anyi*

chapters of meticulous descriptions of the *longtang* in a personified way: the houses are 'sensual', 'a little self-centered', they 'dream' and 'gossip', and 'have no clue of politics'. The *longtang* are in a sense even more 'human' than Wang Qiyao, who serves merely as an archetype embodying the 'soul' of the *longtang*:

> Behind every doorway in the Shanghai longtang a Wang Qiyao is studying, embroidering, whispering secrets to her sisters, or throwing a teary-eyed tantrum at her parents. The *longtang* neighbourhoods of Shanghai are filled with a girlish spirit – the name of this spirit is Wang Qiyao. (25)

Through Wang Qiyao the real protagonist of the novel thus seems to be the *longtang* itself, or, in the words of the Chinese journal *Writer*: 'Shanghai's alleys, Shanghai's atmosphere, Shanghai's thought and spirit', which brings back to mind the earlier quoted words by Luo Xiaowei:

> *Longtang* was a product of Shanghai and belongs to the Shanghai people. There were many types of *longtang* houses, and everyone was a part of the whole. Reading the Shanghai *longtang* is like reading the social history of Shanghai and the Shanghai people.

What is most striking about the novel, however, is how Wang Qiyao's personal experiences and the city's historical events are mirrored in the changing physical appearance of the *longtang*.

During the glorious days of cosmopolitan Shanghai in part I – 'a city of wealth, colours, and stunning women' (45) – the *longtang* are described in the following way:

> First to appear are the dormer windows protruding from a rooftop *tingzijian* of those traditional *longtang* buildings, showing themselves off with a certain self-conscious delicacy; the wooden shutters are carefully delineated, the handmade rooftop tiles are arranged with precision, even the potted roses on the window sills have been cared for painstakingly. (3)

This is the décor against which Wang Qiyao's story begins in 1946, when she is sixteen years old, reaching third place in a Miss Shanghai contest. Leading a glamorous life as a model and mistress of the important Kuomintang officer Director Li, Wang Qiyao is able to escape her humble background. Again, it is also through the portrayals of Wang Qiyao's improving *longtang* residents that the reader comes to understand Wang's improving social status: whereas she grew up in a crowded alley of simple *shikumen*, Wang moves into a 'new-style *lilong*' – 'just off a quiet and secluded main street [...] lined on both sides with two-storey apartment buildings with gardens and garages (49)' – to live with the family of her friend Jiang Lili, and where she discovers that even the nightly lights and sounds are different from her old home:

> Sometimes she thought to herself, *even the moon here is different*. The moon back home was a small courtyard moon, stained by the smell of kitchen smoke and lampblack; the moon here came from a scene in a novel, its light shining on flowers and rambling plants. [...] Back home she could always tell whose baby was crying or which mother was berating her child; she could identify the sounds of rats racing beneath the floor, or the sound of a toilet flushing. Here only one sound had an identity. The lord of all sounds – and that was the sound of the bell tower ringing. (63)

In 1948, Director Li rents an 'apartment *lilong*' for Wang Qiyao in the luxurious Alice Apartments – 'a charming world of satin, gauze, velvet, and tassels' – which provides Wang with yet other sensuous experiences of lights and sounds that reveal much of the people's lives in those apartments:

> Alice Apartments is a quiet island in the midst of the noisy city. [...] As soon as the sun goes down, the iron gate is clanged shut, leaving a small side door illuminated by an electric lamp as the only point of entry. (111)

> Alice Apartments may look quiet on the surface, but underneath it is restive, because the hearts of those who live there are oppressed. You can hear this in the ringing of the telephones behind those heavy window curtains. It reverberates in the large living room, even though, having passed through satin and brocade, the eager sound is muted. The telephone is a crucial item in the Alice Apartments, serving as the artery through which lifeforce flows. [...] Doorbells ringing are of equal significance. Unlike the lingering notes of telephones, however, doorbells tend to be snappy, assertive, overbearing. [...] These two kinds of sound roam Alice Apartments at will with a proprietary air. (113)

However, Wang Qiyao's charmed life ends with Director Li getting killed in a plane crash and Wang being left with only a small box of his gold bars.

Whereas the romantic depiction of a city of beauty contests, movie studios, and fashion confirms the novel's nostalgic image, the narrator does not show an idealized vision of the city's colonizers or colonial power. This is reminiscent of what Shu-mei Shih (2001: 374) names the 'strategy of bifurcating the "colonial West/Japan" and the "metropolitan West/Japan" ': whereas Shanghai intellectuals in the 1920s and 1930s resisted colonial power, they welcomed metropolitan – i.e. cosmopolitan – culture. For example, the narrator's critical attitude becomes evident in the following passage where the protagonist strolls on the Bund:

> With their backs to the water they couldn't help gazing up at the grand fortress-like buildings created by the British during the days of the treaty ports. The overweening style of the architecture could be traced back to the Roman empire; it was designed to look down over everything, impressing viewers with an air of tyrannical power. Fortunately, behind these magnificent buildings was an expanse of narrow streets and alleys that led to the longtang houses, whose spirit was democratic. (274)

So, pursuing Shu-mei Shih's line of thought, one could argue that whereas the Western-style *longtang* represent a modern 'metropolitan Western' lifestyle that the citizens embrace, the majestic buildings on the Bund stand for the suppressive 'colonial Western' power that they reject. Concordantly, all scenes directly related to politics take place on the Bund, while the daily lives of the characters – i.e. the main theme of the novel – take place in the narrow streets behind this grand façade of colonial power. Interestingly, this 'democratic spirit' of the *longtang* becomes even more evident in the second part of the novel, set in the Mao period (1949-1976), where Wang eventually moves back into a simple *shikumen*-style *longtang*, which appears to provide the characters a place of refuge from the world of political violence.

After the death of her lover, Wang Qiyao leaves Shanghai to live in the countryside with her grandmother. To retreat to the countryside has always been a common theme in Chinese literature and film, as exemplified in Ana Moya Pellitero's discussion of the movie *Shanghai Triad* in her chapter in this book. It is mostly depicted as a positive time in which the characters are able to reflect on their confusing life in the city. Furthermore, the retreat often symbolizes a search for roots, which can represent 'personal roots' (practically all Chinese have ancestors from the countryside) or roots in a broader sense standing for (traditional) Chinese culture. 'Miss Shanghai' Qiyao, however, does not feel at home in the countryside and takes a train back to Shanghai: 'the first sign of Shanghai – the illuminated water treatment plant in Zhabei – brought tears to her eyes' (160).

In this part, Wang Qiyao has to start from scratch again, making ends meet as the neighborhood nurse in a rundown *longtang* reminiscent of her childhood. However, in the private space of the *longtang*, daily life runs its normal course, seemingly untouched by the political upheaval surrounding it. Neighbors and friends meet in Wang Qiyao's home, eating, drinking, chatting, gossiping, having afternoon tea, and engaging in even more 'decadent' activities such as dancing and playing mahjong. Apparently, the *longtang* function as a safe haven – as also reinforced by the alley's name 'Peace Lane' – where the characters can continue this quasi-colonial ('metropolitan West') lifestyle that was in fact basically impossible during the Mao period.

All this abruptly ends in 1966, when Wang Qiyao's then lover commits suicide by throwing himself out of the window. The Cultural Revolution (1966-1976) is largely omitted, which is rather striking for a work that deals with forty years of Shanghai history, the city where the Cultural Revolution was instigated and experienced its peak. However, even though the novel does not explicitly narrate the traumatic incidents of this period, it is again through the depiction of the *longtang* that one can painfully sense the atmosphere of overall devastation and indirectly read the city's desertedness after its youth was sent to the countryside, how the remaining citizens were severely restricted in their private lives, and the public humiliations that had taken place:

> *Longtang* alleys of all shapes and sizes ran all over the city, and it was during the summer of 1966 that the red- and black-tiled rooftops riddled with protruding dormer windows and concrete terraces were all pried open suddenly, their secrets, conciliatory or compromising, damp and mouldy, reeking of rat piss, were in the process of rotting away, destined to become so much fertilizer to provide nourishment for new lives – because even the most insignificant of lives must pay the price of sacrifice. (281-2)

In the final part of *The Song of Everlasting Sorrow*, Shanghai embraces the market-economy model. Wang Qiyao, who still lives in the same old *longtang* on Peace Lane, has more difficulties to adapt than her illegitimate daughter Weiwei: 'Aside from its being chaotic and timeworn, what troubled Wang Qiyao about this era of Weiwei and her friends was its vulgarity' (301). As a former Miss Shanghai, Wang Qiyao becomes a symbol of the colonial period and attracts a young boy, who idolizes her because of his 'endless longing for the Shanghai of the forties' (370). Wang Qiyao ironically calls him Old Color, a name people used to refer to young people nostalgic for the semi-colonial past.

However, Old Color's nostalgia for colonial Shanghai reveals itself to be a superficial admiration of only its outer appearance and not its spirit. Accordingly, he soon realizes that his beloved old city and Wang Qiyao are both fading irrevocably away, just like the *longtang* in that period:

> The Shanghai *longtang* have grown gray; there are cracks in the streets and along the walls, the alley lamps have been smashed by mischievous children, the gutters are clogged, and foul water trickles down the streets. Even the leaves of the sweet-scented oleanders are coated with grime. [...] It is only through sheer patience and self-control that it holds itself together, otherwise it would simply explode. It seems to understand that nothing good would come of exploding. (299 and 301)

In a way, Wang Qiyao and the *longtang*, as the symbols of colonial Shanghai, have become no more than empty shells, just like Bracken (2009: 81) remarks on the Xintiandi area:

> Xintiandi is preserving nothing more than a shell – an interesting and attractive one, but a shell nonetheless – the life that once made these places really interesting is gone, perhaps forever.

The Song of Everlasting Sorrow borrows its title from a narrative poem by Bai Juyi (CE 772-846) about the tragic love story between Tang Emperor Xuanzong and his most beautiful concubine Yang Guifei. Being madly in love, the Emperor neglects his state affairs until he has to flee because of an armed rebellion. His royal guards blame Yang Guifei and force the Emperor to have her executed. The poem can be read as an elegy on transience, on fading beauty, and closes with Xuanzong's lamenting words: 'While even heaven and earth will one day come to an end, this everlasting sorrow shall endure'. Wang Anyi's story also ends in the murder of a tragic beauty: Wang Qiyao is murdered for the one possession by which she nostalgically kept the past alive – Li's gold bars, symbols of old Shanghai:

> Long Legs wrapped his large hands around Wang Qiyao's throat. *Look at how thin her neck is, just skin and bones, it's enough to make me sick!* [...] He looked at her face: so ugly and desiccated. Her hair was brittle and the roots were grey, but the rest was dark and shiny with hair dye – how comical! (427)

With the dead Wang Qiyao lying on the floor of her *longtang* apartment on Peace Lane, the narrator zooms out to a bird's eye view of the *longtang* neighborhood, reminiscent of the opening of the novel. But now that the 'girlish spirit' of the *longtang* has died, the aged *longtang* also breathes its last breath:

> Amid the forest of new skyscrapers, these old *longtang* neighborhoods are like a fleet of sunken ships, their battled hulls exposed as the sea dries up. (428)

However, this does not necessary imply that it should be read as a critique of the disappearance of Shanghai's unique *longtang* housing and the traditional lifestyle these houses facilitated. Although the narrator mourns the end of a social life that could be summarized as 'Tönnies' *Gemeinschaft*', she seems very aware of the irreversibility of this process as well. For example, when Wang Qiyao, in the late 1980s, visits a party in an apartment of a newly built high-rise building, she remarks:

> When you first arrive here, the place seems to lack a heart because it is so carefree – but that is because it hasn't yet had time to build up a reservoir of recollections; its mind is blank and has not begun to feel the need to call on its memory. (367)

So, in other words, it might very well be possible that in a hundred years we will read the story of Wang Qiyao's grandchild nostalgically longing for Shanghai's glorious period of mushrooming skyscrapers with its 'tell-it-like-it-is philosophy' (294).

Conclusion

Because of its romantic depiction of a bourgeois lifestyle in the private space of the colonial-built *longtang*, *The Song of Everlasting Sorrow* is commonly regarded as a prime example of 'Shanghai nostalgia'. Certainly, the tragic life story of Wang Qiyao resonates with the collective memory of the city's history: from a young beauty in the glamorous Pearl of the Orient, whose rising social status was reflected in the improving styles of her *longtang* residences, to a common nurse in a rundown *longtang* neighborhood in Maoist Shanghai, until an aging lady echoing a far-gone era who dies in her crumbling *longtang*. In this chapter, however, I have tried to show that this nostalgic mood should not be mistaken for nostalgia for colonial power nor for criticism of the large-scale demolition of the *longtang* houses. Instead, what the narrator mourns, seeing the decay of Shanghai reflected in its *longtang*, is the Shanghai lifestyle that the typology of these houses made possible. Akin to the *longtang*'s hybrid typology (of the traditional Chinese courtyard house and the Western-style terrace), this 'colonial' lifestyle was influenced by both 'traditional' Chinese culture and 'modern' Western culture, as it is precisely this mixed nature that the city's residents take pride in and consider to be Shanghai's unique cosmopolitan identity. But what is perhaps even more important, and what is easily overlooked, is that the novel's author, Wang Anyi, has her own *personal* memories of growing up in a *longtang*. So, couldn't the novel's nostalgic air simply be a reflection of its author's wistful yearning for her own lost youth? The following story Wang Anyi told an audience in Rotterdam seems to suggest this:

> One day I was heading for an appointment but couldn't find the place. I suddenly noticed that I had unconsciously entered a typical Shanghai *longtang* neighborhood. As I walked on, a deeply familiar feeling overwhelmed me. It was a particular smell, but also a particular sound, a particular temperature ... Tears came to my eyes, because these sensations embodied a life that I recognized: my childhood in the *longtang* neighborhood, my *longtang* life when I was a child, when children would play together in the backyards. Most *longtang* have their kitchen windows in the back, so the smells and sounds of cooking are constantly there, while inside the houses, old people chat in the most beautiful Shanghainese ... In 1998, I went to Amsterdam to promote the Dutch translation of one of my novels. The publisher had booked me a room in a small hotel, on a canal. I was lonely, and the murky and overcast sky made things worse, making me feel depressed. But when I got out of bed the next day and opened the curtains, I looked out on a small yard that seemed so similar to the *longtang* of Shanghai that Amsterdam suddenly felt very familiar – and this gave me peace of mind.[25]

Notes

1 See (among others): http://houston.china-consulate.org → 新闻观点.
2 Source: Davis 2002: 244.
3 If one starts counting buildings more than 11 storeys high, the city has built almost 7,000 buildings in this period. New York, by contrast, has managed 5,500 in total. Source: *Asia Times*, 8 April 2006.
4 Source: Laurans 2005: 14.
5 Howard W. French, International Herald Tribune, 6 April 2006.
6 Hou Hanru on www.shanghart.com/text2.htm.
7 After Mao's death, the Municipal Government made the renovated Shanghai Archives, which houses an enormous amount of historical data from pre-1949 files, publicly accessible.

8 Wang Anyi (born 1954) is the author of numerous volumes of essays, short stories, and novels, gaining her increasing recognition around the world, ranging from China's highest literary honor, the Mao Dun Prize (for *Song of Everlasting Sorrow*), to the Los Angeles Times Book of the Year Award (for which *Baotown* was a finalist). Currently Ms Wang is the Chairperson of the Shanghai Writers' Association and a professor of Chinese literature at Fudan University.

9 My interview with Wang Anyi in November 2009 in the Rotterdam Public Library.

10 Quoted in Huang 2004: 122.

11 I prefer to use the term '*longtang*' in this chapter, because this is the word Wang Anyi uses in her novel.

12 'Located at the banks of the Huangpu River between Waibaidu Bridge and Nanpu Bridge, the New Bund has a total length of 4 kilometres. It rests against the Huangpu River on the east and a row of 52 unique buildings integrating the Oriental and Occidental architectural styles on the west, generally known as "buildings in multinational styles of architecture", which, for over a century, has remained a symbol of Shanghai. At night when the floodlights of the buildings are switched on at the same time, the buildings look exactly like crystal palaces, which, set off by the Oriental Pearl Radio and Television Tower on the east bank of the Huangpu River, are even more brilliant and dazzling.' Source: http://lyw.sh.gov.cn/en → Scenic Spot → New Bund.

13 Such as Wang Ban 2002 and Dai Jinhua 1997.

14 *Reading*, March-July 1994. For a book-length discussion of the subject, see Wang Xiaoming 1996.

15 Wang Chaohua (2003: 20) also states that in Shanghai, 'commercialisation ran far ahead of other parts of the country, [Nanjing and Shanghai intellectuals] were among the first to see the turn of the party towards garish popular entertainment as a big blow.'

16 See also Bao Yaming 2001.

17 On 2 July 1993, *Shanghai Star*, for example, praised the 'city government efforts for reviving the past glories of Shanghai'.

18 Cf. Hall and Hubbard (1998).

19 '400 structures and 11 districts have been identified as "fine historic buildings and zones" in the city, including the lavish villas of the former French Concession,' in Bracken (2009: 77).

20 http://www.expo2010.cn/expo/expoenglish/wem/0605/userobject1ai37478.html.

21 Shanghai Daily, 13 April 2009. The World Expo also staged the theater show 'Homeland, Impression Shangsteel' 《家园　印象上钢》 played by 300 former residents who had to move house because of the Expo. The show included a scene entitled '*Longtang* Party 弄堂派对' where the residents showed various '*longtang* life' customs against a big screen with pictures of *longtang* houses. For more information, see http://sh.xinmin.cn/minsheng/2010/05/03/4706964.html.

22 China Daily, 6 May 2010. For a critical study on the displacement of the old residents of the Jianyeli district, I highly recommend Laurans 2005.

23 My interview with Wang Anyi in November 2009 in the Rotterdam Public Library.

24 All citations come from the excellent translation by Michael Berry and Susan Chan Egan (see: Wang 2008).

25 My interview with Wang Anyi in November 2009 in the Rotterdam Public Library. This part of the interview was also quoted in a speech by the Dutch Crown Prince Willem Alexander at the Shanghai World Expo 2010.

ARCHITECTURAL EXPRESSION

8 Urbanization and Housing

Socio-Spatial Conflicts over Urban Space in Contemporary Shanghai

Non Arkaraprasertkul

Abstract

Preserving a city's rich cultural heritage may require a balancing act when weighed against market demand. Shanghai's historic row houses, known as the *lilong* – a legacy of Western-influenced housing during the city's time as a treaty port (1842-1943) – are facing extinction at the hands of post-reform property developers seeking valuable land for high-rise condo development. Once the realm of local servants and Chinese laborers, the *lilong* have come to symbolize the pressures of industrialization as migrants from across the country have settled in – China's first encounter with spatial modernity. Through academic discourse, nostalgia has led the claim that the *lilong* should by all means be preserved even for its historic value *per se*. Here I argue: do we really understand enough about the existence of the *lilong* in the context of the rapidly changing structure of modern Chinese society to make such a claim? All study of contemporary urbanization must begin with a study of its residents' processes of adaptation to their radically modernized identities as buffeted by social and political change, which is different from the study of the image that is being projected about its residents' lives either by scholars on one side or by governments on the other. I will explore the dimensions from which urban housing could be studied in the globalizing processes whereby apparently property-led development is becoming standard urban planning practice, with its concomitant influence on the lifestyle of the Chinese today.

Introduction

Studies of post-reform China from various perspectives have addressed growing societal concerns. The process of post-Mao China's economic reform began in the early 1980s, and China has since experienced massive growth in export revenues and in the development of its domestic market. This development, as all chapters in this volume address, has led to a substantial movement of the population from rural to urban areas to fuel China's industrialized economy.

Urbanization has become one of the key characteristics of contemporary China. The image of today's cosmopolitan, pro-growth, consumer-driven China has fundamentally altered perceptions of pre-reform China.[1] These characteristics are not unique to China, especially when compared to other industrialized East-Asian economies that previously enjoyed rapid growth.[2] Nevertheless, what is unique to China is the sheer scale at which its process of urbanization has occurred.

Fascinated by the process of urbanization in China, my purpose in this chapter is to make sense of this process in a broader sense and to make use of the understanding of this process in a focused case study of local communities in urban Shanghai. By placing my discussions in theoretical frameworks of urbanization studies from various angles – including history, geography, architecture, sociology, and anthropology – I seek to shed light on the conflicts and tensions over urban space brought about by the transformation of urban space. In this chapter, I specifically draw attention to different perspectives on a particular problem of urban housing in China in the context of a market-oriented economy since the economic reforms implemented in the late 1970s. In other words, the central theme of this chapter is the exploration of the importance of community space in the globalizing processes whereby property-led development is apparently becoming standard urban-planning practice, with its concomitant influence on the lifestyle of the Chinese today.

The subject of this chapter is the late low-rise vernacular housing legacy, built in Shanghai by foreigners who occupied Shanghai since the mid-nineteenth century, known as *lilong*. Before the economic reforms of the late 1970s, *lilong* houses were the dominant form of housing in Shanghai. Today, *lilong* houses stand in sharp contrast with the growing trend of property-led growth that favors higher density and higher-return housing development. Life in the *lilong* neighborhoods is inconvenient compared to the modern life in high-rise apartments. Nevertheless, it also has its advantage, which is the sense of community – something the individual room in high-rise apartments cannot provide. On the other hand, whereas many scholars claim that the *lilong* houses and neighborhoods are representations of the history of Shanghai and therefore must be preserved to maintain the identity of the city, there are a number of arguments about the drawbacks of these *lilong* houses, from the perspective both of the local government and of the residents themselves.

Urbanization, urban process, and housing

In market-oriented economies, the 'urban process' is the process by which cities are largely urbanized as a venue for business to take place in order to absorb both labor and capital surpluses.[3] Whereas the 'urbanization process' is the transformational course in which a place becomes urban morphologically, the 'urban process' is a framework that is established to explain the 'capitalistic rationality' of the urbanization process.[4] Fulong Wu argues that rapid economic growth in China owed its continuity to the astute reconfiguration of urban space and market-oriented land development.[5] China's urban process involves densifying the inner-city area and expanding the network of transportation to reach undeveloped parts of the city. High-tech parks and other satellite industrial zones were also included in the plan.[6]

Furthermore, the process of land privatization was the mechanism that made the transfer of land-use rights from socialist to market system smooth and active.[7] As laid out in this sketch, urban development has been a successful tool for economic growth. After housing reform, the real estate markets in urban areas have been dominated by private enterprises and Hong Kong developers. In Shanghai, the real estate market was important in three ways. First and foremost, there was a housing shortage, making the provision of housing crucial to accommodating the growth of the urban population. Second, policy was a means of extracting cash from existing resources; the leasing of land, then, was central to the city's process of capital accumulation.[8] Finally, the expansion of urban areas through the expansion of residential areas was an 'urban process' in which the labor and capital surpluses could be used efficiently.

In reality, by the mid-1990s, Shanghai was dealing with the problem of over-accumulation of capital, galvanized by China's fixed exchange rate and an intensive export-led labor-intensive economy. The lack of effective demand and domestic consumption were also problematic.[9] To address both problems, the city decided to stimulate the housing market. The housing reform process proceeded as follows. In order to provide more housing at a rapid pace, the local government had to be untied from socialist-style housing provision through work-unit distribution and subsidization; therefore, the local government sanctioned both private developers (including joint-ventures between private developers and state-owned enterprises) to have a share in the market by investment. By resorting to private developers, Shanghai could produce a large amount of housing units to accommodate the growing population of the emerging urban center it was building. Not only was Shanghai a destination for Chinese jobseekers (and migrants), it was also a destination for foreign entrepreneurs. The involvement of real estate foreign direct investment (FDI) has subsequently played a crucial role in the spatial restructuring of the city.

Yet, this does not mean that the local government abandoned social housing provision completely. In fact, local government has continued to run a 'dual-track' system; while the real estate market takes care of the upper- and middle-class housing, the local government continues to provide housing to existing residents through relocation and residents tied to the work-unit system through its housing subsidy program. Both tracks necessitated the massive construction of housing units.

Shanghai's *lilong* in context

From this basic overview of urbanization, the urban process, and housing in China, I will now move to the focused subject of this chapter which is the *lilong* houses and neighborhoods. The preservation of a city's rich cultural heritage may require a balancing act when weighted against market demand. In Shanghai, historical row houses, known as the *lilong*, are a legacy of Western influence after China's defeat in the First Opium War and its loss of commercial coastal cities to foreign powers. The *lilong* houses were basically Western row houses transplanted onto Shanghai's soil. British developers first built *lilong* houses to provide basic accommodation for Chinese laborers. A typical *lilong* neighborhood is a walled community composed of a main lane running all or halfway across each block. Smaller lanes branch off, connecting perpendicularly to the main lane in order to provide circulation for other housing units – as many as possible – to be packed into any single neighborhood. The developers saw this layout of *lilong* neighborhoods as the most economical and efficient way to accommodate high densities, foregoing any concern for spatial needs or appropriate sanitary conditions. Architecturally, there was very little reference to the famous Chinese *courtyard houses,* as the purpose of the *lilong* was to create housing of the highest possible density; hence, the conventional luxury of having a courtyard as a communal family space had to be taken away.

The *lilong* houses are also stylistically interesting. Historian Lu Hanchao calls them 'half-breed', as they incorporate both Western and Chinese architectural features.[10] What is special about the houses, however, is the continuity of the way of life of the people who continually adjusted their lifestyle to suit the changing conditions of the *lilong* houses since they were first built in the mid-nineteenth century.[11]

A *lilong* neighborhood, then, is basically a gated community consisting of rows of *lilong* houses. Inside, continuous peripheral *lilong* houses serve as a single wall around the neighborhood and commercial

Figure 8.1 *Aerial photograph of Shanghai in the 1930s*

An aerial photograph of Shanghai (overlooking the original part of the city called *Puxi*) in the 1930s showing the dominating pattern of *lilong* houses. Only along the waterfront (The Bund; by the Huangpu River at the top of the photograph) were other building types located; most of them were foreigners' houses and their business headquarters.

Photo: courtesy of Virtual Shanghai Project, Christian Henriot, IAO – Lyon 2 University

windows to the outside street. Lanes inside the *lilong* are not only for circulation but are a community space where social activity takes place in lieu of the missing courtyard in traditional Chinese courtyard houses. Life in the *lilong* neighborhoods is communal, social, and intimate, as the small size of the houses and the limited availability of social space constrained any other forms of interaction other than intimate ones. Residents have to come out to the lanes to socialize and before long they get to know each other. Once the realm of local servants, the *lilong* houses have come to symbolize the pressures of urbanization as migrants from across the country have settled into them since the reforms and opening up of China in the 1980s.

I have argued elsewhere that there are indeed contesting issues.[12] In this chapter, I want to point out that the *lilong* houses and neighborhoods are in the middle of three contesting issues. First and foremost is a practical problem – i.e. the housing problems in present-day Shanghai (i.e. inadequate supply and displacement) to which the *lilong* has failed to deliver a viable solution. Housing is my main focus of research in this chapter, but this chapter is *not* solely about housing. What comes to contradict the first idea is therefore the second issue: the role of the *lilong* in the image-making process of Shanghai. Having the *lilong* in the city has pros and cons: *lilong* houses and neighborhoods

Figure 8.2 *Diagrams showing the basic structure of a typical lilong neighbourhood*

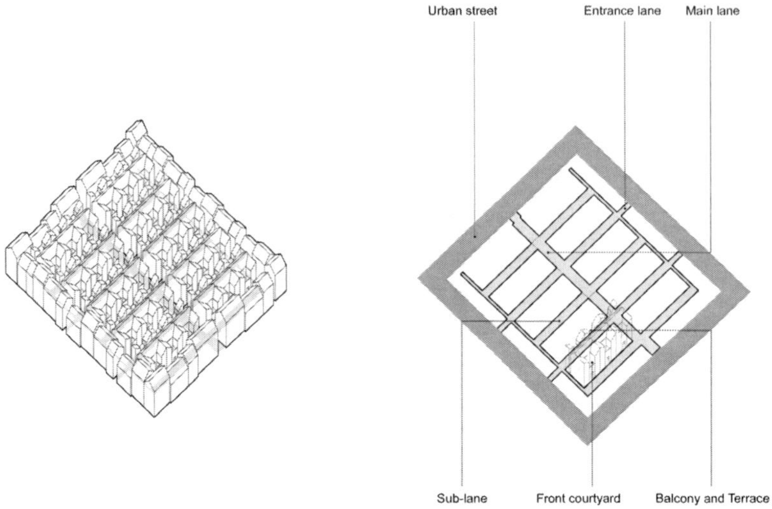

Illustration: Wenjun Ge

in the city could provide Shanghai with some references to the past, but their rundown condition is definitely not eye-pleasing, especially when juxtaposed with the 'postcard image' of the new glittering Shanghai.[13] Finally, the third issue is that the growing preference for other, more modern forms of housing could lead to the voluntary diminishing of the *lilong* housing stock.

As we see in this quick outline of the problem, it is quite obvious that the *lilong* houses and neighborhoods have no 'single location' in present-day Shanghai. Put simply: on the one hand, they should be preserved due to their historical value and their role in making Shanghai a cultural city on a par with Western counterparts;[14] but on the other hand, the attempted preservation of the *lilong* houses and neighborhoods ignores the critical housing condition that affects the quality of urban life. The *lilong* neighbourhoods will help Shanghai maintain its connection to the past; yet most people do not want to live there anymore because of the inconvenience and the better options available among modern accommodation, not to mention, perhaps, a self-conscious rejection of what might be considered an outdated lifestyle. So, where should the *lilong* houses and neighborhoods be? In this chapter, I will try to make sense of the situation through the discussion of several key ideas of urbanization and development as well as my own research. All of these are backed up by my ethnographic fieldwork method, which involves participant observations and semi-structured interviews done in Shanghai from 2009-2010.

Urbanization and housing

Housing issues in Shanghai, in particular, have long been discussed by many scholars from different angles, such as the issues of housing provision, the economy of residents' relocation, migration, the right to the city, and gentrification, to name a few.[15] One example that is central to urban issues in Shanghai is the recent effort of the government to reform housing provision. The interaction between state, market, and society is central to the process of housing development: while the state is obligated to provide housing of adequate standard, it also has an agenda in making space available for economic growth.[16] According to this agenda, a high-rise apartment is a preferred form of investment.

It is useful to understand the historical context of housing provision in Shanghai in conjunction with its urbanization process. In the early stages of the reform, incoming residents were accommodated via several channels with the help of the government through provisions of public housing.[17] Through the work-unit (*danwei*) system, existing urban residents were given the option to stay or to move with reasonable support either in the form of compensation or relocation. Although not entirely equitable, migrants also benefitted from the help of their *danwei* employers and the constant process of negotiation in the system.[18] Such a system, however, had its limit. From an economic and microplanning perspective, this system was nothing more than debt financing, although one could argue that it was reasonably executed in support of other more profitable economic activities for the better of the economic whole.[19] The need for housing is a basic need; hence access to housing is access to a basic need that needs to be fulfilled.

Nevertheless, when the market became more open to competition from private investors and the government decided to take its hands out of the housing market in order to re-balance the losses from the first debt-financing stage, housing became an issue. For example, in Shanghai, the economy took off in the early 1990s and since then the city has resorted to private investors in order to finance the building of housing units. This strategy, according to many scholars, is a double-edged sword.[20] On the one hand, it potentially serves as a viable financial infrastructure, alleviating the burden on the local government and enabling private investors to 'act creatively' in solving the problems of housing shortage. Nevertheless, at the center of the urban residents' discontent is the manipulation of the market due to the lack of transparency in land acquisition.

As Shanghai grows, it needs more space to accommodate its residents. Although the *lilong* houses were by no means low-density houses like the traditional courtyard houses but rather modern medium-density housing designed and built to accommodate large numbers of residents from the mid-nineteenth century onwards, the density – or, to use a planning term, 'plot ratio' – is not enough to lodge the growing population in the era of a market-oriented economy. As housing stock in China is by and large the product of the socialist regime, up until the reforms the state did not resort to the market in the process of housing relocation. Hence, most of the houses were allocated without any real consideration of the market's price.[21] Once the economic reforms were implemented, the local government was responsible for making up the differences between the minimum and the real market price in market-oriented housing situations.[22] With the increasing demand for more space to accommodate new residents who move to Shanghai where there are more employment opportunities, the local government sees handing over the tedious work of housing provision to the developers as a way of achieving the desired density and, ultimately, the high economic development their superiors in the central government want to see.[23]

Given that many *lilong* neighborhoods are a century or at least half-a-century old, they have been razed to the ground, one after the other, at an unprecedented speed, especially in the past ten years, to make way for a much more economically viable solution for accommodating

Figure 8.3 *A poster at the People's Republic of China booth at the United National Human Settlements Program (UNHabitat)* World Urban Forum *in Rio de Janeiro, Brazil (March 2010)*

The poster shows that the government sees traditional settlements as a 'shantytown' and high-rise real estate development as 'renovation'.

Photo: courtesy of Professor Reinhard Goethert, Massachusetts Institute of Technology

the residents of Shanghai.[24] Moreover, sometimes the local government even insists on viewing *lilong* neighborhoods as squatter neighborhoods and therefore dangerous, legitimizing its role in 'cleaning up' to make way for better housing. Whether or not the claim is correct, residents do not usually get the opportunity to speak for themselves and have to watch their houses being razed and be relocated.[25]

In particular, as the pre-reform government housing provision to support residents could only provide subsidies for housing but not maintenance of the houses, many leftover *lilong* neighborhoods were allowed to deteriorate. On top of that, as many *lilong* neighborhoods accommodate a large number of residents, they do not necessarily look as nice or clean as the modern high-rise condos. Some of the *lilong* neighborhoods, in fact, are similar in appearance to squatter settlements. These residents are not wealthy enough to afford better places to stay; hence the question is not whether they do or do not mind living in such conditions because it is the only option they have. Having no money to afford to renovate their places and having to absorb more people in their houses to earn extra much-needed income, squatter-like conditions are inevitable. For sure we know that the projection of such an image is undesirable to Shanghai, a city that is building new and modern skyscrapers day and night to project the image of a new China to the world.

Lilongs were bulldozed many times, usually in prime urban areas, to make space for the building of more profitable high-rises. The former residents were given the option to move back in if they wished. Some research, however, shows that there was only a limited number of people who were 'lucky enough' to receive such compensation. Nevertheless, unless the building process is somehow brought into more of a balance, the imbalanced building of segregated high-rises will lead to the death of the streets and the death of the sense of community as a whole, which is a major social problem. The impact of family displacement has not been well documented, while the growing capacity of Shanghai to economically accommodate more people is praised and emphasized as an achievement.[26] There are clearly negative impacts, namely the weighted changing socio-cultural structure of the city as a whole. That is, if Shanghai only focuses on economic development, welcoming residents who can afford high-rise apartments and continuing to relocate existing residents, the city will soon become less diverse and will lose contact with its original residents, who have lived in these neighborhoods for generations, long before the start of economic reform. Viewed from this angle, as the *lilong* houses and neighborhoods represent a counterbalancing force to the high-rise developments, their existence and right to remain in the city should then be taken into consideration in Shanghai's development plan.

Figure 8.4 *Aerial photographs of Shanghai in the 1930s (left) and 2008 (right)*

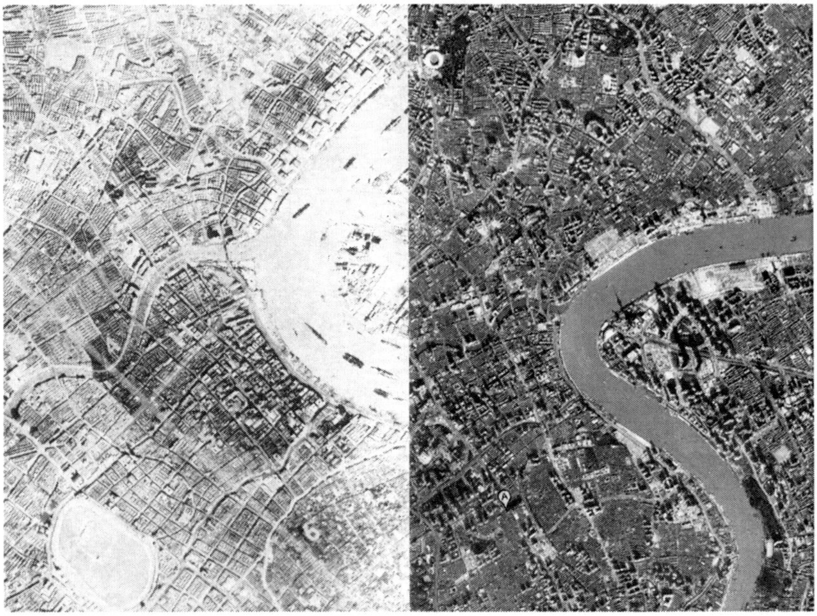

Aerial photographs of Shanghai in the 1930s (left) and 2008 (right) comparing the pattern of urban fabric. A large number of *lilong* houses, which were the dominating fabric of the city in the 1930s, have been razed to the ground since the early 1980s, resulting in a mixed fabric of high-rise buildings and *lilong* houses as shown in the photograph on the right.

Photos: courtesy of Virtual Shanghai Project, Christian Henriot, IAO – Lyon 2 University and Google Earth Image

The Past, Place-Making, and Historical Preservation

Despite the fact that the proponents of the *lilong* houses have made it clear that there are various reasons why they should be protected, preservation alone is not going to help. In fact, what is even more difficult to comprehend is the 'rhetoric' behind historical preservation. Here I would like to present some traces of this rhetoric and then argue for the methodical means of understanding the idea of historical preservation.

In China, the unprecedented speed of urban development and family planning policy also reverse the process and complicate the issue. In Shanghai, the local government may use the discourse of historical preservation to keep the houses it deems representative of the city's history, no matter how derelict they are, as a necessary feature of re-conceiving historical vis-à-vis cultural contents needed for a 'metropolis of the twentieth-first century'. In realizing these contradictory forms and processes of regionalism and globalization within the context of Chinese urbanization, I argue that these attempts to incorporate a particular interpretation of history fall short in terms of foresighted city planning and the omission of actual lived experiences, but also by inadequately explicating the tension that exists behind the façade of a Chinese metropolis. One of the major problems here is the sharp divisions between disciplines of study, which have prevented scholars from understanding the issue from a holistic perspective, let alone reflecting on their experiences in conveying a readable narrative of the place they study. What is worse: authoritative studies of spatial consumerism are often based on painstaking studies in the fields of economics and quantitative sociology. These techniques, however, have proven inadequate when studying the underpinning politics of how 'space' is perceived and consumed. Without a critical analysis of how the change has altered late-socialist spatial restructuring through an ethnographic framework, there is no way to penetrate the reality.

That is to say, as pointed out earlier, although today we know how important *lilong* houses are historically, historical preservation of the *lilong* houses can be superficial if it emphasizes mainly the preservation of the appearance of the building. The first trace of the historical preservation policy is the preservation of the meeting place of the First National Congress of the Communist Party of China, which was, as you might have guessed, held in a *lilong* house (which is now, of course, a museum and a National Heritage Site). It makes a sound case to recognize the importance of such a physical urban constituent, especially when this has a direct link to the history of the Communist Party in China's authoritarian regime context.

Viewed from a distance, I must say, this proto-preservation outlook is hardly deniable. The celebrated renovation project of *lilong* houses known as the Xintiandi, a dilapidated *lilong* neighborhood that has been turned into a multimillion-dollar retail district, is seen by many scholars and professionals as a 'good example' of historical preservation.[27] A Hong Kong mega-developer, Shui-On Land, took the risk of giving this redevelopment project to an American architect, Benjamin Wood, who came up with the idea of designing a retail district that has the humanized feel of small towns in Italy.[28] He asserts strongly:

> I disdain preservation ... I don't believe you should proclaim things dead and turn them into museums. I believe you should

> breathe life into places. That's my goal. I want to make living areas, where people can eat, drink and enjoy themselves.[29]

The success in making Xintiandi one of the must-visit districts in Shanghai exemplifies the superficiality of the preservation. Wood himself mentioned that historical preservation was not his main concern but rather the 'unique quality of the space' that a solely Western-trained architect like him saw as appropriate for this project which would be unique to Shanghai, a city where people have become fed up with air-conditioned department stores.[30]

As Wood himself – a practical architect – admits, the goal of his design is not to preserve the past but to bring some elements of the past to distinguish the project from other retail shopping districts of the present. The cultural claim of restoring a typical neighbourhood is simply false. On the other hand, as one of the goals of this million-dollar development is for it to be something more than merely a self-contained commercial project, to justify this project on the grounds of what we scholars think could have been done better may perhaps have to be rethought. The success of Xintiandi might not be as much in terms of economic or cultural sense, as many argue that the place does not technically generate sustainable incomes given its high development and maintenance costs, and one cannot claim to have rejuvenated the cultural sphere when the displays of high-end products and a hyper-expensive cup of coffee only welcome a certain group of people, most of whom might or might not be residents of Shanghai. However, the project itself is situated at the corner of a gigantic piece of land that the developer is putting efforts into developing into a larger high-end residential and commercial complex. The reason for having Xintiandi might well be argued by the sharp-witted developer who wishes to use it as a cultural landmark for a bigger project that 'will' make money. This argument has been made elsewhere.

In a general sense, the historical preservation campaign of the *lilong* affects the residents' lives in many ways. On the positive side, residents get to remain in the place where they and their ancestors have resided for generations, which is usually the case for the elderly. Many renowned scholars, including the notable urbanist Jane Jacobs, have argued for the maintenance of old neighborhoods as a means of the preservation of the place's livelihood.[31] While it is difficult to stretch that such a claim is a universal one, many scholars have also pointed out that this could well be the case in Shanghai.[32] In my own research, I also found that the sense of community is best maintained by the continuity of the existence of a living community who feels the sense of responsibility in maintaining the social relationship and order among their neighbors.

Among several informants with whom I had discussions and interactions, both formally and informally, there are many similar stories resonating with nostalgia for the good old days when 'everybody knew each other and cared for each other'. Many of my informants have had the experiences of living in both the *lilong* neighborhoods and the new modern housing – they are people from different generations and have different experiences of China. The communal intimacy was also supported by the architectural structure of the neighborhoods. This was, of course, more than what Jane Jacobs calls the 'eyes on the street'[33] that helped to sustain the high level of security in the neighborhood, but a real social intimacy at work that operated like interactive password-screening securities. We can imagine this process as the factor of development of the residents' social life.

On the negative side, many residents are bitter because they cannot renovate their houses simply because their houses are 'registered as an architectural heritage'. One might be able to think about this question holistically if one put oneself in the shoes of the residents: many of them are living in dilapidated buildings without adequate and stable basic infrastructure such as tap water or electricity, yet they cannot make changes to their houses.[34] Despite efforts to rehabilitate some old *lilong* neighborhoods and so-called 'soft densification'[35] to make them more economically viable for the present-day lifestyle by increasing the building density of the neighborhoods, such efforts are still far from being adequate to raise the standard of living of the residents given that they cannot technically do anything to improve the condition of their houses themselves.[36] In addition, as the majority of the tenants are not the high and middle-income groups who work in the financial or service sectors, money to renovate their houses is also an issue as most of the time they can only wait for the local government to help.[37]

In addition, the Historic Preservation Law for both Beijing and Shanghai only took effect in the early 2000s. While one might argue it is better than nothing, the underlying purpose of such a law is questionable. In theory, the law identifies several 'historic relics' that the city wants to preserve, but in practice, these gold-inscribed 'historic relics' plates only give pause to the process of high-rise development in some areas, preserving old houses and neighborhoods that are still in (re)habitable condition.[38] One assumption about the enforcement of this particular law is quite political: as Shanghai tries to re-brand itself to be as important in the way of many successful cities, it would need 'some history' to make it more attractive.[39] The *lilong* houses, with their sophisticated architectural ornaments and form that are unique to China, are seen as an element of history that would make Shanghai a city of not only the present and the future but also the glorious past. The element of history is important in the process of creating the

Figure 8.5 *A Starbucks coffee shop in Xintiandi retail district*

Photo: Gregory Bracken

Figure 8.6 *The famous view of 'Old Shanghai' during the 1930s*

The colonial past as the source of Shanghai nostalgia as claimed by scholar Zhang Xudong.

Photo: courtesy of Virtual Shanghai Project, Christian Henriot, IAO – Lyon 2 University

Figure 8.7 *A typical* lilong *branch lane*

A typical *lilong* branch lane where all types of activities ranging from drying clothes to community gathering are normally taking place.

Photo: Non Arkaraprasertkul

perception of Shanghai as a city with cultural attractions. Recently, the 'preservation and maintenance of historic relics' is one of the key indicators that the local government of Shanghai proudly presents in its *Statistical Yearbook*.[40]

This assumption about the politics behind historical preservation is not new to Shanghai. In fact, it is not new at all. Anthropologist Michael Herzfeld, who has widely conducted research on this specific political agenda in many parts of the world, has pointed out that the use of the two terms 'development' and 'historical preservation' are not always as benevolent and forward-thinking as we think they should be from their literal meanings.[41] The question of 'historical preservation for whom?' is then a very challenging question that can only be answered through the acknowledgment of all other socio-cultural changes in post-reform urban China. The rhetoric of historical preservation is juxtaposed with the city's goal to project its global image representing the contradictions both in terms of ideology of growth and planning.[42]

What make the *lilong* houses and neighborhoods worth preserving is the *combination* of unique architectural form and the dynamism of the community, not just one or the other. Hence, if one is to preserve only the form but not the community, then it is not preservation, but a *Disneyfication*.[43] This marks a condition of post-colonial cities unique to Shanghai, with its two forms of colonial legacy: sophisticated architecture (such as buildings on the Bund) and the run-down *lilong* houses. Whereas the former is seen as the selling point of the city's history, the latter has an ambiguous status. This uniqueness is, of course, based on the history of the city. Had *lilong* houses been houses for the rich, they might hold a similar status as the architecturally sophisticated buildings on the Bund.[44]

Temporary urban residents and population control policy

Another factor that constitutes the change in the organization of space and diverse forms of communal dwelling in the *lilong* is massive migration.[45] As Shanghai has the highest economic growth rate in the country, it attracts migrants from surrounding regions.[46] These migrants do not have the rights to live in the city through the national system of permanent housing registration; hence the solution for their housing choice is basically places where well-off locals would not want to live. The *lilong* neighborhoods are a natural choice in this sense. Therefore, in any of the *lilong* neighborhoods, today we see the mixture of old and new residents, permanent and temporary, fixed and unstable income groups, and so on, all living frugally together in a compound. As the more people there are to share the rent, the better for the residents with unstable incomes, the congestion leads to unsanitary conditions, the dilapidation of infrastructure, and sometimes conflicts between groups, among other problems.

The first area of future research deals with the increasing population and the way in which cities should accommodate them – the hard argument of Housing Studies. There are several aspects to this issue, including inequality and social justice.[47] Since the reform, concerns over housing-related issues have moved to a central position, especially for local governments of major urban areas. What strategy can provide housing for all of the workers in the city? Moreover, an urban-oriented economy and the abundance of labor in rural areas have given rise to a new category of the urban population: the workers who temporarily migrate to urban areas to find jobs and leave when there aren't any: the so-called 'floating population' (*liudongrenyuan*). The migrant workforce, needless to say, is a considerable source of cheap labor that urbanizing areas depend upon.

By simply removing the obsolete old and replacing it with the more economically viable new, however, as shown in a number of studies, the government only generates new problems. In addition, pushing them to marginal areas in order to reserve the more profitable areas for other forms of investment only exacerbates the problems, including social displacement, inadequacy of public and transportation infrastructure, and informal squatter settlements, to name a few.[48] Different groups of people from diverse income groups vary in their ability to afford their accommodations. The lack of urban housing registration on the migrants' side only adds more pressure to their situation; yet all actors, including the government which does not look highly upon their role, depend on their inexpensive labor. The local government's biased investment strategy in favor of the groups that have more purchasing power will not only lead to a severe gentrification problem but also to an artificial bubble-like increase of prices in the properties market.[49] In fact, some studies have shown that this increase in prices of real estate property is the single most controversial political issue in urban areas. This will have an immense impact, manifesting itself as intense socioeconomic and financial problems that someone (i.e. the local government) will have to solve.

Furthermore, policy change can also have an impact on the housing problem. The change in the structure of the family after the enforcement of the One Child Policy has had a profound impact on the reorganization of space in a housing unit.[50] Statistics show that since the reform, the average number of persons per household has consistently declined from 4.6 per household in 1980 to a 'little less than 3 persons' in 2008.[51] With the consistent decline in the number of persons per household (with a projected decline down to 2 or 2.5 persons per household in the next decade), the structure of Shanghai's household is closest to being a modern nuclear family in all of China. With less than three people per household today, residents who no longer need to have large, often multiple-floor living space for their extended families do not want to tolerate the obsolescence of their 'one-hundred-year-old-plus' *lilong* houses, and would prefer a 'mod cons' room in a modern high-rise apartment.[52]

One could argue that given the change in the size of the Chinese family due to the One Child Policy, there have been changes in housing preferences among multi-generational Shanghai residents and immigrants. Younger generations, especially those working in the service sector, tend to prefer the smaller space of an apartment for day-to-day living for a couple and one child.[53] Moreover, as the One Child Policy also allows resources from the entire family to support a single offspring,[54] this generation often has the financial support of the family to purchase apartments in newly built high-rise buildings. These are considered to be a more sound choice for their modern lifestyle as well as being an alternative investment to the shaky stock market. Real estate in China has consistently gone up in value since 1979.[55] It is also worth noting that many of these buyers buy under pressure from their parents. Those of the post-1980s generation are pressured by their parents to divert their money into real estate, often having already benefitted themselves from the high savings rate that finances study abroad and extensive private education programs.[56]

Conclusion

For sure, the living organism of the *lilong* neighborhoods is unique and has been what constituted Shanghai as China's first modern city; yet, the promotion of the *lilong* culture has to be weighed against the skyrocketing housing demand. Here we also recognize the changing preference in housing choice of newer residents. That said, it would make no sense to preserve just the façade of the *lilong* but not the intrinsic quality, as the quality of being a living organism is what makes the *lilong* unique and worth preserving. If the preservation program is to be carried out, then the local government will need more actors to get involved in this program, including residents whose opinions about their living conditions and the present situation in the houses and neighborhoods have to be heard.

To put this in the larger context of the study of contemporary China, what we have learned from the situation of *lilong* houses in Shanghai is the growing social problem that results from the local government's deliberate aim to expedite urban development as a physical terrain of post-reform investment. In this chapter I am not trying to present an argument that there are always conflicts between the two groups – the local government and the people – as most of the previous studies on the topic have done. In fact, what I am trying to do is to present the nuanced nature of the situation. In my introduction, I show that there are a few attitudes towards the existence of the *lilongs* that both the local government and the people do in fact share. Thus, if there is a conflict, it would be 'inside' the terrain of the attitudes themselves; for example, both parties see the dilapidating conditions of the *lilong* neighborhoods as health hazards, but there would be no open talk if one only wants to minimize the cost of the development and one wants the same way of life to be replicated with better infrastructure. That is to say, there are indeed complexities that underpin the situation, but these complexities are not too difficult to overcome.

The handling of history is another related issue; yet the understanding of how history is related to the social context of the present is something that we have yet to see being crystallized. Shanghai, as Gregory Bracken points out, is a city in which the colonial past has played an important role in both establishing and re-establishing its successful economic base.[57] Needless to say, the local government, with its efforts to push forward economic growth, does not seem to believe that it needs to hear from the residents when making a decision that will boost growth qualitatively. As post-reform China is focusing on an export-led economy, labor forces are at the heart of its investment strategy. The housing issue, then, becomes the central social infrastructure that the local government needs to provide. How can it provide housing for all the workers in the city? Here, I argue that the current strategy will defeat the purpose of expediting urban development that the local government set itself from the start simply because the price that it has to pay once all the collective problems explode will be colossal.

As pointed out at the beginning of this chapter, I will not be able to answer whether the *lilong* houses and neighborhoods 'should or should not exist'. What I can answer is whether or not there has been enough study done about the *lilong* houses and neighborhoods to understand the nature of the question. This is the true aim of this chapter. And the answer is a qualified no.

The most recent ethnography of the *lilong* neighborhoods is from the early 1990s, and the only research papers somewhat commensurate to those ethnographies are those of scholars in professional fields such as architecture, urban planning, housing studies, historical preservation, and so on. These papers, although very useful, have the deliberate aim of drawing 'specific conclusions' based upon specific information that scholars trained in the above-mentioned professional fields are capable of acquiring, which obviously does not include ethnography because a recent ethnographic study simply does not exist.

The existing scholarships on the *lilong* neighborhoods today cannot help us to penetrate the reality of urban life in present-day Shanghai.

There is an urgent need to expand research on China. In the study of urban housing and community in Shanghai, I would like to write this chapter to serve as a preliminary study, as the goal of this chapter suggests from the start. I hope that this chapter will provide a marker that will be tested and amplified by other scholars (including myself in the later stage of my academic career) who visit China.

Acknowledgements

I would like to thank Professors James L. Watson and Michael Herzfeld at Harvard University for their guidance and invaluable advice throughout the process of writing this paper. I have been privileged to have both of them as advisers for this project. Both of them have shared with me their research experience and theoretical interest that have shaped me in many ways. I am also grateful to Jacob Dreyer, Reilly Rabitaille, Victor Wong, and Scott Young for reviewing the entire original manuscript of this paper, and for conversations that clarified my thinking on the perceptions of post-reform China and Shanghai from their interdisciplinary perspectives. I owe my gratitude to Professor Michael Keith at Oxford University for his consistent support and encouragement. I owe especially large debts of gratitude to Dr. Gregory Bracken at the International Institute for Asian Studies (IIAS) for all his inclusive comments and eminently practical suggestions over the years. I deeply cherish our shared interest in the urbanism of Shanghai, which came out of our first collaboration in my very first publication on this issue in the journal *Footprint,* of which he was the editor. I would like to also thank Professors Elizabeth J. Perry and Arthur Kleinman at Harvard, Qin Shao at the College of New Jersey, Frank Pieke and Eileen Walsh at Oxford University, Leslie Sklair at LSE, and Tianshu Pan at Fudan University who have also been intellectually and personally supportive of this research project. The financial and institutional support for this project was provided by the Harvard-Yenching Institute, the University of Oxford's China Research Award, and the Anthropology Research and Teaching Unit at Fudan University in Shanghai. The two earlier versions of this chapter appear in 'Debating Interdiscliplinarily, Debating Shanghai Urban Housing', my master's thesis at the University of Oxford, and a conference paper entitled 'Housing and Heritage: Conflicts over Urban Space in Contemporary Shanghai' in *Current Asian Anthropology Conference* at the Chinese University of Hong Kong.

Notes

1 There are several studies that address this issue. I point to a few that are relevant to this chapter. See Deborah Davis, *The Consumer Revolution in Urban China*, Studies on China 22 (Berkeley, 2000); Li May Zhang & Aihwa Ong, eds., *Privatizing China: Socialism from Afar* (Ithaca, 2008); John R. Logan, ed. *The New Chinese City: Globalization and Market Reform* (Oxford, 2002); Fulong Wu, 'Real Estate Development and the Transformation of Urban Space in China's Transitional Economy with Special Reference to Shanghai,' in *The New Chinese City: Globalization and Market Reform*, ed. John R. Logan (Oxford, 2002); John R. Logan, ed. *Urban China in Transition* (Oxford, 2008).

2 See Peter G. Rowe, *East Asia Modern: Shaping the Contemporary City* (London, 2005).

3 See David Harvey, 'Urban Process under Capitalism: A Framework for Analysis,' in *Urbanization and Urban Planning in Capitalist Society*, ed. M.J. Dear & A.J. Scott (London, 1981).

4 See Chris Hamnett, 'Social Polarisation in Global Cities: Theory and Evidence,' *Urban Studies* 31, no. 3 (1994).

5 Fulong Wu, 'China's Recent Urban Development in the Process of Land and Housing Marketisation and Economic Globalisation,' *Habitat International* 25, no. 3 (2001).

6 See Susan M. Walcott, 'Shanghai Pudong: Urban Development in an Era of Global-Local Interaction,' *International Journal of Urban and Regional Research* 33, no. 2 (2009); Yawei Chen, 'Shanghai Pudong: Urban Development in an Era of Global-Local Interaction' (Ph.D. thesis, Technische Universiteit Delft, 2007); Dennis Yehua Wei, Chi Kin Leung, and Jun Luo, 'Globalizing Shanghai: Foreign Investment and Urban Restructuring,' *Habitat International* 30 (2006).

7 See Zhang and Ong (2008).

8 See David Harvey, *A Brief History of Neoliberalism* (Oxford, 2005). See especially his chapter on the process of urban development in China.

9 See Wu in Logan (2002): 161; Chris Hamnett & Yulong Shi, 'The Potential and Prospect for Global Cities in China: In the Context of the World System,' *Geoforum* 33, no. 1 (2002): 132.

10 Hanchao Lu, 'Away from Nanking Road: Small Stores and Neighborhood Life in Modern Shanghai,' *Journal of Asian Studies* 54, no. 1 (1995): 117.

11 This historical and descriptive part is essential to the understanding of this particular societal and housing context. For a more detailed study, see my earlier work: 'Towards Modern Urban Housing: Redefining Shanghai's *lilong*,' *Journal of Urbanism: International Research on Placemaking and Urban Sustainability* 2, no. 1 (2009).

12 See my earlier studies: *Shanghai Contemporary: The Politics of Built Form* (Boston, 2007); 'Politicisation and the Rhetoric of Shanghai Urbanism,' *Footprint*, no. 2 (2008); 'Resilient Lilong: An Ethnography of Shanghai's Urban Housing,' *Working Papers Series: Harvard-Yenching Institute* (2009), http://hyi.scribo.harvard.edu/category/working-paper-series/; 'Beyond Preservation: Rebuilding Old Shanghai,' *Exposition Magazine of the University of Oxford* 3 (Hilary Term, 2010); 'Visualizing Shanghai: The Ascendancy of the Skylines,' *East Asian Studies Journal* 12, no. 2 (2008); 'Leaping Beyond Nostalgia: Shanghai's Urban Life Ethnography,' *The Newsletter of the International Institute for Asian Studies* 55, no. Autumn/Winter (2010).

13 Also in this volume, sociologist Leslie Sklair points out the underlying idea and the impact of the emergence of capitalistic urban form in the context of globalization. For the basic ideas of the concept of globalization in the making of contemporary capitalistic built form and environment, see Leslie Sklair, 'The Transnational Capitalist Class and Contemporary Architecture in Globalizing Cities,' *International Journal of Urban and Regional Research* 29, no. 3 (2005).

14 I would like to invite readers to read the chapters by Lena Scheen and Jacob Dreyer in this volume. They elaborate pertinent points through the view of history and literature (Scheen), and contemporary cultural studies (Dreyer), making connections between Shanghai in the past, present, and especially for Dryer, the 'projected future'. For additional reading, see Jacob Dreyer, 'Shanghai and the 2010 Expo: Staging the City,' in *The Third China Postgraduate Students Conference (CPN)* (Oxford, 2010).

15 There is a plethora of sources on this debate, especially after the early 1980s when Shanghai was granted Special Economic Zone status equal to coastal cities, whose status have been lifted since the early 1980s. See Jean Jinghan Chen & David Wills, *The Impact of China's Economic Reforms Upon Land, Property, and Construction* (Aldershot, 1999): 122; Richard Walker & Daniel Buck, 'The Chinese Road,' *New Left Review* 46 (2007): 49-53.

16 Fulong Wu, 'Residential Relocation under Market-Oriented Redevelopment: The Process and Outcomes in Urban China,' *Geoforum* 35 (2004): 468.

17 See Wu, 'Changes in the Structure of Public Housing Provision in Urban China,' *Urban Studies (Routledge)* 33, no. 9 (1996); Lei Huang, 'Housing Development in the Context of the Modernization, Urbanization and Conservation of Chinese Traditional Cities: Beijing, Shanghai and Suzhou' (Ph.D. Thesis, Harvard University, 2000); Fulong Wu, *Globalization and the Chinese City*, Routledge Contemporary China Series (London, 2006).

18 See Xiaobo Lü & Elizabeth J. Perry, eds., *Danwei: The Changing Chinese Workplace in Historical and Comparative Perspective* (London, 1997); Fei-Ling Wang, 'Conflicts, Resistance, and the Transformation of the Hukou System,' in *Chinese Society : Change, Conflict and Resistance*, ed. Elizabeth J. Perry & Mark Selden (London, 2010).

19 See Ruijue Peng, 'Towards a New Housing Approach: Analysis of Settlement Environment and Housing Policy in Shanghai, China' (Boston, 1986); D.J. Dwyer, 'Urban Housing and Planning in China,' *Transactions of the Institute of British Geographers* 11, no. 4 (1986); Ya Ping Wang & Alan Murie, 'Commercial Housing Development in Urban China,' *Urban Studies* 36, no. 9 (1999).

20 See Zhigang Tang, 'The Urban Housing Market in a Transitional Economy: Shanghai as a Case Study' (Ph.D. Thesis, 2006); Wu, *Globalization and the Chinese City*, Fulong Wu, 'Housing Provision under Globalisation: A Case Study of Shanghai,' *Environmental and Planning* 33 (2001).

21 T.K. Bhaumik, *Old China's New Economy: The Conquest by a Billion Paupers* (Los Angeles, London, 2009): 175; Lin Chun, 'China Today: "Money Dissolves the Commune",' *New Left Review* I, no. 201 (1993): 41-45.

22 Chen & Wills, *The Impact*, 122-36.

23 T.G. McGee, *China's Urban Space: Development under Market Socialism* (London, 2007): 132.

24 See Laurence J.C. Ma & Fulong Wu, *Restructuring the Chinese City: Changing Society, Economy and Space* (London & New York, 2005); Fulong Wu & Shenjing He, 'Property-Led Redevelopment in Post-Reform China: A Case Study of Xintiandi Redevelopment Project in Shanghai,' *Journal of Urban Affairs* 27, no. 1 (2005); Fulong Wu, Jiang Xu & Anthony Gar-on Yeh, *Urban Development in Post-Reform China: State, Market, and Space* (London, 2007); Anthony Gar-on Yeh & Fulong Wu, *The Transformation of the Urban Planning System in China from a Centrally-Planned to Transitional Economy* (Oxford, 1999).

25 In my own study of Shanghai, I also observe a series of changes on the ground responding to the overall projection of the future by the local government. Although my observation is not based on full-scale anthropological fieldwork but rather a survey of existing literature and a light version of ethnography, I can preliminarily see that the physical forms of historical neighborhood *lilong* houses are located within

different realms of perceptions. These perceptions are shaped and re-shaped by forces both from within and from globalization. The pattern of urbanization in Shanghai is more or less that of the removal of the 'economically obsolete' and replacing it with the 'economically viable'. As we learned from many that such taxonomy could be rhetorical and does not always speak of actual needs, we have to be very cautious of any kinds of claims. See my paper presented at the Sixth China Urban Housing Conference, 'Towards Shanghai's Urban Housing: Re-Defining Shanghai's Lilong' (Beijing, 2007) as well as my papers 'Politicisation and the Rhetoric of Shanghai Urbanism' and 'Leaping'. See also Michael Herzfeld, *Divine King or Divine Right: Models of Ritual Authority*; Herzfeld, 'Spatial Cleansing: Monumental Vacuity and the Idea of the West', *Journal of Material Culture* 11, no. 1/2 (2006); Herzfeld, *Evicted from Eternity: The Restructuring of Modern Rome* (Chicago, 2009).

26 Chen & Wills, *The Impact*, 135-36.

27 See Ron Gluckman, 'Shanghai's Stylish Xin Tian Di',(undated), http://www.gluckman.com/XinTianDi.html; Albert Wing Tai Wai, 'Place Promotion and Iconography in Shanghai's Xintiandi', *Habitat International* 30, no. 2 (2006); Fulong Wu & Shenjing He, 'Property-Led Redevelopment in Post-Reform China: A Case Study of Xintiandi Redevelopment Project in Shanghai', *Journal of Urban Affairs* 27, no. 1 (2005); Greg Yager & Scott Kilbourn, 'Lessons from Shanghai Xintiandi: China's Retail Success Story', *Urban Land Asia* 2004.

28 See Yager & Kilbourn, 'Lessons'.

29 Gluckman, 'Shanghai's Stylish Xin Tian Di'.

30 The architect Benjamin Wood was one of the supporters of a research project in Shanghai with which I was involved as a student researcher when I was a graduate student in architecture in the US. I also went back to Shanghai in 2007 to have an interview with him for an architectural magazine in Thailand. Hence, on various occasions, I have had opportunities to have a personal conversation with Wood about his project. Many of the comments I quote from Wood are from my personal communication with him (as cited in the text).

31 See Jane Jacobs, *The Death and Life of Great American Cities* (Harmondsworth, 1964).

32 Among the most comprehensive studies are: D. Louise Morris, *Community or Commodity?: A Study of Lilong Housing in Shanghai* (Vancouver, 1994); Lu, 'Away from Nanking Road: Small Stores and Neighborhood Life in Modern Shanghai'; Qian Guan, 'Lilong Housing, a Traditional Settlement Form' (Master's Thesis, McGill University, 1996); Tianshu Pan, 'Neighborhood Shanghai: Community Building in Five Mile Bridge' (Ph.D. Thesis, Harvard University, 2002); Paul Harley Hammond, 'Community Eclipse and Shanghai's Lilong' (University of Missouri-Columbia, 2006); Samuel Y. Liang, 'Where the Courtyard Meets the Street: Spatial Culture of the Li Neighborhoods, Shanghai, 1870-1900', *Journal of the Society of Architectural Historians* 67, no. 4 (2008). I myself have benefitted greatly from these sources in all of my work on Shanghai.

33 See Jacobs, *Death and Life*.

34 Deborah Pellow, 'No Place to Live, No Place to Love: Coping in Shanghai', in *Urban Anthropology in China*, ed. Gregory Eliyu Guldin & Aidan Southall (Leiden, 1993): 397.

35 Dwyer, 'Urban Housing', 486.

36 See detailed study in Laurence J.C. Ma, 'Urban Housing Supply in the People's Republic of China', in *Urban Development in Modern China*, ed. Laurence J.C. Ma & Edward W. Hanten (Boulder, 1981).

37 See Ruijue Peng, 'Urban Housing Trends in Shanghai: Learning from the Neighborhoods in Shanghai (First Year Paper)', Department of Urban Studies and Planning (Cambridge, MA, 1987).

38 See Wan-Lin Tsai, 'The Redevelopment and Preservation of Historic Lilong Housing in Shanghai' (M.S. Thesis, University of Pennsylvania, 2008).
39 The argument here is that through the process of reinventing history, a community (or a nation at large) could be reconstructed as 'imagined community'. See Benedict R. O'G. Anderson, *Imagined Communities: Reflections on the Origin and Spread of Nationalism* (London, 1983); E.J. Hobsbawm & T.O. Ranger, *The Invention of Tradition*, Past and Present Publications (Cambridge, 1983).
40 *Shanghai Statistical Yearbook*, ed. Shanghai Municipal Statistics Bureau (Shanghai, 2009).
41 See Michael Herzfeld, *Cultural Intimacy: Social Poetics in the Nation-State* (New York & London, 2005); Herzfeld, 'Spatial Cleansing'; Herzfeld, *Evicted from Eternity: The Restructuring of Modern Rome*.
42 See Hamnett & Shi, 'The Potential and Prospect for Global Cities in China: In the Context of the World System'.
43 In fact, the re-building process in Shanghai is quite similar to that of theme park projects, especially those led by property-oriented development per se. For some comparisons and examples, see Sharon Zukin, *Landscapes of Power: From Detroit to Disney World* (Berkeley, 1991).
44 In fact, some of them were and are currently in high demand by wealthy residents. Foreigners and wealthy Chinese still generally prefer to live in high-rise condos whose appearance more or less projects a more *modern*, if not advanced, image of the residents. See the chapters by Sklair and Dreyer in this volume. Also recommended are: Hammond, 'Community Eclipse'; Brook Larmer, 'Shanghai Dreams: China's Global City Tries to Recapture the Glories of Its Past – This Time on Its Own Terms', *National Geographic* 2010; George C. S. Lin, 'Reproducing Spaces of Chinese Urbanization: New City-Based and Land-Centred Urban Transformation',
45 *Urban Studies* 44, no. 9 (2007); Wu, 'China's Recent'; Li Zhang, 'Spatiality and Urban Citizenship in Late Socialist China', *Public Culture* 14, no. 2 (2002).
46 Barry Naughton, *The Chinese Economy: Transitions and Growth* (Cambridge, Mass, 2007): 200.
47 Ibid., 129.
48 See Li Zhang, 'Migration and Privatization of Space and Power in Late Socialist China', *American Ethnologist* 28, no. 1 (2001); Zhang, *Strangers in the City: Reconfigurations of Space, Power, and Social Networks within China's Floating Population* (Stanford, 2001); Wang Feng, Xuejin Zuo, & Danching Ruan, 'Rural Migrants in Shanghai: Living under the Shadow of Socialism', *International Migration Review* 36, no. 2 (2002); Rachel Murphy, *How Migrant Labor Is Changing Rural China* (Cambridge, 2002).
49 See Zhang, *Strangers*; Biao Xiang, *Transcending Boundaries: Zhejiangcun, The Story of a Migrant Village in Beijing* (Leiden, 2005); Yu Chen, 'Migrants in Shanghai's Manufacturing Companies: Employment Conditions and Policy Implications', *Journal of Asian Public Policy* 2, no. 3 (2009).
50 See Wu & He, "Property-Led".
51 See Arkaraprasertkul, 'Resilient Lilong: An Ethnography of Shanghai's Urban Housing'; Arkaraprasertkul, 'Beyond Preservation'; Susan E. Short & Zhai Fengying, 'Looking Locally at China's One-Child Policy', *Studies in Family Planning* 29, no. 4 (1998).
52 This compares to about 3.5 people for one household for China as a whole. See *Shanghai Statistical Yearbook*; The Economist, *Pocket World in Figures 2010* (London, 2010).
53 Though it might seem quite obvious already, geographer Wang Jun re-emphasizes that such changes in housing preference among young professionals working in

Shanghai are inevitable. With a limited budget but the desire to have a contemporary lifestyle and privacy, these young people are much more attracted to the high-rise apartment lifestyle. See Jun Wang, 'Residential Differentiation: The Mapping of Young Professionals' Lifestyle and Their Housing Location Choices in Traditional Shanghai', *Projections: The MIT Journal of Planning* 5 (2006).

54 One could also view this from a point of view of consumerism and changing trends (as do Marxist scholars especially), with some ties to the form of dwelling culture inherited from old traditions. See Bin Zhao, "Consumerism, Confucianism, Communism: Making Sense of China Today', *New Left Review* I, no. 222 (1997).

55 Susan Greenhalgh, *Just One Child: Science and Policy in Deng's China* (Berkeley, 2008); Naughton, *Chinese Economy*, 172-73.

56 I feel that this point could be expanded upon using both qualitative and quantitative data from on-site research. That is, it is obvious that there needs to be more research done in this particular angle.

57 See the editor's introduction. Also see Gregory Bracken, 'The Shanghai Model', *International Institute for Asian Studies (IIAS) Newsletter*, no. 52 (2009), and Bracken, 'Thinking Shanghai'.

9 It Makes a Village

Hong Kong's Podium Shopping Malls as Global Villages

Jonathan D. Solomon

Abstract
As British colonial rule in Hong Kong waned, a plan was drawn up for the future of the city as an interconnected global metropolis. A US$ 20-billion public works project, the Airport Core Program, was implemented to ensure global confidence in the city as it transitioned to Chinese rule. The project, typically described in terms of the ten major infrastructure projects that connected the city to global networks, also resulted in the proliferation of a typology particularly adept at integrating these networks into the local context. A unique spatial product of Hong Kong's post-colonial globalization, these malls represent a mature form of a typology influenced by the city's unique constraints. This paper demonstrates how podium shopping malls form links between Hong Kong's global and local infrastructures, underpinning its transition from colonial city to global metropolis.

Introduction

Hong Kong defies simple solutions. The official slogan 'Asia's World City' suggests a bland and artificial peace with its complex history: junk boats floating serenely past skyscrapers. In fact, Hong Kong's transition from British colony to global city is characterized by rougher waters. 'Asia's World City' has the right idea: it is precisely Hong Kong's relationship to the rest of the world that defines its character and its qualities today, from its unique political and cultural institutions to its continued economic rise. Hong Kong, in contrast to post-colonial cities such as New Delhi, Penang, or Jakarta, is able to achieve cosmopolitan or extra-national status as a world city because of its ability to forge and maintain strong links between local and global populations. It is in the nature of 'Asia', 'World', and 'City' that the smooth and homogeneous marketing tool diverges from a segmented and heterogeneous reality. Exchange systems in Hong Kong force difficult balances at every level, as Tsung-yi Michelle Huang explores in her chapter in this book, which investigates both the historical forces and the cultural effects of Hong Kong's post-1997 regional integration with Mainland China. Borders between cultures and economies and the systems for connecting them figure largely in Hong Kong's formulation of itself as a global city. How do such systems for connection manifest themselves in built form? The answer may help explicate some of the more turbulent urbanism behind the city's post-colonial marketing campaign.

Despite its long colonial history, Hong Kong bears almost no physical trace of its past. A rapacious development environment and a general antipathy towards history under both British and Chinese rule conspired to eliminate all but the faintest trace of the colonial city. Most visibly, the site of Murray House – an 1846 barracks later used as a government office – was vacated in 1982 (the building was eventually reconstructed on the south of the island) to make way for the Bank of China Tower. The Murray Barrack Parade Ground became the site of the Hong Kong Hilton Hotel in 1961, which in turn was cleared in 1995 to make way for a commercial office tower. In 2006, the 1957 Edinburgh Place Ferry Pier from which the Star Ferry had operated was demolished to make way for a new highway despite protests that it should be conserved as part of the city's cultural heritage. Such examples demonstrate the ease with which Hong Kong has historically been willing to replace buildings and fabric rich in historical symbolism – and thus in links to the past – with the accoutrements of globalism. Ironically, it is one of the most conspicuously global of urban typologies – the shopping mall – that ultimately provides Hong Kong with the functional infrastructure for connecting between global and local communities within its borders. In place of symbolic links to its past that could provide the basis for a collective memory, shopping malls provide functional links in the city that bring diverse cultures into propinquity. This unlikely role for a building form widely considered to be fundamentally anti-urban is a unique characteristic of Hong Kong urbanism.

Buying space: ACP and the apotheosis of the Hong Kong mall

In the final years of British colonial rule in Hong Kong, a framework document was drawn up for the future of the city as an interconnected global metropolis. Dubbed the Metroplan, the first goal of the framework was to enhance Hong Kong's role as an international port and airport. A Port and Airport Design Strategy, or PADS, was closely linked with Metroplan, with new development parcels planned along the infrastructure being built to facilitate access to a new airport planned on reclaimed land on outlying Lantau Island. The vision of these developments was clearly laid out in Metroplan. They were to be dense, multi-use communities knitted together by three-dimensional circulation networks.[1]

PADS was ultimately realized as a US$ 20-billion public works project called the Airport Core Program, or ACP. The project comprises ten major infrastructure projects along 34 kilometers that connect the city to the world, including highways, bridges and tunnels, high-speed rail, a new international airport, and prodigious land reclamation for development in the urban core and suburban fringe (see Figure 9.1).[2] The Mass Transit Rail (MTR) Corporation, owner and operator of Hong Kong's intracity rail network, was a major player in the planning of the project and a developer of the properties located over new rail stations. MTR Corporation had utilized the form of the podium mall to maximize the development potential of its other land holdings under Hong Kong's unique constraints.[3] The three-dimensional planning approach and integrated podium became the model for the new properties, fulfilling the vision behind Metroplan.[4]

Some of the MTR-linked podium mall developments have led to enclave communities; others have succeeded in connecting global networks into the local context.[5] This paper demonstrates how podium shopping malls that connect between Hong Kong's global and local infrastructures create different communities from those that remain isolated, and ultimately serve as the urbanism of 'Asia's World City'.

Manuel Castells argues that infrastructure projects serving high-valued spaces for international users constitute a form of neocolonialism, by which economic dominance replaces political dominance.[6] Graham and Marvin have called such projects 'glo-cal bypass' – infrastructure designed to allow the empowered international business class to bypass the local context. Glo-cal bypasses are intended to create redundant and resilient solutions to 'connect local segments of cities to other valued segments in different parts of the globe'. Often involving major physical planning schemes that circumvent the existing fabric, glo-cal bypasses connect selected users and bypass others, creating spatial and social stratification and establishing and reinforcing hierarchies.[7] The podium shopping mall has the potential to reinforce or subvert glo-cal bypasses in proportion to their degree of engagement with the local fabric. This integrated model describes yet another outcome, for which we could use the term 'global villages' as outlined by Marshall McLuhan: a space of discontinuity and division developed out of increased connectivity.[8] Not necessarily leading to greater cohesiveness or tranquillity, a global village describes not a utopian ideal but a contested space, a fractious and messy community in which inequality is not so much eliminated as confronted.

Figure 9.1 *The Airport Core Program*

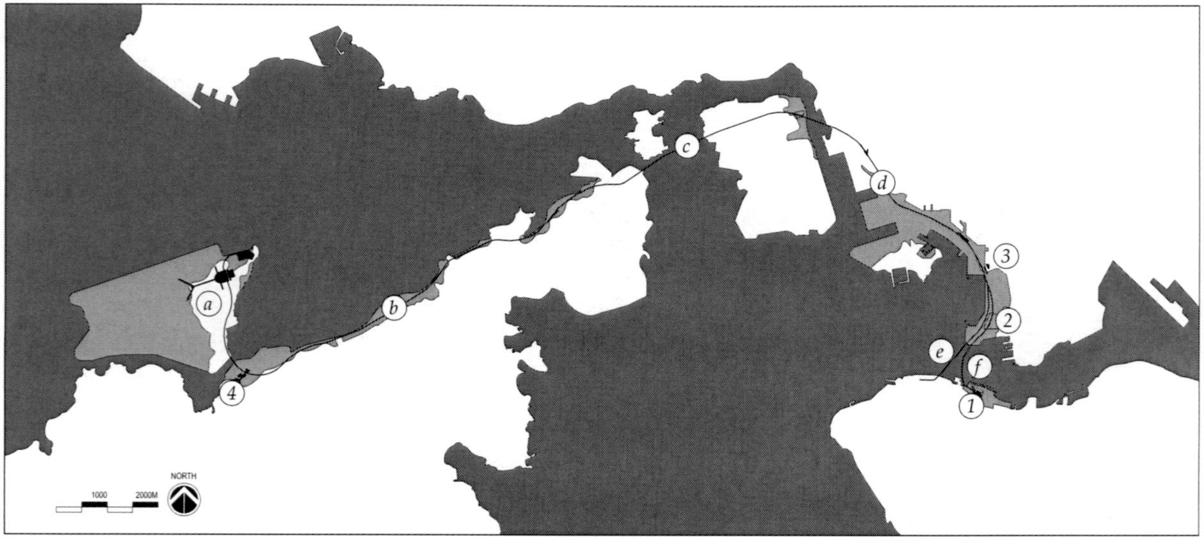

The Airport Core Program, a $ 20-billion public works project for Hong Kong's new international airport, including bridges, tunnels and highways, rail links, and extensive land reclamation works.

1. IFC Mall; 2. Elements Mall; 3. Olympic City Mall; 4. Citygate Mall; a. Hong Kong International Airport; b. North Lantau Expressway; c. Tsing Ma Bridge; d. Western Kowloon Corridor; e. Western Harbour Crossing; f. Airport Express Rail

Image: Jonathan D. Solomon

Taken in its entirety, the ACP satisfies the definition of a glo-cal bypass in three ways. By building new single-purpose rail lines and redundant roadways, it creates a new infrastructure for international and global travel that bypasses existing local networks. By creating integrated, high-end living, working, shopping, and entertainment spaces, it provides a resilient form of infrastructure to target valued users. By allowing international personnel to live in a contained and privileged environment, it creates spatial and social stratification and establishes and reinforces hierarchies. However, when it is appropriately networked to the surrounding local social fabric, the podium shopping mall has the capacity to transform the glo-cal bypass into a global village in two ways: by creating intensive pedestrian links with the local context and, facilitated by these links, allowing the piggybacking of global infrastructure for entrepreneurial local uses. The first breaks spatial hierarchies and the second breaks social hierarchies (see Figures 9.2 and 9.3).

Two malls on the ACP form the basis of a comparison between a glo-cal bypass and a global village. Facing one another across Victoria Harbour, The International Financial Center (IFC) and the Union Square Development are home to Hong Kong's two tallest buildings and two of the city's most prominent malls – IFC Mall and Elements Mall. Built explicitly to facilitate the transition from a colony to a global city, both are elite shopping malls associated with international travel. Yet due to its physical networking, IFC forms a global village, while due to its isolation Elements remains the cap of a larger glo-cal bypass.

A comparison of the transit network at each mall demonstrates that while both serve as hubs for the city's global infrastructure with fast access to the airport, the IFC serves as an intermodal link between global and local networks while Elements does not (see Table 9.1). This statement can be supported by analysing the considerably complex pedestrian networks that surround and penetrate the malls. While some of the differences in quantity in this analysis simply reflect proportion (IFC mall, having more shops than Elements, has proportionally more elevators and escalators), others indicate a disproportionate difference. Indeed, the number of links between the IFC and its surrounding fabric is demonstrably higher than the number from Elements – 76 in the former to only 16 in the latter. The total number of various transit mode connection points, including bus stops, taxi stands, ferry piers, and train platforms is likewise higher in the IFC than Elements. The number of bus lines (used primarily for local travel) serving IFC and its network are 130, while Elements is served by only 60. In fact, the only categories where Elements exceeds IFC are in global connections, boasting a greater number of airport check-in lines and cross-border coach services.

Figure 9.2 *Pedestrian Passage Networks in Elements Mall*

Pedestrian Passage Networks in Elements Mall and the footbridges that connect it to its context, including other malls owned by rival developers.

a. Western Harbour Crossing Bus Stops; b. Kowloon Station for the Tung Chung Commuter Line; c. Kowloon Station for the Airport Express Line; d. Austin Station for the West Rail Commuter Line; e. Mainland Coach Terminal; f. Union Square Bus Terminal; g. Elements Mall; h. ICC Tower. The height scale on this image has been distorted.

Image: Jonathan D. Solomon and Clara Wong

Figure 9.3 *Pedestrian passage networks in IFC Mall*

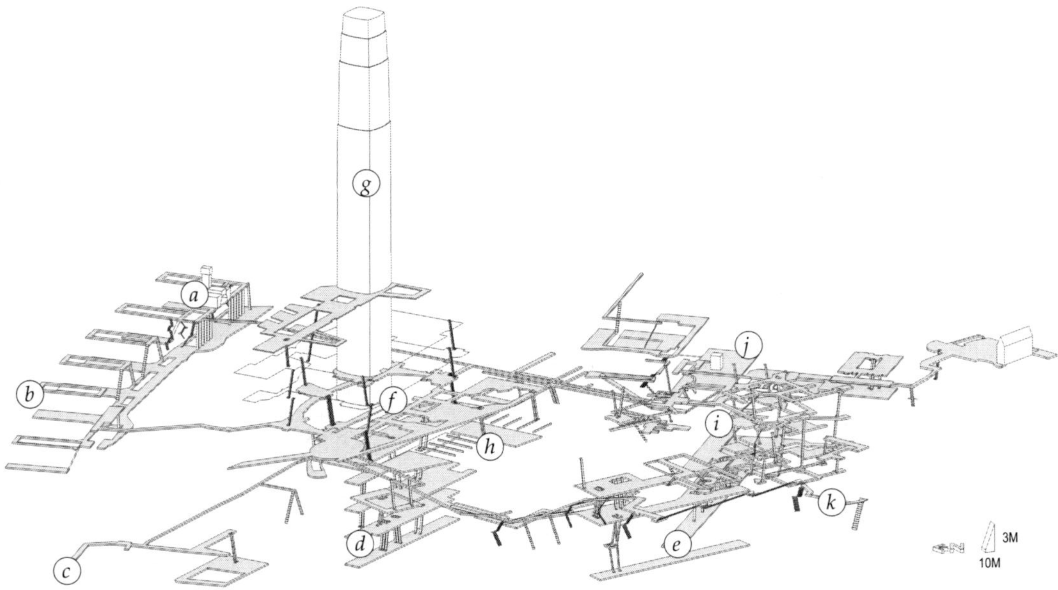

Pedestrian passage networks in IFC Mall and the footbridges that connect it to its context, including other malls owned by rival developers.

a. Star Ferry Pier; b. Central Ferry Piers; c. Footbridge to Macau Ferry Pier; d. Hong Kong Station for the Airport Express and Tung Chung commuter lines; e. Central Station for the Island and Tsuen Wan Lines; f. IFC Mall; g. IFC Tower 2; h. Exchange Square Bus Terminal; i. Landmark Mall; j. Statue Square; k. Central and Midlevel's Escalator. The height scale on this image has been distorted.
Image: Jonathan D. Solomon and Clara Wong

Table 9.1 *A comparison of the transit network between Elements Mall and IFC Mall*

	Elements	*IFC*
Interior Circulation		
Escalators	41	53
Lifts	10	15
Shops	210	264
Exits to street/MTR	3	5
Transit Connections		
Bus lines	60	130
Mini bus lines	4	10
Taxi stand	4	11
Airport bus lines	5	2
Airport check-in lines	34	29
China coaches	5	0
Ferries	0	8
MTR Lines	2	4
External Circulation		
Exits to building/MTR	1	16
Stairs	12	28
Escalators	0	18
Lifts	1	6
Total Exits	16	76

Elements Site boundary: North: Jordan Road; East: Canton Road; South: Austin Road West; West: Western Harbour Crossing
IFC Site Boundary: North: Ferry; East: Man Yiu Street; South: Connaught Road Central; West: Shun Tak Centre

Ultimately it can be concluded that the design of IFC effectively bundles passages from various local and global transit modes to one another and to the city center, while the design of Elements limits access to the city outside but provides smooth connection to global networks.

The glo-cal bypass

Located at the southwest tip of the West Kowloon, Elements Mall is a 334-hectare area reclaimed from Victoria Harbour as part of the Airport Core Program and forms the podium of a megablock complex called Union Square. The mall is topped by some of Hong Kong's tallest residential and commercial towers and several international hotels. It is surrounded by building sites that will one day hold the world's largest performing arts complex and the Hong Kong terminus of China's new high-speed rail network, with service to Shenzhen and Guangzhou expected to take only 12 and 48 minutes respectively. While the eventual development of these parcels – vacant wastelands at the time of this writing – may yield greater pedestrian connectivity, Union Square is currently isolated from all foot traffic from outside (see Figure 9.4).

Easy to access from global networks, Elements is harder to reach by local networks and nearly impossible to approach on foot (see Figures 9.5 and 9.6). The complex does include a single bus terminus and several integrated taxi stands. A direct link to the Airport Express Rail and Tung Chung Mass Transit Rail (MTR), the trunk lines of the ACP, forms an atrium that is a central architectural feature of the mall. A link

Figure 9.4 *The main entrance to Elements Mall*

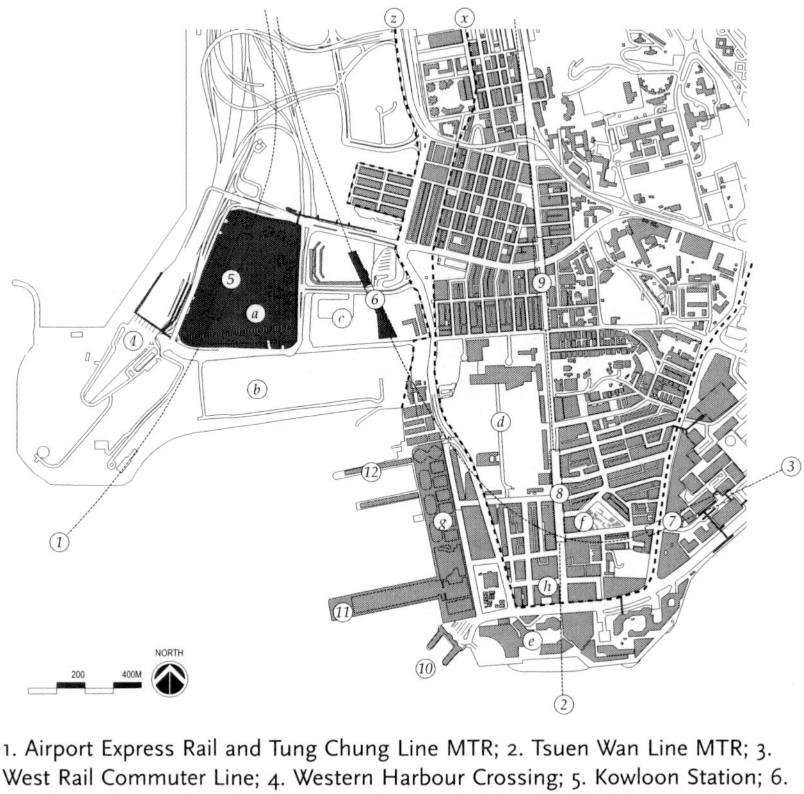

1. Airport Express Rail and Tung Chung Line MTR; 2. Tsuen Wan Line MTR; 3. West Rail Commuter Line; 4. Western Harbour Crossing; 5. Kowloon Station; 6. Austin Station; 7. East Tsim Sha Tsui Station; 8. Tsim Sha Tsui Station; 9. Jordan Station; 10. Star Ferry Pier; 11. Ocean Terminal; 12. China Ferries Pier;
a. Elements Mall and the Union Square Development; b. Site of the Future West Kowloon Cultural District; c. Site of the Future Express Rail Terminus; d. Kowloon Park; e. Hong Kong Cultural Center; f. Chungking Mansions; g. Gateway Mall and Harbour City Mall h. Peninsula Hotel

Image: Jonathan D. Solomon

Figure 9.5 *View from Elements Mall, disconnected from the city*

Photo: Jonathan D. Solomon

Figure 9.6 *Elements Mall: an Atrium leading to the Airport Express Rail*

Photo: Jonathan D. Solomon

by footbridge joins the mall to the Austin Road Station of the city's commuter rail, the West Rail line to the New Territories. Efficient connections to the airport are supplemented by bus services across the border with China, including check-in services and direct routes to Shenzhen's Baoan International Airport. As a result, the mall has become a destination of choice for mainland tourists who utilize direct links to benefit from reduced tariffs on luxury goods without the discomfort of mixing with the local culture, and for expatriate business people who enjoy its smooth integration with the Airport (see Figure 9.7).[9]

Despite its global connectivity, Elements is locally isolated, access on foot to the nearest MTR station on the urban network in Jordan is not practical. A single public entrance at street level is located at the eastern tip of the complex. Of eight planned, two pedestrian footbridges currently connect to beyond the superblock: one westwards to a bus station at the entrance to the Western Harbour Crossing, the other eastward to a park at the border of the nearest populated neighborhood.[10] The

Figure 9.7 *Elevated podium of Elements Mall*

Elevated podium of Elements Mall, serving the surrounding towers but not engaging with the public streets.

Photo: Jonathan D. Solomon

residential properties treat the elevated podium as a new ground level, and do not engage the public street (see Figure 9.8).[11]

The Union Square development was designed as an integrated three-dimensional city with Elements Mall serving to connect the various transport, residential, and commercial programs. Nearly all the facilities necessary for daily life, including grocery stores, convenience stores, cinema, even a school, are available in the mall.[12] It has a high degree of global and internal connectivity but it simply isn't on the way to or from anywhere by foot. Union Square reinforces the Airport Core Program as a glo-cal bypass: an enclave community for the privileged international sector, it is globally connected but locally isolated. Integral

Figure 9.8 *Tsim Sha Tsui, Jordan, and West Kowloon: the vicinity of Elements Mall*

Photo: Jonathan D. Solomon

and resilient, it is both spatially and socially stratified, reinforcing hierarchies in the city.

The global village

In contrast to Union Square, the IFC is both globally connected and well integrated into a local context. IFC Mall has direct pedestrian connections to ferries, buses, minibuses, taxis, and two urban lines on the MTR as well as the Airport Express Rail. Pedestrian footbridges lead to corporate lobbies, hotels, other shopping malls, and adjacent urban fabric. Two major bus terminals serve the complex, and access to numerous taxi stands is available. The IFC is also a part of the network that connects several major ferry lines, including the famous Star Ferry to Kowloon, with the CBD. The IFC's major medium of connectivity is intermodal foot traffic. From an early stage, the form of the mall was conceived of by designers as being fully integrated with public intermodal passage (see Figure 9.9).[13] It is common for office workers to pass through the mall as part of their morning commute from outlying island communities to other parts of the city, or for locals coming to Hong Kong Island on the Star Ferry from Kowloon to use it as an air-conditioned shortcut into the city. Despite being situated on reclaimed land and separated from the older social fabric of the city by a high-speed traffic artery, the IFC manages to not only connect to but also integrate with a neighborhood that is among the most diverse in Hong Kong in terms of the age, form, scale, and use of its buildings, as well as the ethnicity and class of its population (see Figure 9.10).

The IFC enjoys a high degree of connectivity with a pedestrian network already in place at the time of its construction – i.e. with the footbridges and other public passageways that join office lobbies and smaller shopping malls in Central. Unlike the IFC itself or Elements, which were conceived in a master planning exercise that was ultimately government-led, the network of shopping centers and connecting bridges in Central grew piecemeal as a result of developers' desire to link smaller, scattered properties into a more coherent whole.[14] Unlike newly reclaimed sites throughout the territory, where pedestrian connectivity could be achieved through megablock complexes under a single developer, the footbridge network in Central contends with a legacy of the colonial fabric: small plot sizes and multiple owners. The new datum, dense and redundant, proved both convenient and commercially successful, with rents on the footbridge level equalling or even doubling those at ground level.[15] The IFC was planned to connect to and continue this second ground. Stretching from the Macau ferry terminal in the

Figure 9.9 *Public Passage Networks in Central District that connect to IFC Mall*

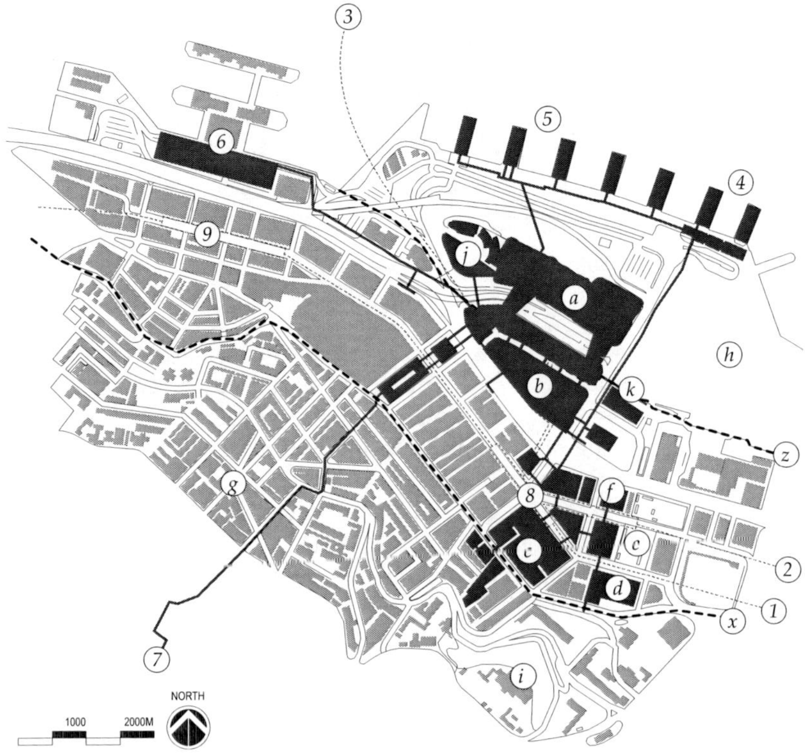

1. Island Line MTR; 2. Tsuen Wan Line MTR; 3. Airport Express Rail and Tung Chung Line MTR; 4. Star Ferry Pier; 5. Central Ferry Piers; 6. Macau Ferry Pier; 7. Central and Midlevel's Escalator; 8. Central Station; 9. Sheung Wan Station; a. IFC Mall and IFC Towers 1 and 2; b. Exchange Square and the Hong Kong Stock Exchange; c. Landmark Mall; d. HSBC Bank Building; e. Statue Square; f. Mandarin Oriental Hotel; g. Soho Neighbourhood; h. Central Reclamation Phase III; i. Chief Executive's Residence; j. Four Seasons Hotel; k. General Post Office

Image: Jonathan D. Solomon

West to Statue Square in the East, this public passage, where global and local flows cross, also serves as an important social space in the city.

The IFC creates a global village out of the glo-cal bypass in two ways: first by creating intensive pedestrian links with its heterogeneous context, both immediate and distant. The IFC's unique architectural contribution is its hybridization of interior circulation with urban transportation systems. It connects the city's financial and corporate center to the

Figure 9.10 *Interior of IFC Mall*

Photo: Jonathan D. Solomon

international airport as well as to outlying islands, public transportation hubs, local urban fabric, and the urban network in an arrangement that breaks spatial hierarchies. IFC creates a global village secondly by allowing the piggybacking of its globally connected infrastructure with entrepreneurial local uses (see Figures 9.11 and 9.12).

The most visible and overtly political of these uses is the occupation of the Central footbridge network by foreign domestic workers on Sundays, their government-mandated day off. Descending from the remarkably cramped conditions of the apartments they service and confronted with Hong Kong's utter lack of public open space, this population (mostly Filipino women) encamp in makeshift shelters across the network, leaving narrow passageways for residents, tourists, and shoppers to pass (see Figure 9.13). An unambiguous political statement by a

Figure 9.11 *Link from IFC Mall to Exchange Square*

View of the dense, layered infrastructure linking IFC Mall and Exchange Square, showing pedestrian footbridges above an access road to a bus terminal and taxi stand.

Photo: Jonathan D. Solomon

Figure 9.12 *IFC Mall's urban context*

View of the network of pedestrian passageways and open spaces that link IFC Mall to its urban context over roads, parking lots, and bus terminals.

Photo: Jonathan D. Solomon

Figure 9.13 *Foreign Domestic Workers gather on the footbridges outside of IFC Mall and Exchange Square*

Photo: Jonathan D. Solomon

service class of their importance to the function of the city, this itinerant public demonstration is in fact the result of a set of very specific local conditions: a culture of hard work and long hours amongst the professional class, and the lack of a large, mobile population within the territory combine to make an attractive market for domestic laborers from poorer neighboring nations. The city's very small apartments – the result of real geographic constraints and of an overheated housing market – provide little excess space. Every Sunday, a government-mandated day off for the highly regulated domestic helper workforce sends a population of approximately 280,000 into a city as lacking in traditional gathering spaces – large public parks, monuments, and squares – as it is in informal public open space.

The occupation of public passageways is as much a necessity as it is an opportunity. That the global economy of IFC Mall and its privileged-sector users confronts a micro-economy of service industries amongst a disempowered segment of society is no accident but rather the result of its diverse network. To the degree that this is integration, it comes in the discontinuity and division formed out of increased connectivity, McLuhan's basis of the global village. The social hierarchies that exist between these communities during the week are not so much broken down as brought into confrontation with one another. This is a unique character of the global village of Hong Kong – it doesn't seek to remedy the inequity of the city, instead it provides a medium in which those inequalities can share space.

Conclusion

Hong Kong is a special case in every category. It can be difficult to argue that with its unique geographical, political, and economic conditions, lessons from the city are applicable elsewhere. Nonetheless, the connectivity of IFC Mall clearly differentiates it from the glo-cal bypass exemplified by Union Square. Close examination suggests that new tools are necessary to analyze, value, and design the podium mall form, particularly in post-colonial cities in Asia where neo-colonial infrastructure is a common development model. 'Global villages' such as the IFC have a profound potential to mix more and less globally connected segments of the population and resist neo-colonial hierarchies while still creating connections between the city and the world. The case of the adaptability of a market-driven strategy for creating continuous pedestrian networks to a government-led design solution, and eventually to unintended uses by diverse sectors of the urban population, suggests that the model has the potential to address matters of social sustainability broadly in Asian cities. In the context of the postcolonial, global city of Hong Kong, it is no surprise that links between local and global networks should exist. What warrants interest is that it is the shopping mall, an iconic space of globalization, that should accomplish this function in the city.

Notes

1 HKG, Metroplan: The Foundations and the Framework, pp. 1, 9, 14.
2 http://www.info.gov.hk/napco/index.html.

3 Stephen S.Y. Lau, R. Giridharan & S. Ganesen, 'Policies for Implementing Multiple Intensive Land Use in Hong Kong', Journal of Housing and the Built Environment 18, 365-378.
4 Steven Smith, *Kowloon, Transport Super City* (Hong Kong, 1998): 30.
5 Barrie Shelton et al. *The Making of Hong Kong: From Vertical to Volumetric* (London, 2011): 110-130.
6 Manuel Castells, *The Information Age: Economy, Society and Culture I, The Rise of the Network Society* (Oxford, 1996).
7 Stephen Graham & Simon Marvin, *Splintering Urbanism: Networked Infrastructures, Technological Mobilities, and the Urban Condition* (London, 2001): 167.
8 Gerald Emmanuel Stearn, ed. *McLuhan: Hot and Cool* (New York, 1968): 314.
9 See Max Hirsh & Jonathan D. Solomon, 'Does Your Mall Have an Airport?' Log 19 Spring/Summer 2010.
10 Smith (1998): 30.
11 Ibid., p. 30.
12 Ibid., p. 25.
13 Greg Pearce, *Arup, Hong Kong Station* (Stuttgart, 2001): 12.
14 Zhang Ziayuan et al., 'The Central District of Hong Kong: Architecture and Urbanism of a Laissez Faire City' A+U Architecture and Urbanism No. 322 July 1997, pp. 3-17.
15 Leslie Lu, 'Asian Arcades Project: Progressive Porosity' in Perspecta 36, The Yale School of Architecture, 2005, pp. 86-89.

Contributors

Non Arkaraprasertkul is a Harvard-Yenching Institute Doctoral Scholar and a PhD candidate in anthropology at Harvard University. He was a Fulbright Scholar and an Asian Cultural Council Fellow at the Massachusetts Institute of Technology (MIT), where he studied history, theory, and criticism of architecture, as well as urban design. He also holds a Master's degree in oriental studies (modern Chinese studies) from the University of Oxford, United Kingdom.

Gregory Bracken is a lecturer and studio master in architecture at the Technical University of Delft (TU Delft). He is also a research fellow of the International Institute for Asian Studies at Leiden University and Project Coordinator for Urban Knowledge Network Asia, a Marie Curie Actions 'International Research Staff Exchange Scheme' (IRSES). He attained his PhD from the Architecture Theory Department of TU Delft in 2009, where he also received an MSc in architecture (with a specialization in urbanism) in 2004 (graduating *cum laude*). He has a BSc in architecture from Trinity College Dublin, Ireland as well as a diploma in architecture from Bolton St College of Technology, Dublin (graduating with distinction in thesis in 1992). Bracken has practiced as an architect in London, Paris, and Berlin as well as Bangkok and Singapore. He is also the author and illustrator of the 'Walking Tour' series of architectural guidebooks to the cities of Asia and Europe and is a board member of *Footprint*, an academic journal dedicated to publishing architecture and urban research.

Jacob Dreyer is currently researching Chinese urbanism at NYU's East Asian Studies department and holds a BA from the College of William and Mary as well as an MRes from the London Consortium. His work as a theorist of contemporary Chinese culture spans the fields of architectural criticism, contemporary art, and branding/brand creation. Additionally, he works as a consultant, largely on projects in Shanghai and New York. His work can be found at http://dreyerprojects.info.

Xiangmin Guo is associate professor of the Harbin Institute of Technology (HIT) at Shenzhen Graduate School. He is also the vice director of the Urban Studies Center at HIT as well as guest professor of IUAV University in Italy. He is an editorial member of the Journal of Asian Architecture and Building Engineering (JAABE). His research interests include urban planning (urban renewal and preservation), urban policies (land use, housing supply, etc.) and urban strategic development (knowledge city development). He is now working on establishing an international urban sustainable development research base in China, which includes the plan of reusing some World Cultural Heritage sites as places for research studios. He received his PhD from the South China University of Technology and successively worked at Tsinghua University and Maryland University before his current position at HIT.

Tsung-yi Michelle Huang is an associate professor of geography at National Taiwan University. She is also the author of *Walking Between Slums and Skyscrapers: Illusions of Open Space in Hong Kong, Tokyo and Shanghai* and *Articulating New Cultural Identities: Self-Writing of East Asian Global City-Regions* (the latter in Chinese). Her work on cinema, cultural studies, cultural geography, and East Asian cities has been published in the *Quarterly Review of Film and Video; the Journal of Narrative Theory*; and *Inter-Asia Cultural Studies*, among others. She received an Academia Sinica research award for junior research investigators (Taiwan) in 2005.

Changtao Liu received his Bachelor's Degree in urban planning from Shandong Jianzhu University and is currently doing a Master's Degree in urban planning and design at the Harbin Institute of Technology at Shenzhen Graduate School. He is also a member of the Center of Urban Design and Landscape Architecture (CULD). His research interests include urban planning (such as urban renewal and preservation) and spatial analysis (like Space Syntax). He is currently working on an analysis of the spatial form of urban villages in Shenzhen based on the Space Syntax model.

Ana M. Moya Pellitero is principal of StudioMEB, office of architecture, planning, and landscape (Portimão-Barcelona) and assistant professor in the architecture Masters program at ISMAT, Grupo Lusófona in Portugal. She conducted her PhD research at the department of architectural history and theory of the Technical University of Eindhoven in the Netherlands. Her PhD research was developed as a transdisciplinary and intercultural study in the field of landscape perception of the urban environment. This phenomenological enquiry involved interrogating topics related with landscape theory, urban culture, psychology of perception, and visual media, both for the European and Chinese urban context. Pellitero currently combines her associate professorship with her responsibility as head of research in StudioMEB, where she is involved in the program GreenEngines, a pedagogic tool on sustainable landscape planning, landscape theory, and urban and visual culture.

Lena Scheen attained her PhD in 2012. Her PhD dissertation was entitled *Shanghai: Literary Imaginings of a City in Transformation*. Together with Dr. Jeroen de Kloet, she has edited the volume *Spectacle and the City: Urbanity in Popular Culture* and *Art in East Asia* (Amsterdam University Press, 2012). She has also worked as project coordinator at the *International Institute for Asian Studies*. Her paper 'City Map: Space, Place and Memory in Short Stories from Shanghai' was shortlisted for the European Association of Chinese Studies (EACS) Young Scholar Award 2010.

Leslie Sklair is emeritus professor of sociology, associate faculty in the Cities Programme at the London School of Economics, associate fellow at the Institute of the Americas University of London, and president of the Global Studies Association (UK). He has been visiting professor at the University of Southern California, New York University, The New School in New York, University of Sydney, Hong Kong University, and Strathclyde University in Glasgow. Editions of his *Globalization: Capitalism and its Alternatives* (2002) have been translated into Japanese, Portuguese, Persian, Spanish, and Korean, with an Arabic edition forthcoming. *The Transnational Capitalist Class* was published in 2001 (Chinese edition 2002, and selections in German, 2009). Papers from his current research project 'Iconic architecture and capitalist globalization' have appeared in *International Journal of Urban and Regional Research* (2005), *City* (2006), *Urban Studies* (2009), and *Theory, Culture & Society* (2010) and have also been translated into Italian and German. He has written on globalization and capitalism for several social science encyclopaedias and served on the editorial boards of *British Journal of Sociology, Review of International Political Economy, Global Networks, Social Forces,* and *Journal of World-Systems Research.*

Jonathan D. Solomon is a founding editor of 306090 Books, a publication series featuring novel developments in architecture, landscape architecture, and urbanism that published its 13th volume, *Sustain and Develop*, in 2009. His essays and criticism have appeared in *Log* (New York), *Footprint* (Delft), *Urban China* (Beijing), and other publications. He is the author of *Pamphlet Architecture #26: Thirteen Projects for the Sheridan Expressway* (Princeton Architectural Press, 2004). Solomon has taught design at the City College of New York and at the University at Buffalo as a Banham Fellow. He is currently acting head of the department of architecture at the University of Hong Kong. Solomon's design work has won awards in the United States and in Hong Kong. Ooi Botos Gallery, a Hong Kong shophouse he renovated as a gallery for contemporary Chinese photography, received an AIA Citation Award in 2009. Solomon is a licensed architect in Illinois and an architect member of the American Institute of Architects.

Bibliography

Abaza, M. (2001), 'Shopping Malls, Consumer Culture and the Reshaping of Public Space in Egypt', *Theory, Culture & Society* 18/5: 97-122.

Abbas, A. (1997), *Hong Kong: Culture and the Politics of Disappearance*. Minneapolis: University of Minnesota Press.

— (1997), 'Hong Kong: Other Histories, Other Politics', *Public Culture* 9: 293-313.

— (2000), 'Cosmopolitan De-scriptions: Shanghai and Hong Kong', *Public Culture* 12.

Anderson, B.R. O'G. (1983), *Imagined Communities: Reflections on the Origin and Spread of Nationalism*. London: Verso.

Anthony, G. et al. (1990), 'Changes in City Size and Regional Distribution, 1953-1986' in *Chinese Urban Reform, What Model Now?*, edited by Grant Blank et al. London: Sharpe, Inc.

Araeen, R. (2000), 'A New Beginning: Beyond Postcolonial Theory and Identity Politics', *Third Text* 50: 3-20.

Arkaraprasertkul, N. (2010), 'Beyond Preservation: Rebuilding Old Shanghai', *Exposition Magazine of the University of Oxford* 3 (Hilary Term): 10-18.

— (2010), 'Leaping Beyond Nostalgia: Shanghai's Urban Life Ethnography', *International Institute for Asian Studies Newsletter* 55: 28-29.

— (2010), 'Power, Politics, and the Making of Shanghai', *Journal of Planning History* 9, no. 4: 232-59.

— (2008), 'Politicisation and the Rhetoric of Shanghai Urbanism', *Footprint* 2: 43-52.

— (2009), 'Resilient Lilong: An Ethnography of Shanghai's Urban Housing', *Working Papers Series: Harvard-Yenching Institute*, http://hyi.scribo.harvard.edu/category/working-paper-series.

— (2009), 'Towards Modern Urban Housing: Redefining Shanghai's *lilong*', *Journal of Urbanism: International Research on Placemaking and Urban Sustainability* 2, no. 1: 11-29.

— (2008), 'Visualizing Shanghai: The Ascendancy of the Skylines', *East Asian Studies Journal* 12, no. 2: 1-39.

— (2007), 'Shanghai Contemporary: The Politics of Built Form', Massachusetts Institute of Technology.

— (2007), 'Towards Shanghai's Urban Housing: Re-Defining Shanghai's Lilong', paper presented at the 6th China Urban Housing Conference, Beijing, China.

Arnold, M. (1993), 'Culture and Anarchy' in *Culture and Anarchy and Other Writings*, edited by Stefan Collini. New York: Cambridge University Press.

Ballard, J.G. (1984), *Empire of the Sun: A Novel*. New York: Simon and Schuster.

Bao Yaming, (ed.) (2001), 包亞明，上海酒吧 空间、消费与想象 [Shanghai Bars: Space, Consumption and Imagination]. 上海：江苏人民出版社.

— (2007), 'Shanghai and the *Shanghai Weekly*: The Problem of Globalization and Localization in Contemporary Chinese Popular Culture' in *Shanghai: Its Urbanization and Culture*, edited by Xuanmeng Yu and Xirong He, 241-256. Washington: The Council for Research in Values and Philosophy.

Baudelaire, C. (1976), *Oeuvres complètes*, Pichois, C. (ed.), Bibliothèque de la Pléiade, vol. 1. Paris: Gallimard.

Benjamin, W. (1997), *Paris, capitale du XIXe siècle: Le livre des passages*, translation of *Das Passagen-Werk* (3rd ed.), Lacoste, J. (trans.), Tiedemann, R. (ed.). Paris: Éditions du Cerf.

Bentmann, R. and Muller, M. (1992), *The Villa as Hegemonic Architecture*, translated by Tim Spence and David Craven. New Jersey: Humanities Press.

Berman, M. (1982), *All That is Solid Melts into Air: The Experience of Modernity*. New York: Simon and Schuster.

Berry, C., et al. (2010), *The New Chinese Documentary Film Movement for the Public Record*. Hong Kong: Hong Kong University Press.

Bhaumik, T.K. (2009), *Old China's New Economy: The Conquest by a Billion Paupers*. London: SAGE.

Boey, M. (2002), '(Trans)national realities and imaginations: the business and politics of Malaysia's Multimedia Super Corridor' in *Critical reflections on cities in Southeast Asia*, edited by Tim Bunnell et al., 185-214. Singapore: Times Academic Press.

Boyer, M.C. (2002), 'Approaching the Memory of Shanghai: the Case of Zhang Yimou and Shanghai Triad (1995)' in *Shanghai: Reflections, Architecture, Urbanism, and the Search for an Alternative Modernity*, edited by Mario Gandelsonas. New York: Princeton Architectural Press.

Bozdogan, S. (2001), *Modernism and Nation Building: Turkish Architectural Culture in the Early Republic*. Seattle: University of Washington Press.

Bracken, G. (2009), *Thinking Shanghai: A Foucauldian Interrogation of the Postsocialist Metropolis*, Ph.D. dissertation, Delft University of Technology.

— (2009), 'The Shanghai Model', *International Institute for Asian Studies Newsletter* 52: 4-5.

— (2006), 'The Interface of Empire', paper presented at the International Forum on Urbanism, Tsinghua University, Beijing, 2006.

Brenner, N. and Keil, R. (eds.) (2006), *The Global Cities Reader*. New York: Routledge.

Broudehoux, A. (2002), *The Making and Selling of Post-Mao Beijing*. London: Routledge.

Bunnell, T. (2004), *Malaysia, Modernity and the Multimedia Super Corridor: A critical geography of intelligent landscapes*. London: Routledge.

Campanella, T. (2008), *The Concrete Dragon: China's Urban Revolution and What it Means for the World*. New York: Princeton Architectural Press.

Canizaro, V.B. (ed.) (2007), *Architectural Regionalism. Collected Writings on Place, Identity, Modernity, and Tradition*. New York: Princeton Architectural Press.

Cantonfair. http://www.cantonfair.org.cn/cn/info accessed on 2010-05-05 and 2010-05-07.

Cartier, C. (2002), 'Transnational Urbanism in the Reform-era Chinese City: Landscapes from Shenzhen', *Urban Studies* 39/9: 1513-32.

Center for Strategic and International Studies & the Institute for International Economics (2006), *China: The Balance Sheet*. New York, PublicAffairs.

Chang, E. (2007), *Lust, Caution and Other Stories*. London: Penguin Books.

Chang S., and R. Yin-Wang Kwok (1990), 'The Urbanization of Rural China' in *Chinese Urban Reform, What Model Now?*, edited by Grant Blank et al. London: Sharpe, Inc.

Chen, J.J., and David Wills (1999), *The Impact of China's Economic Reforms Upon Land, Property, and Construction*. Aldershot: Ashgate.

Chen, X. (2000), 'The Mysterious Other: Postpolitics in Chinese Film' in *Postmodernism and China*, edited by Arif Dirlik and Xudong Zhang. London: Duke University Press.

Chen, Y. (2007), *Shanghai Pudong: Urban Development in an Era of Global-Local Interaction*, Ph.D. dissertation, Delft University of Technology.

— (2009), 'Migrants in Shanghai's Manufacturing Companies: Employment Conditions and Policy Implications', *Journal of Asian Public Policy* 2, no. 3: 279-92.

Chesneaux, J. (1992), *Brave Modern World: The Prospects for Survival*. New York: Thames and Hudson.

Cheung, E.M.K. (2001), 'The Hi/stories of Hong Kong', *Cultural Studies* 15 (3/4): 564-90.

China. http://www.china.com.cn/economic/zhuanti accessed on 2007-07-25, 2009-10-01 and 2010-05-09.

Chinanews. http://www.chinanews.com.cn/news accessed on 2005-08-17, 2005-08-26 and 2010-05-07.

Chow, R. (1998), 'King Kong in Hong Kong: Watching the "Handover" from the U.S.A', *Social Text* 55: 93-108.

— (1993), 'Things, Common/Places, Passages of the Port City: On Hong Kong and Hong Kong Author Leung Ping-kwan', *Differences* 5 (3): 179-204.

— (1993), 'Male Narcissism and National Culture: Subjectivity in Chen Kaige's *King of the Children*' in *Male Trouble*, edited by Constance Penley and Sharon Willis. Minneapolis: University of Minnesota Press.

— (1992), 'Between Colonizers: Hong Kong's Postcolonial Self-Writing in the 1990s', *Diaspora* 2 (2): 151-70.

Chu, Y. (2002), 本土神話　全球化年代的論述生產 [Myth-making of the local: the production of discourse in the age of globalization]. Taipei: Student.

Chun, L. (1993), 'China Today: "Money Dissolves the Commune"', *New Left Review* I, no. 201: 34-45.

Chung, C.J. et al. (2001), *Great Leap Forward*. Cambridge, Massachusetts: Harvard Design School.

Cnns. http://www.cnss.com.cn/article accessed on 2009-10-03 and 2010-05-08.

Cohen, M.L. (1993), 'Cultural and Political Inventions in Modern China: the Case of the Chinese Peasant', *Daedalus*, 122(2).

Comité invisible (2009), *The Coming Insurrection* [*L'insurrection qui vient*]. Semiotext(e) Intervention Series, 1. Cambridge, Massachusetts: Massachusetts Institute of Technology Press.

Cornelius, S., and Ian Haydn Smith (2002), *New Chinese Cinema, Challenging Representations*. London: Wallflower.

Crinson, M. (2003), *Modern Architecture and the End of Empire*. Aldershot: Ashgate.

Currie, K. (1996), *Beyond Orientalism: An exploration of some recent themes in Indian history and society*. Calcutta: KP Bagchi & Company.

Curtis, W. (1996), *Modern Architecture since 1900*. London: Phaidon.

Dai, J. (1997), 'Imagined Nostalgia', *Boundary* 2, vol. 24: pp. 143-161.

Damisch, H. (2001), *Skyline: The Narcissistic City*. Stanford: Stanford University Press.

Davis, D.S. (2002), 'When a House becomes His Home' in Link, P., Madsen, R.P. and Pickowicz, P.G. (eds.), *Popular China: Unofficial Culture in a Globalizing Society*, edited by Perry Link, Richard P. Madsen and Paul G. Pickowitz, 231-250. Lanham: Rowman & Littlefield Publishers.

— (2000), 'The Consumer Revolution in Urban China', *Studies on China* 22. Berkeley: University of California Press.

Davis, M. (2006), *Planet of the Slums*. London: Verso.

Deckker, Z.Q. (2001), *Brazil Built: The Architecture of the Modern Movement in Brazil*. London: Spon Press.

Dreyer, J. (2010), 'The Metropolis and the Capital: Shanghai and Beijing as Paradigms of Space', *International Institute for Asian Studies Newsletter* 55: 20-21.

— (2010), 'Shanghai and the 2010 Expo: Staging the City', paper at the 3rd China Postgraduate Students Conference, the University of Oxford, United Kingdom.

Dwyer, D.J. (1986), 'Urban Housing and Planning in China', *Transactions of the Institute of British Geographers* 11, no. 4: 479-89.

Economist, The (2010), *Pocket World in Figures 2010*. London: Economist Books.

Edensor, T. (2001), *Tourists at the Taj: Performance and Meaning at a Symbolic Site*. London: Routledge.

Eggener, K.L. (2007), 'Placing Resistance: A Critique of Critical Regionalism' in *Architectural Regionalism: Collected Writings on Place, Identity, Modernity, and Tradition*, edited by Vincent B. Canizaro, 395-407. New York: Princeton Architectural Press.

— (1999), 'Towards an Organic Architecture in Mexico' in *Frank Lloyd Wright: Europe and Beyond*, edited by Anthony Alofsin, 166-83. Berkeley: University of California Press.

Eijkelboom, H. (2007), *Paris – New York – Shanghai: A Book about the Past, Present, and (Possibly) Future Capital of the World*. New York: Aperture.

Feng, W. et al. (2002), 'Rural Migrants in Shanghai: Living under the Shadow of Socialism', *International Migration Review* 36, no. 2: 520-45.

Fishman, T.C. (2005), *China, Inc*. New York: Scribner.

Fong, V.L. (2004), *Only Hope: Coming of Age under China's One-Child Policy*. Stanford: Stanford University Press.

Fraser, V. (2000), *Building the New World: Studies in the Modern Architecture of Latin America, 1930-1960*. London: Verso.

Friedmann, J. (2005), *China's Urban Transition*. Minneapolis, University of Minnesota Press.

— (1986), 'The World City Hypothesis', *Development and Change* 17 (1): 69-83.

Gamble, J. (2003), *Shanghai in Transition: Changing Perspectives and Social Contours of a Chinese Metropolis*. London: Routledge.

Gardiner, J. (1971), 'Educated Youth and Urban-Rural Inequalities 1958-66' in *The City in Communist China*, edited by John Wilson Lewis. Stanford: Stanford University Press.

Gibson, K. et al. (2001), 'Beyond Heroes and Victims: Filipina Contract Migrants, Economic Activism and Class Transformations', *International Feminist Journal of Politics* 3 (3): 365-86.

Gluckman, R. (undated), 'Shanghai's Stylish Xin Tian Di', http://www.gluckman.com/XinTianDi accessed on 2009-11-09.

Goldman, R. and Stephen Papson (1996), *Sign Wars: the cluttered landscape of advertising*. New York: Guilford Press.

Greco, C. (2008), *Beijing: The New City*. Milan: Skira Books.

Greenhalgh, S. (2008), *Just One Child: Science and Policy in Deng's China*: Berkeley: University of California Press.

Guan, Q. (1996), 'Lilong Housing, a Traditional Settlement Form', M.Arch. thesis, McGill University.

Guldin, G.E. and Aidan Southall (eds.) (1993), *Urban Anthropology in China*. Leiden: Brill.

Hall, T. and Phil Hubbard (eds.) (1998), *The Entrepreneurial City: Geographies of Politics, Regime and Representation*. Chichester: John Wiley.

Hammond, P.H. (2006), *Community Eclipse and Shanghai's Lilong*. Missouri: University of Missouri-Columbia.

Hamnett, C. (1994), 'Social Polarisation in Global Cities: Theory and Evidence', *Urban Studies* 31, no. 3: 401-24.

Hamnett, C. and Yulong Shi (2002), 'The Potential and Prospect for Global Cities in China: In the Context of the World System', *Geoforum* 33, no. 1: 121-35.

Harvey, D. (2008), 'The Right to the City', *New Left Review* 253: 23-40.

— (2005), *A Brief History of Neoliberalism*. Oxford: Oxford University Press.

— (1981), 'Urban Process under Capitalism: A Framework for Analysis' in *Urbanization and Urban Planning in Capitalist Society*, edited by Michael J. Dear and Allen J. Scott, 91-122. London: Methuen.

— (1973), *Social Justice and the City*. London: Edward Arnold.

— (1972), *Society, the City, and the Space-Economy of Urbanism.* Washington: Association of American Geographers.

Hayes, J. (1983), *The Rural Communities of Hong Kong: Studies and Themes.* Hong Kong: Oxford University Press.

Herrie, P. and Erik Wegerhoff (eds.) (2008), *Architecture and Identity.* Berlin: Lit Verlag and Habitat-International.

Herzfeld, M. (2009), *Evicted from Eternity: The Restructuring of Modern Rome.* Chicago: University of Chicago Press.

— (2005), 'Spatial Cleansing: Monumental Vacuity and the Idea of the West', *Journal of Material Culture* 11, no. 1/2: 127-49.

— (2005), *Cultural Intimacy: Social Poetics in the Nation-State.* New York: Routledge.

— (1973), 'Divine King or Divine Right: Models of Ritual Authority', *Journal of the Anthropological Society of Oxford,* vol. 4, issue 3: 68-76.

Herzog, L. (1999), *From Aztec to High Tech: Architecture and Landscape across the Mexico-United States Border.* Baltimore: Johns Hopkins University Press.

Hitchcock, H. and Philip Johnson (1996), *The International Style.* New York: Norton (updated reprint of the 1932 edition).

Hobsbawm, E.J. and Ranger, T.O. (1983), *The Invention of Tradition: Past and Present Publications.* Cambridge, United Kingdom: Cambridge University Press.

Holston, J. (1989), *The Modernist City: An Anthropological Critique of Brasilia.* Chicago: University of Chicago Press.

Hu, B. (2007), *Informal Institutions and Rural Development in China.* New York: Routledge.

Huang, L. (2000), 'Housing Development in the Context of the Modernization, Urbanization and Conservation of Chinese Traditional Cities: Beijing, Shanghai and Suzhou', D.Des. Thesis, Harvard University.

Huang, M.T. (2004), *Walking Between Slums and Skyscrapers: Illusions of Open Space in Hong Kong, Tokyo, and Shanghai.* Hong Kong: Hong Kong University Press.

— (2000), 'Hong Kong Blue: *Flâneurie* with the Camera's Eye in a Phantasmagoric Global City', *Journal of Narrative Theory* 30 (3): 385-402.

Huang, Q. (2007), 'The External Trade of Guangdong in Two Thousand Years: Guangzhou as the Center', *Shenzhen University Journals* 24 (2): 150-157. Shenzhen: Humanity Social Science Press.

Huang, S. and Yang W. (1983), *Beijing*: 35-45. Beijing: China Construction Industry Press.

Huang, Y. (2008), *Capitalism with Chinese Characteristics: Entrepreneurship and the State.* Cambridge, United Kingdom: Cambridge University Press.

Hugo, V. (1957), *Les Misérables,* Guyard M. (ed.). Paris: Garnier Frères.

— (2008), *Les Misérables.* Julie P. Rose (trans.): 487. London: Modern Library.

Hung, W. (2005), *Remaking Beijing: Tiananmen Square and the Creation of a Political Space.* London: Reaktion Books.

— (2003), 'Monumentality of Time: Giant Clocks, the Drum Towers, the Clock Towers' in *Monuments and Memory, Made and Unmade,* edited by Robert S. Nelson and Margaret Rose Olin. Chicago: University of Chicago Press.

Iovine, J.O. (2006), 'Our Man in Shanghai: Ben Wood Takes on History', *The New York Times.* http://www.nytimes.com accessed on 2006-08-13.

Ishiguro, K. (2000), *When We Were Orphans.* London: Faber & Faber.

Jacobs, J. (1964), *The Death and Life of Great American Cities.* Harmondsworth: Penguin Books (in association with Jonathan Cape).

Kalia, R. (2006), 'Modernism, modernization and post-colonial India: a reflective essay', *Planning Perspectives* 21: 133-56.

King, A.D. (2004), *Spaces of Global Cultures: Architecture, Urbanism, Identity*. London: Routledge.

Koolhaas, R. (1978), *Delirious New York: A Retroactive Manifesto for Manhattan*. New York: Oxford University Press.

Kraicer, S. *Little Cheung*. http://www.chinesecinemas.org/littlecheung.html.

Kusno, A. (2000), *Behind the Postcolonial: Architecture, Urban Space, and Political Cultures in Indonesia*. New York: Routledge.

Larmer, B. (2010), 'Shanghai Dreams: China's Global City Tries to Recapture the Glories of Its Past – This Time on Its Own Terms', *National Geographic*: 124-41.

Laurans, V. (2005), 'Shanghai: Modern Conveniences as an Argument for Displacing Residents', *China Perspectives*, vol. 58: 10-21.

Law, L. (2002), 'Defying Disappearance: Cosmopolitan Public Spaces in Hong Kong', *Urban Studies* 39 (6): 1625-45.

Lee, L.O. (2010), *Shanghai mo deng: Yi zhong xin du shi wen hua zai Zhongguo (1930-1945)* [Shanghai Modern: The Flowering of a New Urban Culture in China, 1930-1945]. Beijing: Ren min wen xue chu ban she.

Lee, Y. (1992), 'Rural Transformation and Decentralized Urban Growth in China' in *Urbanizing China*, edited by Gregory E. Guldin. New York: Greenwood Press.

Lefebvre, H. (1991), *The Production of Space* (Nicholson-Smith, D. trans.). Cambridge, United Kingdom: Blackwell.

Levin, M. (1991), 'Regional Aspects of the International Style in Tel Aviv and Jerusalem' in *Critical Regionalism*, edited by Spyros Amourgis, 240-57. Pomona: California State Polytechnic University.

Liang, S.Y. (2008), 'Where the Courtyard Meets the Street: Spatial Culture of the Li Neighborhoods, Shanghai, 1870-1900', *Journal of the Society of Architectural Historians* 67, no. 4: 482-503.

Lin, G.C.S. (2007), 'Reproducing Spaces of Chinese Urbanization: New City-Based and Land-Centred Urban Transformation', *Urban Studies* 44, no. 9: 1827-55.

Ling, H. (1997), 'The Political Economy of the Privatisation of the Land Market in Shanghai', *Urban Studies* 34, no. 2: 321-35.

Little Cheung (2000), Fruit Chan (dir.). Hong Kong: Nicetop Independent Ltd.

Logan, J.R. (ed.) (2008), *Urban China in Transition*. Oxford: Blackwell.

— (2002), *The New Chinese City: Globalization and Market Reform*. Oxford: Blackwell.

Lu, H. (1995), 'Away from Nanking Road: Small Stores and Neighborhood Life in Modern Shanghai', *Journal of Asian Studies* 54, no. 1: 93-123.

Lu, X., and Elizabeth J. Perry, (eds.) (1997), *Danwei: The Changing Chinese Workplace in Historical and Comparative Perspective*. London: M.E. Sharpe.

Luo Q., and Tao W. (2004), 'Research about the Relationship of Exhibitions and Urban Economical Social Development: Guangzhou Fair as example', *Journal of Beijing International Studies University*, no. 3: 30-37.

Luo, X., and Wu J. (eds.) (1997),上海弄堂 [Shanghai Longtang]. 上海: 上海人民美术出版社.

Ma, L.J.C. (1981), 'Urban Housing Supply in the People's Republic of China' in *Urban Development in Modern China*, edited by Laurence J. C. Ma and Edward W. Hanten, 222-59. Boulder: Westview Press.

Ma, L.J.C., and Fulong Wu (2005), *Restructuring the Chinese City: Changing Society, Economy and Space*. London: Routledge.

Marcuse, P. (2006), 'Space in the Globalizing City' in *The Global Cities Reader*, edited by Neil Brenner and Roger Keil, 361-9. London: Routledge.

Marshall, R. (2003), *Emerging Urbanity: Global urban projects in the Asia Pacific Rim*. London: Spon Press.

Mbembe, A. (1992), 'Prosaics of Servitude and Authoritarian Civilities', *Public Culture* 5 (1): 123-45.

McGee, T.G. (2007), *China's Urban Space: Development under Market Socialism*. London: Routledge.

McGrath, J. (2007), 'The Independent Cinema of Jia Zhangke: From Postsocialist Realism to a Transnational Aesthetic' in *The Urban Generation: Chinese Cinema and Society at the Turn of the Twenty-first Century*, edited by Zhen Zhang. London, Duke University Press.

Morris, D.L. (1994), *Community or Commodity? A Study of Lilong Housing in Shanghai*. Vancouver: Centre for Human Settlements, School of Community and Regional Planning, University of British Columbia.

Murphy, R. (2002), *How Migrant Labor Is Changing Rural China*. Cambridge, United Kingdom: Cambridge University Press.

Nalbantoğlu G.B., and C.T. Wong. (eds.) (1997), *Postcolonial Space(s)*. New York: Princeton Architectural Press.

Naughton, B. (2007), *The Chinese Economy: Transitions and Growth*. Cambridge, Massachusetts: Massachusetts Institute of Technology Press.

Pal, P. (ed.) (1989), *Romance of the Taj Mahal*. Los Angeles: Los Angeles County Museum of Art and Thames and Hudson.

Pan, T. (2005), 'Historical Memory, Community-Building and Place-Making in Neighborhood Shanghai' in *Restructuring the Chinese City: Changing Society, Economy, and Space*, edited by Laurence J. C. Ma and Fulong Wu, 122-37. London: Routledge.

— (2002), *Neighborhood Shanghai: Community Building in Five Mile Bridge*, Ph.D. dissertation, Harvard University.

Pang, L. (2001), 'Death and Hong Kong Cinema', *Quarterly Review of Film and Video* 18 (1): 15-29.

Parish, W.L., and Martin King White (1978), *Village and Family in Contemporary China*. Chicago: The University of Chicago Press.

Pelli, C., Thornton, C., and Joseph, L. (1997), 'The World's Tallest Buildings', *Scientific American* 277/6: 64-72.

Pellow, D. (1993), 'No Place to Live, No Place to Love: Coping in Shanghai' in *Urban Anthropology in China*, edited by Greg Guldin and Aidan Southall. Leiden: Brill.

Pemberton, J. (1994), 'Recollections from "Beautiful Indonesia" (Somewhere Beyond the Postmodern)', *Public Culture* 6: 241-62.

Peng, R. (1987), 'Urban Housing Trends in Shanghai: Learning from the Neighborhoods in Shanghai', first-year paper: 1-42. Cambridge, Massachusetts: Massachusetts Institute of Technology Press.

— (1986), 'Towards a New Housing Approach: Analysis of Settlement Environment and Housing Policy in Shanghai, China', M.S. thesis. Cambridge, Massachusetts: Massachusetts Institute of Technology.

Pridmore, J. (2008), *Shanghai: The Architecture of China's Great Urban Center*. New York: Abrams.

Querrien, A. (1986), 'The Metropolis and the Capital', *Zone 1/2*: 219-221. Cambridge, Massachusetts: Massachusetts Institute of Technology Press.

Ren, X. (2011), *Building Globalization: Transnational Architecture Production in Urban China*. Chicago: University of Chicago Press.

Rossi, A. (1982), *The Architecture of the City*, Eisenman P. (ed.), Arts Graham Foundation for Advanced Studies in the Fine and Studies Institute for Architecture and Urban. Cambridge, Massachusetts: Massachusetts Institute of Technology Press.

Rowe, P.G. (2005), *East Asia Modern: Shaping the Contemporary City*. London: Reaktion.
Rowe, P.G. and Seng Kuan (eds.) (2009), *Shanghai: Architecture and Urbanism for Modern China*. London: Reaktion Books.
— (2002), *Architectural Encounters with Essence and Form in Modern China*. Cambridge, Massachusetts: Massachusetts Institute of Technology Press.

Sassen, S. (1996), 'Cities and Communities in the Global Economy', *American Behavioral Scientist* 39 (5): 629-39.
— (1991), *The Global City*. Princeton: Princeton University Press.
Shang, C. (2007), 'From Forbidden Overseas Activity to Seclusion: The Evolution of External Trade Rules in the Ming and Qing Dynasties', *Hubei Institute of Economics Journals* 4 (10): 63-64.
Shanghai Statistical Yearbook (2009), Shanghai Municipal Statistics Bureau. Shanghai: China Statistics Press.
Shen, H. (1993), 上海里弄民居 [Shanghai Lilong Dwelling], (北京：中国建筑工业出版社.
Shih, S. (2001), *The Lure of the Modern: Writing Modernism in Semicolonial China, 1917-1937*. Berkeley: University of California Press.
Short, S.E. and Zhai Fengying (1998), 'Looking Locally at China's One-Child Policy', *Studies in Family Planning* 29, no. 4: 373-87.
Sidaway, J., and M. Power, (1995), 'Sociospatial transformations in the 'postsocialist' periphery: the case of Maputo, Mozambique', *Environment and Planning A* 27: 1463-91.
Skinner, W. (1977), 'Urban and Rural in Chinese Society' in *The City in Late Imperial China*, edited by William Skinner, 253-273. Stanford: Stanford University Press.
— (1977), 'Urban Social Structure in Ch'ing China' in *The City in Late Imperial China*, edited by William Skinner, 521-553. Stanford: Stanford University Press.
— (1964), 'Marketing and Social Structure in Rural China: Part I', *The Journal of Asian Studies* 24, no. 1: 3-43.
Skinner, W. and Baker, H.D.R. (eds.) (1977), 'The City in Late Imperial China', *Studies in Chinese Society*. Stanford: Stanford University Press.
Sklair, L. (2009), 'The emancipatory potential of generic globalization', *Globalizations* 6/4: 523-537.
— (2006), 'Iconic architecture and capitalist globalization', *City* 10/1: 21-47.
— (2005), 'The transnational capitalist class and contemporary architecture in globalizing cities', *International Journal of Urban and Regional Research* 29/3: 485-500.
— (2002), *Globalization: Capitalism and Its Alternatives*. Oxford: Oxford University Press.
— (2001), *The Transnational Capitalist Class*. Oxford: Blackwell.
Smith, R.G. (2003), 'World City Topologies', *Progress in Human Geography* 27 (5): 561-82.
Southcn. http://www.southcn.com/news/gdnews accessed on 2010-05-09.
Southcn. http://www.southcn.com/news/gdnews accessed on 2010-05-08 .
Stockman, N. (2000), *Understanding Chinese Society*. Cambridge, United Kingdom: Blackwell.

Tang, Z. (2006), *The Urban Housing Market in a Transitional Economy: Shanghai as a Case Study*, Ph.D. dissertation, Indiana University.
Tombesi, P. (2001), 'A true south for design? The new international division of labour in architecture', *Architectural Research Quarterly* 5/2: 171-79.
Tombesi, P., Dave, B., and Scriver, P. (2003), 'Routine production or symbolic analysis? India and the globalization of architectural services', *Journal of Architecture* 8: 63-94.
Tsai, W. (2008), 'The Redevelopment and Preservation of Historic Lilong Housing in Shanghai', M.S. thesis, University of Pennsylvania.

Vale, L. (2008), *Architecture, Power, and National Identity*. London: Routledge.
— (1999), 'Mediated monuments and national identity', *Journal of Architecture* 4: 391-408.

Virilio, P. (2006), *Speed and Politics*, translated by Mark Polizzotti. Cambridge, Massachusetts: Massachusetts Institute of Technology Press.

Wai, A.W. (2006), 'Place Promotion and Iconography in Shanghai's Xintiandi', *Habitat International* 30, no. 2: 245-60.

Walcott, S.M. (2009), 'Shanghai Pudong: Urban Development in an Era of Global and Local Interaction', *International Journal of Urban and Regional Research* 33, no. 2: 585-86.

Walker, R., and Buck, D. (2007), 'The Chinese Road', *New Left Review* 46: 39-66

Wang, A. (2003), 长恨歌 [Song of Everlasting Sorrow]. 海口：南海出版社.

— (2008), *The Song of Everlasting Sorrow: A Novel of Shanghai*, translated by Michael Berry and Susan Chan Egan. New York: Columbia University Press.

Wang, B. (2002), 'Love at Last Sight: Nostalgia, Commodity, and Temporality in Wang Anyi's Song of Unending Sorrow', *Positions: East Asia Cultures Critique*, vol. 10, no. 3: 669-694.

Wang, C. (2003), 'Introduction' in *One China, Many Paths*, edited by Chaohua Wang, 9-49. London: Verso.

Wang, F. (2010), 'Conflicts, Resistance, and the Transformation of the Hukou System' in *Chinese Society: Change, Conflict and Resistance*, edited by Elizabeth J. Perry and Mark Selden, 80-100. London: Routledge.

Wang, H. (2003), 'The New Criticism' in *One China, Many Paths*, edited by Chaohua Wang, 55-86. London: Verso.

Wang, J. (2008), *Brand New China: Advertising, Media, and Commercial Culture*. Cambridge, Massachusetts: Harvard University Press.

Wang, J. (2006), 'Residential Differentiation: The Mapping of Young Professionals' Lifestyle and Their Housing Location Choices in Traditional Shanghai', *Projections: The MIT Journal of Planning* 5: 68-88.

Wang, X. (2003), 'A Manifesto for Cultural Studies' in *One China, Many Paths*, edited by Chaohua Wang. London: Verso: 274-291.

Wang, X. (1996), 人文精神寻思录 [Thoughts on the Humanist Spirit]. 上海：文汇出版社.

Wang, Y. and Murie, A. (1999), 'Commercial Housing Development in Urban China', *Urban Studies* 36, no. 9: 1475-94.

Wasserstrom, J.N. (2009), *Global Shanghai, 1850-2010: A History in Fragments*. London: Routledge.

Wei, D.Y., Leung, C.K., and Luo, J. (2006), 'Globalizing Shanghai: Foreign Investment and Urban Restructuring', *Habitat International* 30: 230-44.

Weizman, E. (2007), *Hollow Land: Israel's Architecture of Occupation*. London: Verso.

Welsh, F. (1996), *A Borrowed Place: The History of Hong Kong*. New York: Kodansha International.

Wharton, A.J. (2001), *Building the Cold War: Hilton International Hotels and Modern Architecture*. Chicago: University of Chicago Press.

Wilson, D. (1996), *China, the Big Tiger*. London: Little Brown.

Wong, J.K.Y. (2002), 'The Distance between Hong Kong and China: Hong Kong People's Perception of Their Identity', paper presented at the Crossroads in Cultural Studies: Fourth International Conference, Tampere, Finland.

Woods, M. (2007), 'Engaging the Global Countryside: Globalization, Hybridity and the Reconstitution of Rural Place', *Progress in Human Geography* 31 (4): 485-507.

Wright, A.F. (1977), 'The Cosmology of the Chinese City' in *The City in Late Imperial China*, edited by William Skinner, 33-73. Stanford: Stanford University Press.

Wu, F. (2009), 'Globalization, the Changing State, and Local Governance in Shanghai' in *Rising Shanghai: State Power and Local Transformations in a Global Megacity*, edited by Xiangming Chen, 125-144. Minneapolis: University of Minnesota Press.

— (2006), *Globalization and the Chinese City*, Routledge Contemporary China Series. London: Routledge.

— (2004), 'Residential Relocation under Market-Oriented Redevelopment: The Process and Outcomes in Urban China', *Geoforum* 35: 453-70.

— (2002), 'Real Estate Development and the Transformation of Urban Space in China's Transitional Economy with Special Reference to Shanghai' in *The New Chinese City: Globalization and Market Reform*, edited by John R. Logan, 154-166. Oxford: Blackwell.

— (2001), 'China's Recent Urban Development in the Process of Land and Housing Marketisation and Economic Globalisation', *Habitat International* 25, no. 3: 273-89.

— (2001), 'Housing Provision under Globalisation: A Case Study of Shanghai', *Environmental and Planning* 33: 1741-64.

— (1996), 'Changes in the Structure of Public Housing Provision in Urban China', *Urban Studies* 33, no. 9: 1601-28.

Wu, F. and He, S. (2005), 'Property-Led Redevelopment in Post-Reform China: A Case Study of Xintiandi Redevelopment Project in Shanghai', *Journal of Urban Affairs* 27, no. 1.

Wu, W. (2002), 'Migrant Housing in Urban China: Choices and Constraints', *Urban Affairs Review* 38 (1): 90-119.

Xiang, B. (2005), 'Transcending Boundaries: Zhejiangcun: The Story of a Migrant Village in Beijing' in *Zhejiangcun: The Story of a Migrant Village in Beijing*, edited by Jim Weldon. Leiden: Brill.

Xu, G.G. (2007), *Sinascape, Contemporary Chinese Cinema*. Maryland: Rowman & Littlefield.

Xu, J. and Yeh, A.G.O. (eds.) (2007), *Urban Development in Post-Reform China: State, Market, and Space*. London: Routledge.

Yager, G. and Kilbourn, S. (2004), 'Lessons from Shanghai Xintiandi: China's Retail Success Story', *Urban Land Asia*: 34-37.

Yau, E. (1994), 'Border Crossing: Mainland China's Presence in Hong Kong Cinema', in Browne, N. (ed.), *New Chinese Cinema: Forms, Identities, Politics*: 180-201. Cambridge, United Kingdom: Cambridge University Press.

Yau, K. (2001), 'Cinema 3: Towards a "Minor Hong Kong Cinema"', *Cultural Studies* 15 (3/4): 543-63.

Yeh, A.G.O. (1999), *The Transformation of the Urban Planning System in China from a Centrally-Planned to Transitional Economy*. Oxford: Pergamon.

Yusuf, S., Wu, W., and the World Bank (1997), *The Dynamics of Urban Growth in Three Chinese Cities*. Oxford: Oxford University Press.

Zhang, L. (2005), 'Migrant Enclaves and Impacts of Redevelopment Policy in Chinese Cities' in *Restructuring the Chinese City, Changing Society, Economy and Space*, edited by Laurence J. Ma and Fulong Wu. London: Routledge.

— (2002), 'Spatiality and Urban Citizenship in Late Socialist China', *Public Culture* 14, no. 2: 311-34.

— (2001), 'Migration and Privatization of Space and Power in Late Socialist China', *American Ethnologist* 28, no. 1: 179-205.

— (2001), *Strangers in the City: Reconfigurations of Space, Power, and Social Networks within China's Floating Population*. Stanford: Stanford University Press.

Zhang, L.M. and Ong, A. (eds.) (2008), *Privatizing China: Socialism from Afar*. Ithaca: Cornell University Press.

Zhang, X. (2009), 'Competitiveness and International Growth: The External Trade and Construction Development of Guangzhou (1912-1936)', *The Research of Chinese Social Economy History* (4): 91-102.

— (2008), *Postsocialism and Cultural Politics: China in the Last Decade of the Twentieth Century*. Durham: Duke University Press.

Zhang, Y. (1996), *The City in Modern Chinese Literature and Film: Configurations of Space, Time and Gender.* Stanford, Stanford University Press.

Zhao, B. (1997), 'Consumerism, Confucianism, Communism: Making Sense of China Today', *New Left Review* I, no. 222: 43-59.

Zhao, C. (2004), 'From shikumen to new-style: a rereading of lilong housing in modern Shanghai', *The Journal of Architecture*, vol. 9, no 1: 49-76.

Zukin, S. (1991), *Landscapes of Power: From Detroit to Disney World.* Berkeley: University of California Press.

Index

IIAS
International Institute
for Asian Studies

Publications Series

Josine Stremmelaar and Paul van der Velde (eds.)
What about Asia? Revisiting Asian Studies
2006 (ISBN 978 90 5356 959 7)

Monographs

Alex McKay
Their Footprints Remain. Biomedical Beginnings Across the Indo-Tibetan Frontier
Monographs 1
2007 (ISBN 978 90 5356 518 6)

Masae Kato
Women's Rights? The Politics of Eugenic Abortion in Modern Japan
Monographs 2
2009 (ISBN 978 90 5356 793 7)

Jeroen de Kloet
China with a Cut. Globalisation, Urban Youth and Popular Music
Monographs 3
2010 (ISBN 978 90 8964 162 5)

Rituparna Roy
South Asian Partition Fiction in English. From Khushwant Singh to Amitav Ghosh
Monographs 4
2010 (ISBN 978 90 8964 245 5)

Chaiyakorn Kiatpongsan
The EU-Thailand Relations. Tracing the Patterns of New Bilateralism
Monographs 5
2011 (ISBN 978 90 8964 164 9)

Olena Mykal
The EU-Japan Security Dialogue. Invisible but Comprehensive
Monographs 6
2011 (ISBN 978 90 8964 163 2)

Kah Seng Loh, Edgar Liao, Cheng Tju Lim and Guo-Quan Seng
The University Socialist Club and the Contest for Malaya. Tangled Strands of Modernity
Monographs 7
2012 (ISBN 978 90 8964 409 1)

Eka Srimulyani
Women from Traditional Islamic Educational Institutions in Indonesia. Negotiating Public Spaces
Monographs 8
2012 (ISBN 978 90 8964 421 3)

Edited Volumes

Gijsbert Oonk (ed.)
Global Indian Diasporas. Exploring Trajectories of Migration and Theory
Edited Volumes 1
2007 (ISBN 978 90 5356 035 8)

Wen-Shan Yang and Melody Chia-Wen Lu (eds.)
Asian Cross-border Marriage Migration. Demographic Patterns and Social Issues
Edited Volumes 2
2010 (ISBN 978 90 8964 054 3)

Margaret Sleeboom-Faulkner (ed.)
Frameworks of Choice. Predictive and Genetic Testing in Asia
Edited Volumes 3
2010 (ISBN 978 90 8964 165 6)

Birgit Abels (ed.)
Austronesian Soundscapes. Performing Arts in Oceania and Southeast Asia
Edited Volumes 4
2011 (ISBN 978 90 8964 085 7)

Dipika Mukherjee and Maya Khemlani David (eds.)
National Language Planning and Language Shifts in Malaysian Minority Communities
Edited Volumes 5
2011 (ISBN 978 90 8964 271 4)